BLUE NOTES AND SAD CHORDS

Color Coded Harmony In

THE BEATLES

27

Number 1 Hits

Brian Hebert

Blue Notes and Sad Chords

Copyright © 2018 by Brian Hebert

All rights reserved. No part of this book may be reproduced or transmitted in any form or by any means without written permission of the author.

Keywords: The Beatles, Musical Cartography, Music Education

ISBN 978-0-692-10479-8 (paperback)
ISBN 978-0-692-10483-5 (eBook)

Published by:
ScribeKey, LLC

DEDICATION

This book is dedicated to my mom and dad, especially for letting me watch the Ed Sullivan Show on Sunday night, February 9, 1964.

ACKNOWLEDGMENTS

I would like to thank my friends Rich Grady, Fletcher Brock, Bill Carrier, Jeff Donze, Bill Tufts, Forrest McCluer, Jim Moore, and especially Jessica Williams and my son Liam, for so much helpful feedback and encouragement.

I'd also like to thank the countless people, friends and family alike, who put up with me endlessly describing this book and making them look at miniature colored song maps and chord palettes on my cell phone.

Thanks to my editor Jess Shulman, for her wonderful eagle eyes (and ears).

Special thanks to Stephanie Anderson at Jera Publishing, for her patience, help, and incredible insight on this book's layout and design, and so many other things.

Most importantly, very special thanks to my daughter Emily for playing all the singles and every song on every Beatles album, over and over again, on our long rides to and from Montreal, and listening for energy, vocal harmony, and contrasting song parts.

FAIR USAGE

This work is intended for music education. In no instance have full lyrics, musical scores, or chord progressions been shown for any songs. As such, no rendition of any song, its melody, or its accompaniment can be reproduced from its description in these pages. Rather, vocal arrangements and the sets of chords used in a song have been suggested in a highly generalized manner, using colored diagraming techniques, along with small snippets of lyrics to help describe a song's main characteristics. This is in keeping with the intent of fair usage, where references to copyrighted works may be used for purposes such as criticism, comment, news reporting, teaching, scholarship or research.

CONTENTS

Preface i
SECTION 1: Introduction 1
    Overview 3
        Another Beatles Book? 4
        Who This Book Is For 4
        What This Book Is Not About 4
        Sections 5
        Musical Pep Talk 6
    Why Were the Beatles So Successful? 6
    About the Song Maps 7
        Listening Skills 7
        Mixing Voices, Mixing Colors 8
        The Write-Ups 10
        Using the Number 1s 11
        Who's Singing and Playing What? 11
    Music 101 12
        The Parts of a Song 12
        Notes and the Scale 14
        Keys 15
        Chords 15
        Harmony 16
        Blue Notes 17
        Some Common Musical Terms 18
        Wrap Up 19
    Seeing and Hearing 20

SIDEBAR: How It Came to Be 21

SECTION 2: The Songs 23

   1 Love Me Do 25
   2 From Me to You 29
   3 She Loves You 33
   4 I Want to Hold Your Hand 37
   5 Can't Buy Me Love 41
   6 A Hard Day's Night 45
   7 I Feel Fine 49
   8 Eight Days a Week 53
   9 Ticket to Ride 57
  10 Help 61
  11 Yesterday 67
  12 Day Tripper 71
  13 We Can Work It Out 77
  14 Paperback Writer 81
  15 Yellow Submarine 85
  16 Eleanor Rigby 91
  17 Penny Lane 97
  18 All You Need Is Love 103
  19 Hello, Goodbye 109
  20 Lady Madonna 115
  21 Hey Jude 121
  22 Get Back 127
  23 The Ballad of John and Yoko 133
  24 Something 137
  25 Come Together 143
  26 Let It Be 149
  27 The Long and Winding Road 155
      Song Map Patterns over Time 159

SIDEBAR: Out of Phase Stereo (OOPS) 165

SECTION 3: Blue Notes and Sad Chords 169

  Music 201 171
  Mapping Colors to Chords 171
  Happy and Sad Chords Continued 172
  Other Chords 174
  There's More to It 175
  The Full Set of Chord Colors 176
  Choosing the Colors 176

- Chord Palettes ... 178
- Beatles Number 1-Hits Chord Palettes ... 182

SIDEBAR: Chord Progressions and the Wistful 4 ... 185

- The Beatles and Chord Progressions ... 186
  - The Wistful 4 ... 187
  - The 4 Chord and 4 Note ... 187
- Essential Early Beatles: Song Map and Chord Palette Together ... 189
- Blue Notes and Sad Chords ... 190
- A Music Genome for the Beatles ... 191
- Early and Late Beatles Musical Word Clouds ... 192
- The Albums ... 193
  - #1 Please Please Me ... 193
  - #2 With the Beatles ... 194
  - #3 A Hard Day's Night ... 194
  - #4 Beatles for Sale ... 194
  - #5 Help ... 195
  - #6 Rubber Soul ... 195
  - #7 Revolver ... 195
  - #8 Sgt. Pepper's Lonely Hearts Club Band ... 196
  - #9 Magical Mystery Tour ... 196
  - #10 The White Album ... 196
  - #11 Yellow Submarine ... 197
  - #12 Abbey Road ... 197
  - #13 Let It Be ... 197
- Album Charting ... 198
- The Beatles and Other Artists ... 199
  - 1960s Hit Singles ... 199
  - The Beatles and the Rolling Stones ... 205

SIDEBAR: Synesthesia and Colored Music ... 208

- The Clavier à Lumières ... 208
- Song Maps and Chord Palettes ... 210
- The Beatles and Color ... 210
- Light and Sound ... 210
- So Where Did It Come From? ... 212
  - Merseybeat ... 212
- Blue Notes and Sad Chords: A Deeper Look ... 214
  - Music and Contrast ... 214

  Black and White 215
  The Genesis of Rock 'n' Roll and Charting Crossover 217
  Yank and Brit 218
  Music, Evolution, and the Beatles 219
 Conclusion 220
 Performance Energy, Vocal Harmony, and Song Quality 220
 And in the End 221
  A Last Personal Note 222

APPENDIX **225**
 Music 301 225
  Notes, Harmonic Ratios, and Overtones 225
  The Relative Minor Key and the Church Modes 227
  Blue Notes and Extended Chords 228
  Chord Degrees and Function 228
  Understanding Musicology 229
  The B Chord in I Want to Hold Your Hand 231
 Full-Lyrics Song Maps 233
 Wrap Up 234

About the Author 237
About the Graphics 237

PREFACE

In late 2013, I got the idea to do a book on the Beatles' hits, color coding the lyrics to the twenty-seven songs on the *1* album, to help show who was singing and when they were harmonizing. I especially wanted to highlight how the Beatles constantly switched in and out of harmony, which is an essential ingredient of their wonderful sound.

So, I reached out to Sony/ATV, who owns the rights to the Beatles' published songs, and was granted permission to use the lyrics in my book, on a fee-per-song basis. I then set out on my journey, listening to the songs over and over, writing about them, writing computer programs to generate colored song maps of the lyrics, and just thinking about the Beatles and their music a lot. I easily spent over a thousand hours, working mostly on weekends for over three years.

When I started working on the last part of the book, I checked in again with Sony/ATV to make sure I could still use the lyrics. They informed me that they now used Hal Leonard, the big music book publisher, to handle all the reprint rights. So, I contacted Hal Leonard and they said that, yes, I could still secure reprint rights. But a few months later, in a sudden and startling about face, the people at Hal Leonard informed me that they had changed their minds (I suppose they have their reasons, but they never said why), and that I could no longer include the lyrics in my book. Ouch.

But the show must go on. So, onward to Plan B. I changed gears and created a simpler version of the song maps, showing only the song parts and no lyrics, but still using the same color scheme I had developed to show which Beatles were singing.

These Plan B song maps are not as easy to follow along with while you're listening to the music—they take a little more work. But I believe that the main message still comes across, and that fans, old and new, can still gain a new appreciation and understanding of what made this most amazing band so successful and enduring, and why their music is still so loved today by millions the world over.

"These rules, the sign language and grammar of the Game, constitute a kind of highly developed secret language drawing upon several sciences and arts, but especially mathematics and music (and/or musicology), and capable of expressing and establishing interrelationships between the content and conclusions of nearly all scholarly disciplines. The Glass Bead Game is thus a mode of playing with the total contents and values of our culture; it plays with them as, say, in the great age of the arts a painter might have played with the colours on his palette."

– Hermann Hesse, *The Glass Bead Game*

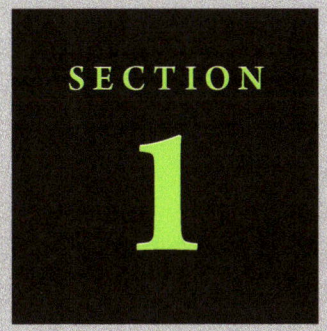

INTRODUCTION

OVERVIEW

This companion volume to the Beatles' *1* CD shows the vocal arrangements for the full set of the Beatles' twenty-seven all-time greatest hits, using brightly colored *song maps*. By assigning a primary color to each of the singing Beatles' voices and applying the simple color-mixing formulas we all learned as children in art class, the song maps show which Beatles are singing on the different parts of a song, and whether they are singing alone or together, in unison or in harmony.

The Beatles' vocal arrangements, and the beautiful harmonies they used in so many of their songs, are a quintessential element of the band's amazing sound. By following along with the song maps while listening to the music, fans can gain a new appreciation and a deeper and more detailed understanding of what made the Beatles and their music so special.

Along with each colored song map is a write-up. Each write-up includes release and recording dates, a description of the song map, charting info, the song's back story, some personal memories and thoughts on the Beatles and related topics, a detailed walk-through of the song, and a few important Beatles time-line events.

While the main body of the book is focused on vocal arrangements, a shorter section at the end shows a set of colored *chord palettes* for the twenty-seven hit songs, using the analogy of an artist's palette of paints. These chord palettes show how the Beatles combined different musical styles in their songs, another key element of their sound. The palettes especially show how the band, at the height of their early fame, uniquely blended bluesy rock 'n' roll and heartstring-tugging pop sounds together in the same songs, as well as how this genre-blending changed over the course of their career.

Another Beatles Book?

Hundreds of books in all sizes and shapes have been written about the Beatles. Many are biographical, describing the Beatles' childhoods, their early interest in music, how they came together, stories about their friends and families, how their lives were intertwined with events of the 1960's, and so forth. Some books are primarily collections of photographs. Still other books help readers peer behind the curtains, such as Mark Lewisohn's wonderful body of work, which describes all the Beatles' recording sessions in a highly detailed manner and is a treasure to hard-core fans.

A smaller number of books actually describe the music in detail. Typically written by musical experts, most of these books require the reader to possess a detailed understanding of music theory and a very specialized vocabulary, and as such are generally inaccessible to the average fan, and even quite challenging for many rock musicians, many of whom can't read music. One goal of this book is to bridge this gap, and provide lovers of Beatles music with a unique and enjoyable way to understand some of the key musical elements that made the four lads from Liverpool so successful, without needing to be a musician or possess any specialized knowledge of music theory.

Who This Book Is For

This book was written for:

- Baby-boomer fans who experienced the Beatles first hand, during the crazy 1960s. Hopefully, as in Marcel Proust's classic work *Remembrance of Things Past*, when the narrator takes a bite of a cookie and is magically transported back through time to his childhood, hearing and seeing the music in this new way will help bring it all back.
- The children of baby boomers, or other younger fans, who love the Beatles and want to know more about their music and the 60s scene, and perhaps gain a new understanding of the times their parents grew up in.
- Students taking a course on the Beatles or the music of the 1960s. There are now hundreds of courses like this being taught at colleges and universities.
- People interested in music visualization, synesthesia, and music classification systems like the Music Genome.
- Anybody else, non-musician and musician alike, who just likes the Beatles and wants to learn more about the special qualities in their music using a highly simplified and visual approach to explain some basic concepts of music theory.

What This Book Is Not About

Unlike so many other books on the Beatles, which include details of every single song, or recording session, or concert, or calendar day, etc., this book is not exhaustive. Only the twenty-seven number 1 hits are covered in detail.

And while many have explored the subject, this book is also not about trying to analyze or interpret the Beatles' lyrics.

Sections
This book is divided into three main sections:

Section 1 introduces the book's main theory, which is that, in addition to the Beatles' looks and charm, their incredible popularity was also due to three key musical ingredients: 1) performance energy, 2) vocal harmony, and 3) song quality. This is followed by a general description of the colored song maps and the write-ups that follow in Section 2, along with a highly simplified Music 101 review of song parts and the elements that constitute musical harmony.

Section 2 the main body of the book, contains the set of colored song maps showing vocal arrangements for the twenty-seven hit singles, and in particular, highlights how harmony comes in and out of the picture. Each song map is accompanied by a multi-section write-up describing the song, including release and recording info, charting in the US and the UK, a back story, a description of the song map, some personal memories and reminiscences about the times and the Beatles by the author (me), a detailed description of the song, and lastly a condensed Beatles timeline.

Section 3 presents a set of colored chord palettes, again for each hit single, in order to show a key element of how the Beatles constructed their songs. There is an additional Music 201 review of more harmonic elements to explain how different chords evoke different feelings. This is followed by a discussion of the hit-single chord palettes and how the Beatles changed over time. The end of Section 3 includes a review of the Beatles' albums and the music of other chart-topping songs and artists of the 1960s in the context of the main energy, vocal harmony, and song quality theory. This is followed by a look at the roots of the Beatles' music, the Liverpool Merseybeat scene, and rock 'n' roll, all as descendants of the rich mixing of black African and white European musical elements throughout the history of popular music. Section 3 also contains several colored word clouds to describe the two halves of the Beatles' career, and another to depict the many elements of popular song and dance over the course of American history. This is all followed by a conclusion, some suggestions for next steps, and a final personal note.

The Appendix contains a Music 301 section that provides a more detailed look at some fundamental elements of music theory that were highly simplified in the Music 101 and 201 sections, along with a few other odds and ends, including what full-lyrics song maps look like.

Musical Pep Talk

Some non-musician readers/listeners may initially think that the simplified reviews of song parts, harmony, and chord feelings presented in these pages are still too complex to understand. But do please give it a try—one of the key ideas this book hopefully gets across is that these musical concepts can be conveyed, and understood intuitively, using relatively simple, color-rich graphics, which do not at all require an in-depth understanding of music theory.

Everyone can basically hear the difference between singing solo or singing in unison vs. singing in harmony. So, after a basic review of song parts, the song maps that make up the main body of the book should be fairly easy to follow along with while listening to the music. The material in Section 3 does require a bit more understanding of how chords work, but hopefully the Music 201 review and the colored chord palettes can be generally understood and appreciated by non-musician and musician alike, in much the same way that complex sets of facts and figures can be simplified and readily understood using colored charts and graphs. So, all readers/listeners are encouraged to work through Section 3, as it explains the book's title, *Blue Notes and Sad Chords*, in more detail, and hopefully sheds light on what really did make the Beatles' music so very special and enduring.

WHY WERE THE BEATLES SO SUCCESSFUL?

Released in November 2000, the Beatles' *1* CD includes the twenty-seven number 1 singles that hit the top of the charts in either the UK or the US from 1962 to 1970. The album, which was produced by George Martin and Phil Spector, runs for about eighty minutes. Even though it was released thirty years after the Beatles broke up, the CD became the bestselling album of the decade worldwide and sold more than 31 million copies. How can a phenomenon like that be explained?

Many people, including manager Brian Epstein, have said that the Beatles had something so special that it can't be explained. And when people talk about the amazing impact the Beatles had on the music world, they credit them with inventing the music video and the concept album and call attention to their unparalleled chart success, being the first band to fill large stadiums, and, of course, their brilliance in the recording studio. But much less has been said about the Beatles' more basic musical elements like vocal harmony, at least not in a way that is understandable to the average fan. That's what this book is about.

Yes, the four mop-topped British boys from Liverpool were young and good-looking. They had a special charm and a great sense of humor. They had playful and biting wit, individually and together. They wore cool clothes and said quirky things. All of this drove millions of teenage girls totally crazy—the images of the band's fans screaming, crying, and fainting are iconic. And the events that led to the band's formation—John and Paul meeting one fateful July 6 in 1957, George joining the band, their stints playing in Hamburg, getting Brian Epstein as a manager, Ringo joining the band, and, so very importantly, getting a recording shot with EMI's George Martin and having him become their producer—will continue to be talked about for decades to come.

But there have always been, and there always will be, good-looking, charming, lucky musicians that make it big. There had to be something more, something very special, to turn a rock 'n' roll band from Liverpool into the Beatles. That something can be found in the music itself.

The simple theory put forth in this book is that, in addition to the Beatles' profound likability, looks, and charm, there were three main *musical* reasons behind their incredible success and popularity:

1. **Performance Energy:** Call it what you want—spirit, moxie, musical chutzpah—the Beatles had a musical energy like nobody else. Originating in their natural abilities and inspired by their enthusiasm for early rock 'n' roll stars like Elvis and Little Richard, and then honed over countless hours playing, night after night, in Hamburg, Germany and later at the Cavern Club in Liverpool, their energy was tight, powerful, unique, and infectious.
2. **Vocal Arrangements and Harmony:** Whether it's John's lower and soulful baritone, Paul's Little Richard–inspired rocker or higher sincere-choirboy voice, or George's sharper but sometimes whispery mid-range, the Beatles had amazing voices. And while each Beatle singing on his own was great, it was when they combined their voices in beautifully arranged harmonies, that the full brilliance of their music really came out.
3. **Song Composition and Quality:** The Beatles wrote incredible songs. They have been covered by hundreds, and in some cases thousands, of artists, from Alvin and the Chipmunks to Joe Cocker. Their songs contain beautiful melodies and unusual chord progressions, and often combine contrasting moods and feelings within the same song or even song *part*, and especially in several important early hits, mix hard-driving bluesy rock 'n' roll with sentimental heartstring-tugging pop. This blending of genres inspired this book's title, *Blue Notes and Sad Chords* (see Section 3 for a detailed explanation).

And while each of these three elements, on its own, would be enough to make a band great, it was all three of them *in combination* that defined the Beatles' irresistibly magic formula, particularly in their earlier work.

ABOUT THE SONG MAPS

Listening Skills

To follow along with the twenty-seven song maps, you need to sharpen two basic listening skills that you already possess. The first the is the ability to hear the difference between singing in unison, when two or more people are singing the same notes, and singing in harmony, when two or more people are singing different notes. For example, when John, Paul, and George are singing the title words to *She Loves You* together, they are all singing the same notes, in unison. But when John and Paul are singing the opening verse to *Love Me Do*, they are both singing the same words, but each using different notes, in harmony. Greater than the sum of its parts, harmony adds an extra energy and a more pleasing sound to music, vocal and instrumental alike.

The second skill is the ability to recognize the different parts of a song, including the intro, the chorus or refrain, the verse, the bridge, instrumental breaks, and the outro. There's a basic primer on song parts in the Music 101 section. Additionally, as you'll see, the song maps are broken up by song part, and each part is labeled with a minute:second time tic and an identifying label, allowing you to know exactly which part is playing as you listen along or study the song map on its own.

Mixing Voices, Mixing Colors

We all learned as children that red mixed with blue makes purple, blue with yellow makes green, and red with yellow makes orange. Red, blue, and yellow are called the primary colors; purple, green, and orange are the secondary colors. If we assign a primary color to each singing Beatle voice (John red, Paul blue, and George yellow) and color code the parts of a song, we can see where they were singing alone, using a primary color, or together in unison or harmony, using secondary colors, or rich vertical blends of primary colors. Because Ringo did not sing as much as the others and is featured on a single number 1 hit, *Yellow Submarine*, he gets his own special *Sea-of-Green* color.

As a simple example, look at the opening verse from the *Ticket to Ride* song map shown below. Because John is singing the first and last lines by himself, the first and last sections of this song part are shown in red, but when Paul comes in to harmonize, in the middle of the verse, the color changes to a red-blue blend, showing a richer mixture of colors, visually mirroring the rich mix of the two harmonizing voices.

First Verse in *Ticket to Ride*

But it's of course not quite that simple. The Beatles didn't just sing alone or as pairs in harmony—sometimes all three of them would sing in unison, as in parts of *She Loves You*, or sometimes they sang in three-part harmony, as in parts of *I Feel Fine*. Or sometimes a single Beatle sang lead vocals and two others sang backup, with different words, like when John sings lead in *Help* and Paul and George sing backup vocals in harmony. So, to create a colors-to-voices mapping scheme, while we can rely on the basic primary and secondary formula as a foundation, we need a few extra color shades to account for the additional variations.

To show unison when two Beatles are singing the same notes, a single, and simpler, lighter secondary color is used, such as in the following snippet, again from *Ticket to Ride*, where John and Paul are singing the first lines of the refrain in unison, shown as light purple, and then finish in two-part harmony, shown in a red-blue blend:

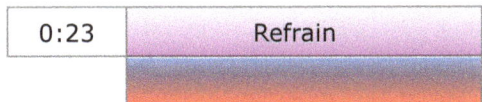

First Refrain in *Ticket to Ride*

Background vocals, when the words don't match the lead vocals but are sung at the same time, and some instrumental passages, are labeled with the squiggle character ~, as in the following snippet from a verse in the *Paperback Writer* song map, where Paul is singing lead vocals, and John and George are singing *Frère Jacques* in harmony in the background:

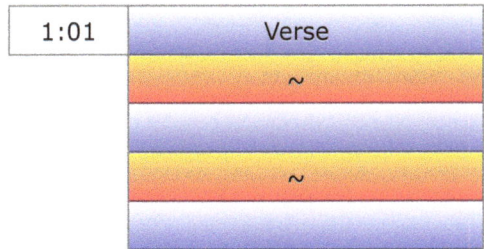

Lead and Harmonized Backing Vocals in a *Paperback Writer* Verse

As stated in the preface, the original song maps showed the full lyrics for each song, but because SONY/ATV and Hal Leonard reversed their decision about granting any rights, a simpler technique showing only song parts had to be used. (See the Appendix for an example of a full lyrics song map.) Because these original full lyrics versions were used as a starting point for the simplified song part versions, there are frequently sections of song maps shown as multiple lines, suggesting stanzas, such as in the *Paperback Writer* verse shown above.

Even without the full lyrics, the main purpose of the song maps is to portray vocal arrangements, and in particular, when harmony comes in and out of the mix. So, things that will stand out in a song map are, for example, seeing that the first time a song part is sung it's solo or in unison, while the next time it's harmonized, or that harmonized backing vocals have come in and been interspersed between solo lines.

The song maps also show prominent guitar riffs and to a lesser extent, drums. Other spots show where keyboards, string quartets, orchestras, or choirs come into the mix, in a variety of uniform colors and blends to show combinations of instruments. While the song map technique is used primarily to portray vocals, instruments have been added in to provide a loosely suggested visual hint of a prominent aspect in the song's mix. Instrumental sections are also sometimes shown in more detail at the beginning of a song. Additionally, in several McCartney numbers, where there are only blue vocals, more guitar, string quartet, piano, and orchestra parts have been added in to fill out the maps and make them more visually interesting. Lastly, the song maps in the second half of the set often show more complex colors and blends, as the mapping technique evolved to accommodate the Beatles' changing style.

Each song map also has a legend to indicate which colors are used to represent Beatle voice combinations and instruments. There are also four pages at the end of section 2 that show simplified and reduced renderings of each song map, without song part labels or time tics, so that they can be seen as a single series over time, as well as a full legend of all colors, voice combinations, and instruments.

When you really think about it, a perfect mapping of colors, primary and secondary, to an arrangement of song parts, voices in unison and harmony, along with instruments, is impossible. So, while the song maps are somewhat generalized, sometimes inconsistent, and most often more art than science, they still hopefully provide a good, easy-to-follow idea of what's going on in a song.

Note: The layout size of the song maps is somewhat larger than what might be expected, but this was to make them look a bit like posters.

The Write-Ups

The writing that accompanies each song map is broken into the following sections:

The Number, Song Name, and Headline
A sequential number matching the order of the song as it appears on the *1* CD, its name, and a brief one- or two-liner describing key aspects of the song.

Release and Recording
The dates of both the UK and US releases along with the recording dates, the song's length, and what its B-side was.

Charting
The dates and number of weeks each song spent at the top of the charts, in both the US and the UK, along with information for the songs that were number 1s before and after the Beatles' hit.

Note: There are different release, recording, and charting dates, depending on whether you look at the CD liner notes, pages on Wikipedia, or book sources. In cases where there are differences, the Wikipedia page for the song is used for release and recording dates, and the Wikipedia pages *List of Billboard Hot 100 number 1 singles from 1958 to 1969* and *List of UK Singles Chart number 1s of the 1960s*, for charting.

The Back Story
Background information on the song, typically a condensed version of what you might find on a Wikipedia page or some other source.

The Song Map
A brief description of the song map's visual elements.

Personal Notes
Typically, one or two nostalgic memories the song conjures up, some opinions about a Beatle's musical talents, or some other aspect of being a young guitar player in the 1960's, written in first person by the author (me).

The Details
A detailed walk-through of the song, describing the vocals and instrumental parts, how they're combined, and how they come in and out of the mix.

Timeline
A condensed list of dates and events that took place in the Beatles' lives since the previous hit.

Note: For double A-sides, the Charting and Timeline sections are repeated.

Using the Number 1s

The official Beatles canon, consisting of the full set of singles and albums recorded and released between 1962 and 1970, includes about 220 songs. It's an amazingly rich and varied collection of both covers and original material. Looking at only the number 1 hits, of course, doesn't really capture the full measure of the band's amazing work. However, the number 1s are some of their very important and most successful songs—they are the songs that the Beatles and George Martin thought the fans would like the best when they were released. The progression of songs and styles in the set also tells an important story about how the Beatles evolved over time.

Who's Singing and Playing What?

Most of the time, it's pretty easy to tell who's singing or playing what instrument in the different parts of the songs. There are also lots of videos and written descriptions of performances and recording sessions available to help us figure it out. But there are certain cases where it's not so easy to be certain about the exact lineup, especially in certain spots where George Harrison might be singing along. For an authoritative source, I've used the author Ian MacDonald's lists that appear on Wikipedia pages, taken from his famous book *Revolution in the Head*.

In some cases, Beatles pundits disagree about who is singing or playing on what part. For example, some people think that John and George are not singing backing vocals on *Eleanor Rigby*, although they are listed as such in many sources. In other cases, the Beatles may have changed the lineup as time went on, resulting in different versions of songs. For these situations, the song maps and descriptions were developed as well as possible after lots of listening, watching videos, reading different material, etc. and sometimes using a technique called *out of phase stereo* (OOPS—see the related Sidebar). OOPS changes what you can hear in a recording and can sometimes unearth or isolate some sounds that you wouldn't normally notice in the official release's mix.

In any case, with such a high volume of information to cover, there are no doubt details which some readers may have different ideas about. So if you think there's a more accurate depiction, description, date, or have other comments, feel free to send an email (please be polite) to bnasc27@gmail.com (an acronym for *Blue Notes and Sad Chords* and the 27 songs).

This book is not intended as a scholarly work. You won't find footnotes or a list of references, and Wikipedia has been used as a main source for many facts, lists of songs, and other interesting links. Given the incredible volume of information that has been compiled about the Beatles over the years, actually finding an authoritative source for almost anything is next to impossible. And while Wikipedia has its critics, it should be pointed out that, because it is crowdsourced, and there are thousands of people who know every little detail about the Beatles, the pages describing the songs and albums are generally pretty accurate. Additionally, Wikipedia has some wonderfully rich content describing music theory concepts and music history. Where else could you find a single source that lists all of the number 1 singles and albums in the US and UK in the 1960s (these were cross checked from other sources), a list of hundreds of pop songs that use a classic 1950's chord progression, or as you'll see in the Sidebar *Colored Music and Synesthesia*, nice musical graphics and a history of composers trying to map light to music?

MUSIC 101

In order to appreciate how special the Beatles were, and to understand how their music is presented and described in this book, you'll need a simple primer on song structure and some basic musical concepts. This overview is very simple and is designed specifically to avoid the complex and highly specialized jargon one typically encounters when studying formal music theory. You don't need to be a musician to understand this material, but if you are, whether you read music or not, you'll no doubt already have an intuitive sense for most of these things.

The Parts of a Song
When you hear a nursery rhyme, a limerick, or some other word ditty, you're hearing a miniature and condensed story, primarily rhythmic in nature, with separate parts, which builds suspense and ends with a

release of tension. While only lightly suggesting a musical melody, these little multi-act word plays, which have undoubtedly existed since the dawn of human language, can be thought of in part as the structural ancestors of modern folk, blues, rock, and pop songs. Fast forward to the twentieth century, and these structures have evolved into elaborate and ritualistic patterns, and while more complex than simpler rhymes and ditties, still perform the basic job of telling a rhythmic, melodic, emotionally interesting, and dramatic story.

The basic parts that make up a song, providing repeated mounting and released tension along with variation to keep things interesting, are described below. These parts are used to break up each song map.

Intro

The intro is usually a short instrumental section. It might be unique, or it might use material that will be repeated throughout the song. Many Beatles songs start with instrumental intros. For example, *Love Me Do* and *From Me to You* start off with harmonica intros, and *I Feel Fine* and *Day Tripper* start off with guitar intros. However, there are plenty of exceptions. *She Loves You* and *Paperback Writer* both start off with vocals. Some songs don't have any intro at all, like *Yellow Submarine* or *We Can Work It Out*.

Verse

A song is like a little story, and the main chapters of the story are delivered through the verses. While using the same music as its siblings, each verse typically contains different lyrics, although many songs end with a repeat of the first verse. Repetition and variation are an essential aspect of music, and verses exemplify this by using the same music to deliver continually changing lyrics and ideas.

Refrain or Chorus

Unlike a verse, a refrain or chorus is generally the same music and the same words, interspersed between the verses, and repeated throughout the song. The distinction between a refrain and a chorus is a little fuzzy, but refrains are typically shorter than choruses. For example, the title lyrics *I Wanna Hold Your Hand* sung twice could be considered a refrain, while the three repetitions of the title lyrics *She Loves You* followed by three *yeahs* might be considered a chorus. For simplicity, the word *refrain* is used consistently to name these sections in the song map write-ups.

When you find yourself remembering and singing the most memorable part of a song, it's usually the refrain. Refrains are usually more energetic and emotional than verses. The back-and-forth between the verses and the refrain is one of the things that keeps a song interesting.

For a little added detail, shorter refrains have been broken out in some of the song maps.

Bridge

A bridge, or middle eight (British) as the Beatles called it, is a section of a song where the melody and feeling change, like a mini-song within a song, serving to vary and contrast with the main material in the verses and refrain. Bridges are very important in Beatles music. They put laser-beam focus on Lennon/McCartney collaboration, frequently contain more vocal harmony than the rest of the song, and highlight how the Beatles often mixed musical genres within the same song.

Solo
A solo is a break that features a single instrument for its own little show. It can use the same underlying music as the verse or refrain or add some entirely new material. A lot of rock and pop songs feature guitar and keyboard solos, once in a while a drum solo, and very rarely a bass solo. (Ringo never really took a drum solo, except maybe for a few great minutes on the *Abbey Road* album.)

Outro
The outro brings an end to a song, very often repeating and fading into the distance, but sometimes a song ends distinctly on one last chord or note. The last chord or note can be instrumental, vocal, or a combination of both. A fade-out can sometimes give the impression that the song just keeps going on forever, and that you just can't hear it anymore.

Hook
You'll also hear the word *hook* used when describing song parts. The hook is supposed to be a short catchy bit of music to get your attention, get you interested. The instrumental and vocal intros described above can all be considered hooks. Hooks are not labeled in the song maps, but it's good a good term to know about.

Notes and the Scale

If you have access to a piano or organ keyboard, or an app like Garage Band on your iPad, do feel free to test out the ideas presented in this section.

Remember the eight notes of the major scale you learned as a child, *do-re-mi-fa-so-la-ti* and then *do* again? The first and the eighth notes in the scale are the same, but an octave apart, so there are really only seven distinct notes. A note one octave above another vibrates twice as fast, but sounds the same to us, just higher. A familiar example of an octave is found at the beginning of the song *Somewhere Over the Rainbow*, where the first syllable *some* and the second syllable *where* are an octave apart.

In Western music, the set of distinct musical pitches we hear in a single octave is actually divided into twelve notes, but five of them are not used in the major scale. In the following graphic, you can see the seven notes of the scale as the white keys on a piano; the five that aren't used in the major scale are the black keys.

27 : INTRODUCTION

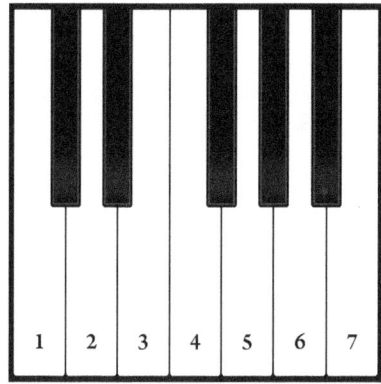

Seven White Keys and Five Black Keys

Keys

A scale can start on any of the twelve notes in the octave, creating twelve possible major scales. We say that each one of these twelve scales is in a specific *key*, and named using a letter from A to G, with the symbols # (sharp) or *b* (flat) used if the scale starts on a black key. If you start a scale on the white note just below the group of two black keys on a piano, and hit only white keys as you move up the keyboard, you're in the key of C. We won't be referencing specific keys in this book. Instead, we'll use a simpler and more generic system using only numbers like 1-2-3 (*do-re-mi*) to identify the notes in a scale, which applies to all keys.

Chords

The simplest way to think about a chord is that it is made up of three notes, stacked together, and played at the same time. You can build a chord on each of the seven notes in the scale. To build the three-note stack for a given scale note, you start with the note itself, skip a note, use the next note, skip a note, and use the next note. So, a chord built on the 1 note has the notes 1-3-5, the chord built on the 2 has the notes 2-4-6, and so on. The figure below shows the set of seven stacks for each chord in the major scale.

5	6	7	1	2	3	4
3	4	5	6	7	1	2
1	2	3	4	5	6	7

The Seven Three-Note Chord Stacks in the Scale

Sometimes these chord stacks get rearranged, and the order of the three notes is changed. For example, a chord based on the 1 note could have a stack like 5-1-3. In other cases, there can be a doubling of the same note, an octave apart. When you play the well-known E-major chord on a guitar, in first position, the full stack from the lowest sounding string on up is 1-5-1-3-5-1.

15

As you can see from the section of the piano keyboard shown earlier, and more clearly in the figure below, the spacing between the seven notes of the scale, within the full twelve that make up the octave, is uneven. For example, there is a black-note gap between the 1 the 2 and the 3, but the 3 and 4 are right next to each other, and there is a black-note gap between the 5 the 6 and the 7, but the 7 and 1 are right next to each other.

The Spacing of the White Scale Notes and the Non-Scale Black Notes in the Octave

Because of this uneven spacing, we end up with three different-sounding types of chords. The chords built on the 1, 4, and 5 notes are called major, and they have a stronger, happier sound. The chords built on the 2, 3, and 6 notes are called minor, and they have a weaker, sadder sound. The chord built on the 7 is sort of an oddball—it would be a minor chord, except that the top note of its stack is a notch lower than in the other chords, and so it sounds a little jarring to our ears.

When people say that for rock 'n' roll you only need to know three chords, they're talking about the three strong happy chords, the 1, 4, and 5. The three sad chords, the 2, 3, and 6, get added in with the three happy ones in lot in sentimental pop songs and folk ballads. In some pieces of music, the sad chords are used by themselves, resulting in a gloomier or sadder kind of feeling.

Harmony

When people sing in harmony, they're usually just singing different notes from the same chord stack at the same time, because the notes sound good together. For example, you can see in the following graphic, that when two people sing *Row Row Row Your Boat*, and start the second and fourth lines at the same time, they're singing a series of two-note chord stacks, shown here with a colored note for each syllable. So, when the second-line voice is singing *gent* with a 3 note, the fourth-line voice is singing *life* with a 5 note, which makes a 3-5 two-note stack. And even though there is no 1 in the stack, our ears wondrously tend to want to hear it as a three-note 1-3-5 stack, and, in a way, fill in the missing note.

Harmony as Two-Note Chord Stacks in *Row Row Row Your Boat*

When people sing harmony using small spaces between the notes in the stack, for example, only a single white key on a piano separating them, it's called *close* harmony. In contrast, when they sing notes that are further apart, say by three or more keys on a piano, they're singing *broad* harmony. You can hear John and Paul singing in close harmony on *I Want to Hold Your Hand* and in broad harmony on *Love Me Do*.

Blue Notes

Some types of music use more than just the simple set of notes and chords from the seven-note *do-re-mi* scale described so far. In the blues and rock 'n' roll, two of the black-key notes on the piano, shown in blue in the diagram below, are used a lot. Black-key notes just below white key notes are called flat and those just above white keys are called sharp. (Technically, the same black key note can be described as both flat to the note above it, and sharp to the note below it, although typically only one description is used.) The two notes highlighted in blue below, the flat-3 and the flat-7, are called *blue notes*, and they can give music a low-down, swampy, or lonesome feeling. They're often the notes you hear emphasized when a slide-guitar player or blues harmonica is wailing away. (The flat-5 is sometimes included in a discussion of blue notes, but we are leaving it out here—it's mostly used as a *passing* or leaning note, always wants to go to up to 5 or down to 4, rarely if ever is held on a strong beat, and is never really used as the root note in a *blue* chord, the way the flat-3 and flat-7 can be, as you'll see in Section 3.)

Two Blue Notes in the Octave

Some Common Musical Terms

This section explains a few more common musical terms that appear in the number 1-hit write-ups accompanying the song maps.

Backbeat

Backbeat is an essential rhythmic element of many different types of music. It is especially prominent in rock 'n' roll and in the Beatles' music. Typically, in a regular rhythmic pattern, the first beat in the group is stressed. For example, in military marching, the first step in each group of two, the left, is called out with the familiar *left left left-right left*. Applying a backbeat to this familiar pattern would have the stress moved "back" to the right steps. There are so many up-tempo Beatles' songs that have a backbeat that it would be easier to identify the ones that didn't. For good examples of backbeat in the number 1 hits, listen to the tambourine whacks in a *Day Tripper* verse or the hand claps in an *Eight Days a Week* verse. Slower ballad-type songs like *Yesterday, Something*, or *Let It Be* generally don't have a backbeat.

Falsetto

Falsetto occurs when someone sings artificially higher or lower than their normal vocal range, and it's a prominent feature in Beatles music. You'll find it in songs like *Paperback Writer* when John and George sing *Frère Jacques* in the backing vocals, or in many songs that use the Little Richard–inspired *woohs* that the early head-shaking Beatles became famous for.

Tempo

Tempo, typically stated as the number of beats per minute (bpm), describes the pace of a song, how slow or fast it moves along. Classic rock 'n' roll numbers like *Long Tall Sally* and *Roll Over Beethoven* are very fast or *up-tempo* songs. Some early high-energy Beatles songs, the ones where it sounds like they can't get the words out fast enough, are very up-tempo, for example, numbers like *From Me to You* and *Help*. Others are at a slower pace, like *Love Me Do* or the floaty *Ticket to Ride*. Over the Beatles' career, the tempo of their songs generally slowed down.

Time Signature and Waltz Time

The *time signature* refers to the pattern of beats in a piece of music. Just about all music has beats broken into multiples of two or three, with groups of two being the most common. But pieces of music like waltzes and Irish jigs are broken into groups of threes and sixes. Waltzes use what's called a 3/4 time signature, where, if you were counting out the beats, you'd say *1* 2 3 *1* 2 3 and so on, accentuating the first beat in each group of three. The rhythmic pattern of a limerick is based on a 6/8 time signature, like an Irish jig. In the phrase *There **Once** Was A **Man** From Nan-**tuck**-et*, the syllables *Once* and *Man* occur on the stressed 1 and 4 beats in the first group of 6. The vast majority of Beatles songs use groups of two and four, often referred to by musicians as *cut* time, but there are some rare waltz-time songs, like *Baby's in Black, Norwegian Wood,* and *Lucy in the Sky with Diamonds*. The temporary switching in and out of waltz time in *We Can Work It Out* is a notably creative Beatles effect, and it's the only place where we hear 3/4 time in the number 1 hits.

Arpeggio
When a chord is played note by note, instead of all at once with a single beat or brush strum on a guitar, it's called an *arpeggio*. Arpeggios can move upward or downward and are very common in guitar playing. When a guitar player plays the common E-major chord, and hits each note separately, moving up from the lowest pitched bottom string to the highest pitched top string, that's an arpeggio.

Home Key and Modulation
Most songs use the notes from a single scale, identified by its bottom note, or Home Key. For example, the song *From Me to You* has a home key of C. However, in some cases, particularly in bridges, the song will temporarily change its home key, and move it to another note, go through a few passages, and then return home to the scale it started in. The bridge in *From Me to You* switches up the F, or the 4 note in the original scale, and then returns back to the home key of C. In many Beatles' songs, and other pop music, this temporary switch up to the 4 in a bridge is fairly common. In musical terms, this key switching is called *Modulation*. In some cases, such as in a song like *Penny Lane*, towards the end, there is a permanent key switch, which gives the song a very uplifting feeling.

12-Bar Blues Chord Progression
Most blues and rock 'n' roll songs, like *Johnny B Goode*, use a basic chord progression, commonly referred to as the *12-bar blues*. The progression uses only the three chords of rock 'n' roll and looks something like: 1-1-4-1-5-1. There are also lots of variations on this basic formula used in songs like *Roll Over Beethoven*, *Wipeout*, and *Kansas City*.

Wrap Up
The simplified descriptions of song parts, happy and sad chords, harmony, blue notes, and a few musical terms presented here should help you better understand the song maps and the written descriptions that accompany them. The main things to keep in mind are:

- The different parts of a song are the intro, verse, refrain, bridge, solo, and outro.
- Bridges are prominent and very important in early Beatles music.
- There are seven notes in the familiar major scale, taken from the twelve that make up the octave.
- Basic chords are built using three-note stacks, using a 1-3-5 pattern. There are three happy chords, the 1, 4, and 5; three sad chords, the 2, 3, and 6; and one oddball, the 7.
- Harmony is based on singing different notes from the same chord stack at the same time.

- Blue notes are the flat-3 and flat-7 in any major scale. They can be identified as two black keys in the all-white-key C scale on a piano. Blue notes give music that swampy, low-down sound that we hear in slide-guitar or blues-harmonica playing.
- Backbeat and falsetto are important elements of Beatles music.
- Most songs stay in a single home key, but on some occasions, both temporary and permanent key changes occur, in what is called *modulation*.

Music theory is of course much more complicated than what's been described here. There are many more types of scales with different spacings between the notes, and there are extended chords, especially in jazz and classical music, that have four, five, or even more notes in their stacks. You'll find a more accurate and detailed explanation of these ideas in the Appendix at the end of the book.

SEEING AND HEARING

It's time to put the music on.

To go through the song map section of the book while listening to the music, it's best to make at least two separate passes. The first time through each song, just follow the song map as you listen, and then read the brief description in the Song Map section of the write-up. Listening to all twenty-seven songs takes about an hour and twenty minutes. This will give you a good overview of what the song maps are all about and hopefully give you a more detailed understanding of how the Beatles arranged their hit songs, how they mixed the instruments in, and in particular, how much they switched in and out of harmony.

The second time around, especially if you're a die-hard fan that really wants the particulars, read the Details section and then listen to each song again. You may want to stop and restart a song at specific spots to check things out.

NOTE: If you're not that interested in the minutiae of each hit song, the Details section may be a bit too much. If that's the case, then just skip over them.

HOW IT CAME TO BE

We begin our story with the Beatles' first number 1 hit in 1962. Before we dive in, let's briefly review some key milestones in early Beatle history.

1940 – July 7: Richard Starkey, aka Ringo Starr, is born ~ October 9: John Lennon is born ~ **1942** – June 18: Paul McCartney is born ~ **1943** – February 25: George Harrison is born ~ **1956** – October 31: When he is fourteen years old, Paul McCartney's mother Mary dies from illness ~ **1957** – March: John Lennon forms a Skiffle group that will become the Quarrymen ~ July 6: John Lennon, playing a Quarrymen gig, meets Paul McCartney at a church fair in Liverpool ~ August 7: The Quarrymen perform at the Cavern Club in Liverpool ~ October 18: Paul McCartney appears with the Quarrymen for the first time ~ **1958** – In the early part of the year, a very young George Harrison auditions for John Lennon on top of a double-decker Liverpool bus, and plays the cool and twangy guitar part for the song *Raunchy*, which passes muster with Lennon ~ July 9: The Quarrymen record Buddy Holly's *That'll Be the Day* and a Harrison/McCartney number *In Spite of All the Danger* ~ July 15: When he is seventeen years old, John Lennon's mother, Julia, is killed by a speeding car ~ **1959** – March 25: Richard Starkey becomes the drummer for the band that will become Rory Storm and the Hurricanes ~ **1960** – May 5: The Quarrymen become the Silver Beetles ~ May 10: After an unsuccessful audition for Larry Parnes to back up Billy Fury, the Silver Beetles are offered a tour of Scotland to back Johnny Gentle, with Stuart Sutcliffe on bass and Tommy Moore on drums ~ August 12: Pete Best becomes the drummer for the Silver Beetles ~ August 17: The Silver Beetles change their name to the Beatles and start a forty-eight-day gig at the Indra Club in Hamburg, Germany ~ Oct 4: The Beatles start a fifty-eight-day gig at Hamburg's Kaiserkeller ~ November 21: George Harrison is deported from Germany for being under age and having no work permit ~ December 1: Paul McCartney and Pete Best are deported from Germany for an arson charge (they lit a condom taped to a wall on fire) ~ **1961** – Feb 9: The Beatles do their first lunchtime show at the Cavern Club in Liverpool ~ March 15: Stuart Sutcliffe returns to Hamburg and is engaged to Astrid Kirchherr ~ April 1: The Beatles return to Germany, and start a ninety-two-gig stint at the Top Ten Club in Hamburg ~ June 22: The Beatles, aka the Beat Brothers, record backing vocals for Tony Sheridan's *My Bonnie* album in Germany ~ November 9: Brian Epstein and assistant Alistair Taylor see the Beatles perform at the Cavern ~

SECTION 2

THE SONGS

#1 Love Me Do

With the bluesy harmonica and John's and Paul's droning voices, *Love Me Do* has a lazy, almost country-western feel. It's definitely not early high-energy Beatles, and you'd never know from hearing just this where they were headed, but it's still a great song with a nice easy swing. And it's fitting that the very first words we hear on the band's very first record are sung by John and Paul in full trademark harmony.

Release and Recording

UK Release: October 5, 1962
US Release: April 27, 1964
Recorded: September 4 and 11, 1962
Length: 2:22
B-Side: *P.S. I Love You*

Charting

US: On May 30, 1964, *Love Me Do* knocked *My Guy* by Mary Wells out of the top spot, which it had held for 2 weeks. It stayed at number 1 for a week and was then replaced by the Dixie Cups' *Chapel of Love*, which held for 3 weeks.

What's unusual is that *Love Me Do* hit number 1 in the US over a year and a half after it was first released, just after the Beatles had skyrocketed to fame and launched the British Invasion.

UK: The song never hit number 1 but did make it up to 17 in December 1962. (One story has it that Brian Epstein bought up hundreds of copies himself to make sure that the song would chart.)

The Back Story

Love Me Do was written primarily by Paul several years before its release, with John helping on the bridge.

In a famous Beatles rarity, Ringo didn't actually play drums on the version of the song that appears on the 1 CD, although he did play tambourine. George Martin had brought in studio drummer Andy White to fill in. This was because when the Beatles first auditioned at EMI, Pete Best was still their drummer, and George Martin didn't think he was steady enough. The version of the song with Ringo playing drums can be heard on *Past Masters Volume 1*, and the Pete Best version can be heard on *Anthology 1*.

If you look at the famous photo shot at EMI's Abbey Road studios around this time, with the Beatles standing in the background behind their instruments (George's guitar is in the middle and upside down), you'll see that George has a black eye. The story has it that some Cavern fans were angry about Ringo replacing Pete Best, and George ended up getting punched by one of them.

Love Me Do

Time	Section
0:00	Intro
0:14	Verse
0:27	Refrain
0:35	Verse
0:49	Refrain
0:56	Bridge
1:09	Verse
1:23	Refrain
1:31	Solo
1:50	Verse
2:03	Outro
	Fade Out

Song Map Legend

Harmonica
John, Paul, Harmony
Paul

The Song Map

There's lots of red-blue blend in this one, with John and Paul singing in harmony together for all the verses. Paul sings the refrains and the outro alone, but the short bridge alternates between Paul alone and harmonizing with John. This alternating between harmony and a single solo voice is a fundamental hallmark of Beatles songs. What's a little unusual about this one is that we hear the harmony first and then the solo voice. As we'll see in many of the other songs, it's usually the other way around, with a solo voice or unison sung first and the brighter harmony coming in after. The song is laced with harmonica throughout—in the intro, during all the refrains, at the end of the bridge, and in a solo toward the end. This number uses only the three solid and simple chords of rock and blues, which was common in the band's early covers but is otherwise rare in the Beatles' songbook; it happens in only two other number 1s, *Paperback Writer* and *The Ballad of John and Yoko*.

Personal Notes

The First Album
We didn't hear *Love Me Do* in the US until it showed up on the album *Introducing the Beatles*, released in January 1964 on the Vee-Jay label. As crazy as it seems today, Capitol Records wasn't too hot on the Beatles, and so the big music firm EMI, which the Beatles had signed with in England, worked out some deals with other labels to get the music played in the US. *Introducing the Beatles* was a slightly repackaged version of the Beatles' first UK album *Please Please Me*, although oddly enough, it didn't have the title song *Please Please Me* on it. The subtitle on the album cover said ENGLAND'S No.1 VOCAL GROUP. The Beatles are shown in a very staged pose with John in the center, his hands folded daintily on his crossed knee, and each Beatle's hair looking a little too short. I first heard the album about a month after the Beatles had first appeared on Ed Sullivan, at a friend's birthday party (she was turning nine). We were all dying to hear more Beatles music and I remember how incredible that album sounded and what an amazing discovery it was. Like the *Please Please Me* album, this one did start and end with the bookends *I Saw Her Standing There* and *Twist and Shout*. Some say this album is the closest thing to the great early Beatles—the music John said was their best stuff and that never got recorded.

The Teaberry Shuffle
The tail end of the bouncy little harmonica part that's played in both the intro and solo in *Love Me Do* always reminded me of the *Teaberry Shuffle*, a crazy little song and dance that people did on the Clark's TV gum commercial, featuring none other than Herb Alpert on trumpet (you can find it on YouTube). Herb Albert went on to become a major chart success story with three Billboard number 1 albums in 1966.

The Details

The song starts out with a bluesy harmonica riff, a little hook with just a few descending notes. You can hear John bite into a few of the notes as they're repeated, distorting them by pulling harder on the harmonica, as blues players do.

For the verse, John and Paul sing a few simple lines in harmony, making *please* a multi-syllable word on the last line. Then Paul solos on the short and simple refrain, with the harmonica coming back in behind him. (This refrain, sounding a little too low for Paul's voice, was originally intended to be sung by John, but he needed to play the harmonica at this spot, so Paul ended up doing it.) They repeat the short verse a second time, without variation.

The bridge is a very simple four-line passage, ending with two drum beats, suddenly stopping the song in its tracks. After another verse and refrain, the bridge passage is repeated as an instrumental break.

After the harmonica solo, there's a last time through the verse, followed by Paul repeating and varying the two-line refrain, with a little burst of energy on the *yeah*, followed by the fade-out. If you listen carefully, you'll hear Paul sing a very cool and laid-back bluesy sounding *yeah* toward the end of the outro at around 2:16.

The harmonica that John plays, and that would be heard on many of these earlier songs, was not the simple type of harmonica blues players typically use. Instead it's a larger chromatic harmonica, the type played by Bruce Channel's bandmate, Delbert McClinton, on the 1962 hit, *Hey! Baby*, said to have inspired John. The Beatles actually ended up on the same bill as Channel and his band, during a UK tour, in the summer of 1962.

Timeline

1962—January 1: The Beatles do a fifteen-song audition at Decca studios, outside of London, but are not offered a record deal, with A&R (Artists and Repertoire) man Dick Rowe supposedly saying, "Guitar groups are on the way out" ~ January 24: The Beatles sign their first contract with manager Brian Epstein ~February 5: Ringo fills in for drummer Pete Best, who is sick, for two shows at the Cavern in Liverpool ~April 10: Stuart Sutcliffe, who had been the Beatles' bass player during their Hamburg, Germany, gigs, dies from a brain hemorrhage ~April 13: The Beatles return to Hamburg, Germany, to play at the Star-Club ~June 4: The group signs with EMI on the Parlophone label ~June 6: The Beatles visit Abbey Road for the first time, to work with producer George Martin ~August 18: Ringo Starr becomes the Beatles' drummer ~August 19: George gets a black eye from a disgruntled fan loyal to former Beatles drummer Pete Best ~August 22: The band is filmed playing *Some Other Guy* at the Cavern in Liverpool by Granada Television ~August 23: John Lennon and Cynthia Powell are married in Liverpool ~September 4: The band records *Love Me Do* and *How Do You Do It* at Abbey Road

#2 From Me to You

This is the one that put the Beatles on the map. Like *Love Me Do*, it's got harmonica, but this one is much more pop than blues sounding, with some sad chords mixed in, great high-pitched and harmonized Beatle *oohs*, and a lot more energy. It's really their first number 1, and in a similar style to *P.S. I Love You*, the title is the ending of a love letter.

Release and Recording

UK Release: April 11, 1963
US Release: May 27, 1963
Recorded: March 5, 1963
Length: 1:56
B-side: *Thank You Girl*

Charting

US: The Beatles version did not chart at all, but a cover by Del Shannon (who sang the April 1961 hit *Runaway*), released in June 1963, did make it into the top 100.

UK: On May 2, 1963, it replaced *How Do You Do It* by Gerry and the Pacemakers, which had been at the top spot for 3 weeks. It stayed at number 1 for a whopping 7 weeks, and was then replaced by *I Like It*, again by Gerry and the Pacemakers, which stayed on top for 4 weeks.

The Back Story

John and Paul supposedly wrote this song at the back of the bus while on a musical tour in the UK with Helen Shapiro, who had had two number 1 hits in the UK, *You Don't Know* and *Walkin' Back to Happiness*. The authorship of *From Me to You*, and songs before it, was credited to *McCartney-Lennon*, but after this song it switched to *Lennon-McCartney* and stayed that way until the end. Right around this time, George Martin had tried to get the Beatles to do the song *How Do You Do It*, written by Mitch Murray, but they wanted nothing to do with it. (Mitch Murray also wrote *I'm Telling You Now*, for Freddie and the Dreamers.) It must have been one of the happiest times for the Beatles, with their first album, *Please Please Me*, going to number 1 on the UK charts.

From Me to You

0:00	Intro

0:07	Verse

0:21	Verse

0:35	Bridge

0:49	Verse

1:03	Verse

1:17	Bridge

1:31	Verse

1:44	Outro

Song Map Legend

John, Paul, Unison
Harmonica
John, Paul, Harmony

The Song Map

This one is loaded with unison purple and the harmonizing red-blue blend; John and Paul singing together for the entire song. They alternate throughout, singing the beginnings of the verse lines in unison and finishing them in harmony. The first time through the bridge they only sing the very last phrase in harmony, but the second time they use harmony for the beginning as well. There's no real refrain, but all the verses end with the title lyrics. Like *Love Me Do*, this song features harmonica. Ringo's drum fills at the end of the verses and bridges are great in this one. There's a classic early pop/rock sentimental sad chord in the verse, and some interesting chord changes in the bridge that they later use for the bridge in *I Want to Hold Your Hand*. In the *Anthology* film documentary, Paul demonstrates the happy-to-sad chord change in the verse, sitting at the piano, saying that it was something new for them.

Personal Notes

Thank You Girl

I really loved the B-side to this one, *Thank You Girl*, and I remember letting it spin around again and again while I read Isaac Asimov's *Fantastic Voyage*, which was also made into a 1966 movie, staring Raquel Welch. In the story, a medical swat team is put into a very cool futuristic submarine, then shrunken down to microscopic size and injected into a world renowned scientist's body to try to repair damage to his brain after he's shot in the head by a would-be assassin. The microscopic scenes inside the body are truly fantastic, and to this day when I hear *Thank You Girl* I still think about the book and the movie, and I can still see the beautiful Rachel Welch in that white wet suit and scuba gear, swimming around in the light-green plasma, and getting attacked by those nasty gangly yellow antibodies, all against an amazingly colorful backdrop of big bubbly blue-and-red corpuscles.

Beatles Moments

There are some spots in Beatles songs where everything amazing about them—the energy, the harmony, the song quality—all just comes together for a wonderful fleeting moment. In *From Me to You* there's a spot like this right when Paul comes in to harmonize with John on the words *I can do,* the first time at about 0:11.

The Details

The intro to this song starts off with a couple of lines of scat-nonsense syllables to create the hook, doubled by the harmonica and sung to a standard happy-to-sad pop chord change, with Ringo's fills leading into the first verse. It's early-Beatles high energy right from the start, singing in unison and then very quickly switching to beautifully blended harmony, all against a backdrop of Paul's slightly bouncy bass lines. At 0:11 there's a high-emotion harmony moment on the words *I can do,* with Paul singing on top and in falsetto. John really bites into the word *just* at 0:14. Then there's a little turnaround change, with guitar notes sliding down to a sad chord. At 0:27 you can hear that John and Paul sing different words, *just* and *so.* It's interesting to think that George Martin kept the recording as is, probably because it was such a good take. Another verse is repeated, this time John biting into the words *I got.*

At the bridge the feeling changes, the music a little softer and less intense, the band backing off the energy a little. It's John and Paul in unison first, and then in harmony, building up and ending with a very quick trademark *ooh,* which sounds like they had to rush a little to get it in. At the end of the bridge, the words *you satisfied* are sung with broader harmony, a bit like some of the harmonies in *Love Me Do.*

After a repeat of the first verse there's a short harmonica solo, which mimics the verse, but with an interesting alternating between harmonica notes and the title words *From Me* and *To You.* Then at 1:17, we come to the second time through the bridge, but with John and Paul also harmonizing the opening lines this time, which builds up more energy and emotion. The words here are delivered in very rich Everly Brothers country-western style harmony.

At 1:31 they sing the basic verse a third and last time, then three more repeated lines, alternating between harmonica and words as they did in the break earlier, and building up to the ending. The harmonica plays the hook theme underneath the last words, and the song finishes with a last downward change to a sad minor chord.

Timeline

1962—October 26: *Love Me Do* enters the UK Singles Chart ~December 17: George Martin sees the Beatles perform at the Cavern in Liverpool ~December 18: The band goes to Hamburg, Germany, again, for twelve shows at the Star-Club ~**1963**—January 11: The single *Please Please Me/Ask Me Why* is released ~February 22: *Please Please Me* spends 2 weeks at the top of several UK singles charts ~March 22: The Beatles' first album, *Please Please Me,* is released in the UK, hits the top spot, and stays for an unprecedented 30 weeks ~April 5: The Beatles are awarded a silver record for the single *Please Please Me* ~April 8: Julian Lennon is born ~

#3 *She Loves You*

This is the quintessential early-period hit that rocketed the Beatles into stardom in the UK. It gave rise to *Beatlemania* and forever associated the four lads from Liverpool with the three words *yeah, yeah, yeah*.

Release and Recording

UK Release: August 23, 1963
US Release: September 16, 1963
Recorded: July 1, 1963
Length: 2:18
B-side: *I'll Get You*

Charting

US: March 21, 1964, six months after it was released, *She Loves You* replaced the Beatles' own *I Want to Hold Your Hand*, which had been on top for 7 weeks. It stayed 2 weeks, and was then replaced by yet another one of their songs, *Can't Buy Me Love*, which held for 5 weeks, their third number 1 hit in a row.

UK: September 12, 1963, the first time the song went to the top, it replaced *Bad to Me*, by Billy J. Kramer and the Dakotas (written by John Lennon), which had been on top for 3 weeks. It stayed 4 weeks, and was then replaced by Brian Poole and the Tremeloes' *Do You Love Me*, which stayed on top for 3 weeks. *She Loves You* came back to the top a second time, on November 28, for another 2 weeks, replacing Gerry and the Pacemakers *You'll Never Walk Alone* (which became the anthem for the Liverpool F.C. soccer team), which had been on top for 4 weeks. *She Loves You* stayed in the UK charts for a total of 31 weeks.

The Beatles were rocketing to stardom. Their first album, *Please Please Me*, remained at number 1 for 30 weeks on the UK album chart only to be replaced by their next album, *With the Beatles*. *She Loves You* would become the bestselling Beatles single of all time and the bestselling single in the UK for all of the 1960s.

The Back Story

Like *From Me to You*, John and Paul supposedly started *She Loves You* on the bus, and then continued working on it later in the hotel, while they were touring with Roy Orbison and Gerry and the Pacemakers. They recorded it a week later. They also made a German-language version, *Sie Liebt Dich*, as they did for *I Want to Hold Your Hand*, because EMI Germany thought that was the only way it would sell in Germany.

George Martin supposedly didn't care for the last jazzy chord that *She Loves You* ends with, thinking it was too outdated and corny, but the Beatles convinced him otherwise.

She Loves You

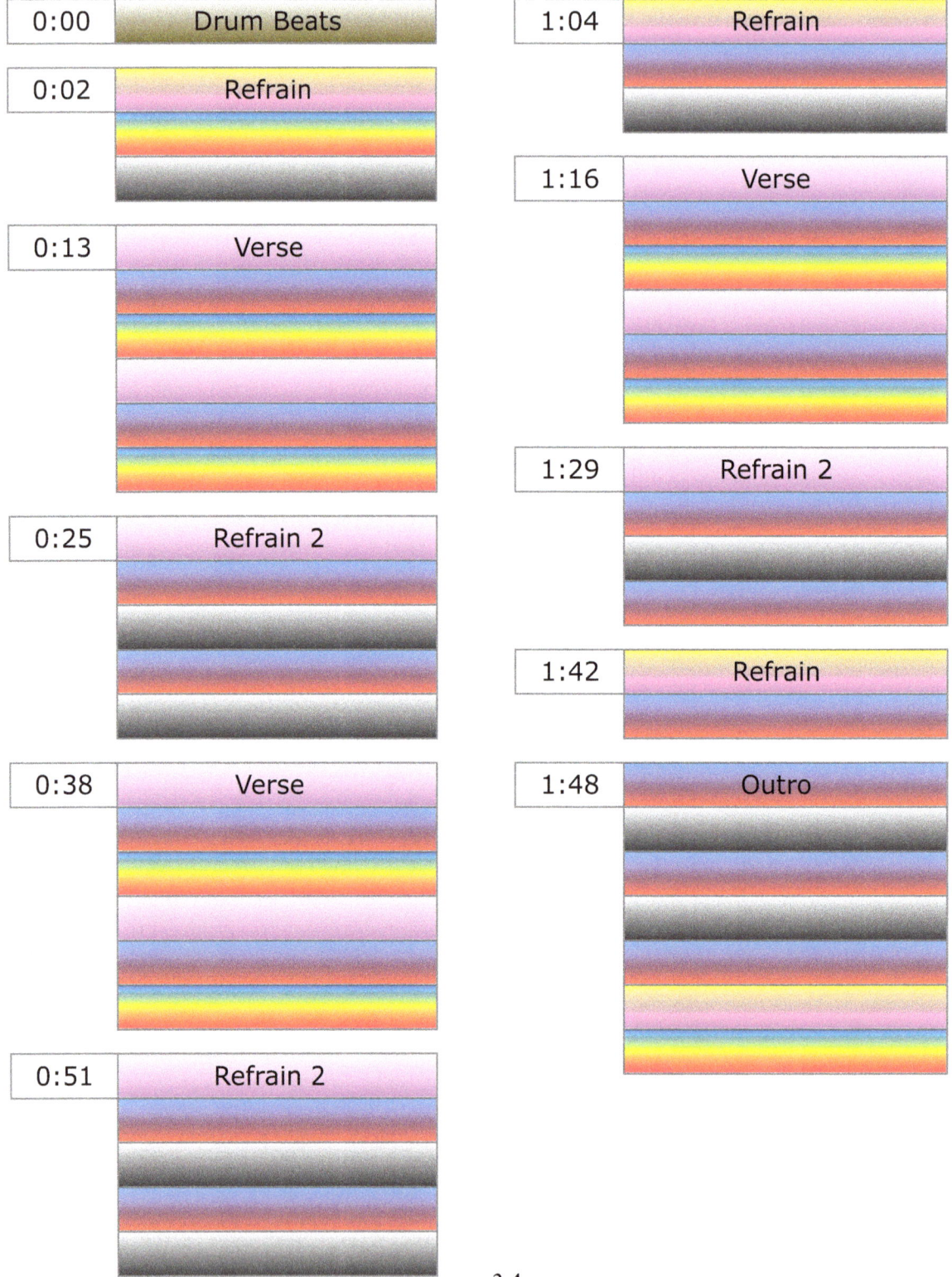

Song Map Legend

The Song Map

A look at the colors and recurring patterns in the song map show that this song was finely chiseled and very well thought out. Like in *From Me to You*, there's a lot of alternating between John and Paul in unison, and then in harmony, typically on a single word ending the line. But for this one, George comes in on the ending lines of the verse sections, resulting in brilliant and beautiful three-part harmony. There are lots of great guitar riffs and chords added in at just the right moments, and the song uses a full set of pop chords with constant, quickly paced shifting back and forth between happy energetic chords and sad sentimental ones. This song has no bridge and is shown here with two refrains, the main one being when they sing the title words and the three *yeah*s.

Personal Notes

She Loves You
I can still see the orange and yellow spiral on that Capitol 45 going around and around on our record player, with the little yellow plastic spider inserted into hole in the middle so we could play it on a 33-sized platter. Using the auto-replay feature on the record player, my brother and I played *She Loves You* over and over, never stopping it, and drove my parents and especially our poor babysitter totally crazy. We even made the babysitter sit and watch us lip synch the song while we air strummed away on brooms and baseball bats, over and over.

The Details

After a few quick pick-up beats on Ringo's tom-tom, John, Paul, and George jump right in, singing in unison, and belt out three repeated refrain lines. At 0:10, the last time around, the three voices finish with a beautiful third *yeah*, in three-part harmony (that's a lot of threes). They're really singing their hearts out and it's very high-energy from the start.

There's a great rocker-style guitar riff in this classic mix of pop and blues sounds, which leads John and Paul into the first verse. It's kind of a question-and-answer, call-and-response format, with a very specific and purposefully designed pattern. John and Paul sing most of a line in unison, but then harmonize on the last word, which, in the first verse, is *love*. Then George joins in, and they sing an answer in full harmony, using three syllables to sing the end of the word *yesterday-ee-yay*.

The harmonies are very rich and packed closely together. At 0:55, in the second refrain, there's a different and richer harmony on the word *bad* this time around. There's that little trademark stagger to Ringo's drum fills then three descending guitar chords, echoing the three *yeahs*, with the third and last chord a sad minor.

The second time through the verse, instead of ending with a moderate-energy guitar riff as they did the first time, they sing a high-energy harmonized Beatles *ooh*, which leads into a couple of refrain lines, then a few calm-down lines, with John and Paul holding to the close harmony.

After the third time through a verse, they sing two full refrain lines, and then repeat three *yeahs*, three times. The last time around, after a heartfelt multi-syllable buildup on *shou-ooh-ould be*, John, Paul, and George all join in to sing the word *glad* in high-energy unison. They finish things up with the guitar doing the three descending *yeah* chords, and then a brightly colored high-energy *yeah*, delivered in a jazzy sounding chord, and leaving us with only their richly harmonizing voices as the last sustained note in the song.

There are a lot of threes in this song. There are of course the three *yeahs*, and their echo in the three descending guitar chords, but the Beatles also begin the song with three refrain lines, sing three verses, and sing three repeated sections of the last verse, before the outro, which, with the guitar chords, has three last lines, ending on a word with three-part harmony.

This is a finely tuned and planned-out song, with very specific places chosen to sing in unison and then switch to bright harmony. The refrain and verse construction is varied and more sophisticated than in the previous hits. Ringo also gives a slight stagger on the drums throughout, which helps give the song a great beat.

Timeline

1963—April 14: The Beatles see the Rolling Stones at the Crawdaddy Club in London ~April 18: Paul meets Jane Asher ~April 28: Paul, George, and Ringo vacation in Tenerife; John and Brian Epstein go to Spain ~June 18: Paul's twenty-first birthday party ~August 3: The Beatles play their last show at the Cavern in Liverpool ~Summer: The Beatles move to London ~

#4 *I Want to Hold Your Hand*

The Beatles' first number 1 in the US, *I Want to Hold Your Hand* was the song that brought Beatlemania across the Atlantic, started the British Invasion, and launched the Beatles onto the world stage.

Release and Recording

UK Release: November 9, 1963
US Release: December 26, 1963
Recorded: October 17, 1963
Length: 2:24
UK B-side: *This Boy*
US B-side: *I Saw Her Standing There*

Charting

US: On February 1, 1964, *I Want to Hold Your Hand* replaced Bobby Vinton's *There I've Said It Again*, which had held the top spot for 4 weeks. It stayed a full 6 weeks, only to be replaced by *She Loves You*, (recorded and released before *I Want to Hold Your Hand*) which held for 2 weeks.

UK: On December 12, 1963, *I Want to Hold Your Hand* replaced the Beatles' own *She Loves You*, which had held the top spot for 2 weeks (its second time on top.) It stayed on top for 5 weeks, and was then replaced by the Dave Clark Five's *Glad All Over,* which held the top spot for 2 weeks.

The Back Story

I Want to Hold Your Hand was supposedly written in London, at the piano in the basement of Jane Asher's house where Paul was staying. Paul and John found and settled on an unusual sad-to-tragic chord change, which gave the song so much of its feeling. It was a monumental breakthrough moment for the band when they first heard, while in Paris, that *I Want to Hold Your Hand* was their first number 1 hit in the US. And as with *She Loves You*, they also recorded this one in German as *Komm Gib Mir Deine Hand.* There's also a story that Bob Dylan, and probably many others, thought they were singing *I get high*, instead of *I can't hide* at the end of the bridge.

I Want to Hold Your Hand

0:00	Intro
0:07	Verse
0:22	Refrain
0:28	Verse
0:43	Refrain
0:51	Bridge
1:10	Verse
1:26	Refrain
1:33	Bridge
1:53	Verse
2:08	Refrain
2:11	Outro

Song Map Legend

The Song Map

The arrangement is similar to *From Me to You*, with John and Paul singing the entire song together, alternating between unison and harmony, and again harmonizing at the end of each line. The first time through the bridge, they harmonize on just the last lines, but then they fully harmonize on all lines the next time. The twangy guitar intro and the catchy riffs after the first line in each verse are shown in gray. With the alternating unison and harmony pattern, the great guitar and bass riffs between the lines, and the heavy use of sentimental pop chords delivered in high energy, *I Want to Hold Your Hand* is very similar to *She Loves You*. These two songs together define the blockbuster formula that put the Beatles on the world stage.

Personal Notes

The Ed Sullivan Show
I'll never forget the buildup to the *Ed Sullivan Show* that had been going on all week, and I just couldn't wait. Beatles songs were flooding the radio air waves, and there were pictures of the band in all the newspapers and magazines (I remember my father saying they looked like girls). And on that magical Sunday night, February 9, they opened their first set with *All My Loving*, which always seemed like an odd choice to me, but they did end their second set with *I Want to Hold Your Hand*, after playing *She Loves You*. While we all saw them on our TVs in black and white, all the magazines and the flood of Beatle cards that came out afterward were in color, showing the bright blue stage in the Ed Sullivan theater in New York City. Even though they had appeared on the *Jack Paar Show* a month earlier, it was really the first time everybody saw them here in the US, and we heard all the stories about the huge TV audience of 70 million, and supposedly how no crime took place during their appearance. To be sure, music and so many other things were just never really the same again.

The Details

This one starts up with medium energy and builds up using a back-and-forth between two guitar chords that sound more rock than pop. After the intro, John and Paul break into the first verse in unison, against a steady backbeat to which handclaps have been added. If you try to count a regular beat off the intro, you get thrown off, as it's not quite a regular set of four or eight—it feels like there's an extra beat or two inserted just before the lyrics start.

The guitar chords and the first lyrics give the very beginning of the verse a rocker feeling, but then there's a quick shift to more of a pop sound, using a transition riff on the guitar and bass, followed by a twangy higher-end downward slide on lead guitar, before landing on a darker minor chord at 0:10, which does a lot to set the mood. After singing a few more lines in unison they hit a signature-Beatles high-pitched *hand*, and there's a whole new burst of energy. Then against a backdrop of some great drum fills they hit one of the most amazing Beatles passages of all time, singing a descending multi-syllable *ha-a-a-and*, in bright and fully colored harmony, with John's voice slightly prominent.

They repeat another verse, and then go into the bridge, more romantic pop than rocker, with John and Paul singing in unison. The energy drops way down in the bridge, backing off the guitars and drums and introducing a more personal, intimate feeling. But then at the end of the bridge, we hear the same chords from the into, with the same buildup of energy as John and Paul again join their voices in harmony.

After the first bridge, there's another verse-refrain-verse, but unlike in the first half of the song, they skip a refrain before going into the bridge again, which is a common technique to avoid monotony and increase a song's overall intensity.

The second time through the bridge, John and Paul sing all the lines in full harmony, adding more romantic energy and intimacy.

They sing one last verse (a repeat of the third verse) and then at 2:11, with John really biting into the words *I Wanna*, you can feel from the different chord and repeated higher-energy drum beats, that the end is coming. Against a backdrop of repeating and heavier drum beats, they sing the word *ha-a-a-a-a-and*, a full seven syllables, and finish, with a long-lasting fading chord, that tapers off, leaving a faint but sustained sound of ringing guitar strings.

Like *From Me to You* and *She Loves You*, this is another early and amazingly successful John and Paul collaboration, with high energy, beautiful harmonies, slick guitar riffs, and great drumming. The guitar and bass riffs between the verse lines really create a nice space and help build up energy. John's voice sounds a bit louder in the mix, with Paul's coming in very clear and adding a beautiful, youthful high energy to the two-part harmony sections.

This is a hallmark early-Beatles mix of rock 'n' roll/pop sounds and vocal arranging, with lines beginning in medium-energy unison, and finishing in beautiful high-energy harmony.

Timeline

1963—September 16: George Harrison visits his sister in the US ~October 13: The Beatles appear at the London Palladium ~October 31: After a tour in Sweden, the Beatles return to London's Heathrow Airport and thousands of fans where Ed Sullivan just happens to be passing through, which leads to the band playing on his show a few months later ~November 2: A headline in the UK *Daily Mirror* reads "BEATLEMANIA! It's happening everywhere…" ~November 4: The Beatles play for the Queen Mother, Princess Margaret, and other members of the Court at the *Royal Variety Performance* ~November 22: The second album, *With the Beatles*, is released ~November 29: The single *I Want to Hold Your Hand* is released ~December 4: US Capitol Records signs the Beatles ~

#5 Can't Buy Me Love

This first number 1 with only Paul singing is another classic mix of rock 'n' roll and pop. With a masterful guitar solo by George Harrison, it will forever recall the crazy soccer-field romp in the hit movie *A Hard Day's Night*.

Release and Recording

UK Release: March 20, 1964
US Release: March 16, 1964
Recorded: January 29, 1964
Length: 2:11
B-side: *You Can't Do That*

Charting

US: On April 4, 1964, *Can't Buy Me Love* replaced the Beatles' own *She Loves You*, which had been on top for 2 weeks, stayed for 5 weeks, then was replaced by Louis Armstrong's *Hello Dolly* which stayed on top for 1 week.

UK: On April 2, 1964, the song replaced *Little Children* by Billy J. Kramer and the Dakotas (also from Liverpool and managed by Brian Epstein), stayed for 3 weeks and was then replaced by Peter and Gordon's *A World without Love,* which stayed for 2 weeks and which incidentally John and Paul also wrote.

When *Can't Buy Me Love* hit number 1, the Beatles had the five top spots in the Billboard Hot 100 and fourteen in the top 100, something no other artist had ever done.

The Back Story

Most of *Can't Buy Me Love*, a Paul song, was written and recorded in Paris, on a piano in the band's room at the Hotel George V. The Beatles were doing an eighteen-show run at the Olympia theater. They supposedly tried the song with harmony first (I would *love* to hear what that sounded like) but then settled on having only Paul sing. They recorded part of the song in Paris, then finished it back in London. While they were in Paris, the band also worked on the German versions of *She Loves You* and *I Want to Hold Your Hand,* which they supposedly didn't want to bother with, but George Martin had insisted.

Can't Buy Me Love

Time	Section
0:00	Refrain
0:09	Verse
0:25	Verse
0:41	Refrain
0:54	Verse
1:11	Solo
1:28	Refrain
1:40	Verse
1:56	Outro

Song Map Legend

The Song Map

The lyrics here are all blue, with Paul singing everything on his own, and complemented by George's great guitar solo. Because there are no other Beatles singing, guitars are shown behind Paul's voice in the opening refrain, and then guitars and drums are shown in the rest of the song parts. The refrain, used to start the song, uses sad heartstring-pulling chords, but then ends with a happy uplifting change before settling into a classic rock 'n' roll verse. This is again a classic early-Beatles high-energy switch-up between driving rock 'n' roll and pop sentimentality in the same song.

Personal Notes

Guitars
This is one of the rare times on Beatles recordings that George plays a solo guitar break to a classic 12-bar rock 'n' roll progression, and he really nails it. Unlike so many other Beatles songs before and after, this one was actually pretty easy to learn, the break included, so as aspiring musicians, we could play along.

It was early 1964, and one of the best times ever to be alive, because after that first Ed Sullivan Show just about every kid in the US went out and got a guitar, or a bass, or drums, and started a band. For kids like me, guitars became just like hot cars—we could identify them by make and model, and we knew how much they cost. We had all the catalogs from Fender, Gibson, Epiphone, Gretsch, and others, and I remember just sitting and staring at all those beautiful pictures for hours at a time, and wanting those guitars *so bad*.

The Details

The song starts with Paul's heavily double-tracked voice, really belting out the words to the refrain, with no intro at all. There's a high-energy backdrop of John's big full strums on acoustic guitar and George's sparser and more fractured chords on electric. The drums come in on the verse, and the band settles into a classic three-chord 12-bar rock 'n' roll progression with a solid backbeat. This song, along with *The Ballad of John and Yoko,* are the only two Beatles hits that use a progression like this. There's a great stop-start gimmick the first time around, at 0:20, where Paul sings the word *too* followed by an abrupt pause and then *much for money.* Then there's another little pause before he gets back into the swing of things.

The refrain is unlike the main body of the song—these are not rock 'n' roll chords, but in classic early-Beatles fashion, they switch to a more emotional pop-chord progression with some sad minors in the mix. Then things transition smoothly back to the rock 'n' roll vibe at the end, building up the energy with the string of *nos*, and Paul biting into the word *say* when the third verse begins. It's interesting to listen to how simple Paul's bouncy bass lines are in this song, as many other bass players would have loaded up this classic rock 'n' roll number with a lot more notes.

Paul takes us one more time through the verse and then gives a raw crazy scream at 1:10, which launches George into one of his best early guitar solos. The much sharper tone of his guitar cuts deep through the backdrop wash of drums and rhythm guitar. This wonderful rockabilly break is a nice mix of both lead notes and chords, with lots of note-bending and finishing off with a great bluesy slide and riff at 1:26. If you listen carefully you can hear the ghostly echoes of an older and similar guitar break, recorded earlier in Paris, especially around 1:19, that stayed in the mix. You can also just barely hear the word *hey* around 1:27.

There's another refrain after this, Paul singing only *Buy Me Love*, without the *Can't*, to change things up just a little. After a fourth time through the verse, and a slightly altered refrain with different chords, the band ends the song with Paul singing a bluesy *oh* at the tail end of the world *love*.

The use of rock 'n' roll–sounding verses in this high-energy number, contrasting with the more pop-sounding emotional bridge, is a yet again a classic characteristic of the early Beatles. And oddly enough, there's no harmony at all in this one and there's only one Beatle singing. It's also the first of only a few number 1s with a guitar solo.

Timeline

1964—January 10: The album *Introducing the Beatles* is released in the US ~January 16: *I Want to Hold Your Hand* reaches the number 1 spot in the US ~January 20: The album *Meet the Beatles* is released in the US ~February 4: German versions of *She Loves You* and *I Want to Hold Your Hand* are released ~February 7: The Beatles land at JFK Airport in New York City to thousands of screaming fans ~February 9: The Beatles make their first appearance on the *Ed Sullivan Show* ~February 11: The Beatles perform in Washington, DC ~ February 12: The Beatles perform at Carnegie Hall in New York City ~ February 18: The Beatles visit Cassius Clay ~March 2: The filming of *A Hard Day's Night* begins ~

#6 A Hard Day's Night

The chord heard round the world, played (mainly) on George's beautiful 12-string electric red-to-yellow sunburst Rickenbacker, will forever be associated with the beginning of a great black-and-white movie in which we really get to spend a day in the life with the four lads from Liverpool.

Release and Recording

UK Release: July 10, 1964
US Release: July 13, 1964
Recorded: April 16, 1964
Length: 2:32
UK B-side: *Things We Said Today*
US B-side: *I Should Have Known Better*

Charting

US: On August 1, 1964, *A Hard Day's Night* replaced *Rag Doll* by the Four Seasons, which had been on top for 2 weeks. It stayed for 2 weeks, and was then replaced by Dean Martin's *Everybody Loves Somebody*, which was on top for 1 week. The song ended up winning a Grammy for Best Performance by a Vocal Group.

UK: On July 23, 1964, the song replaced *It's All Over Now* by the Rolling Stones, which had been on top for 1 week. It held for 3 weeks, and was then replaced by Manfred Mann's *Do Wah Diddy Diddy*, which stayed for 2 weeks.

This was also the first time a group had both a top single and a top album on both sides of the Atlantic.

The Back Story

A Hard Day's Night was John's first time singing solo on a number 1. The title was inspired by something funny Ringo had said (he was supposedly always saying things like this), and the song was said to have been written in just one night. The band needed one last song for the film: the title number. That they could bang out a song of this quality on demand goes to show how incredibly creative and productive the band was at this time.

George Martin played the electric-piano break, which seems crazy—a music producer sitting in and playing along with a group like this. (Martin also did this on *In My Life* and a few other numbers.) And because the tempo of the song was so fast, he played it at half the speed, an octave lower, then doubled the playback speed and spliced it in.

A Hard Day's Night

Time	Section
0:00	Guitar Chord
0:02	Verse
0:23	Verse
0:43	Bridge
0:58	Verse
1:19	Solo ~
1:33	Verse
1:39	Bridge
1:54	Verse
2:15	Outro / Fade Out

Song Map Legend

Guitar
John
John, Paul, Harmony
Paul
Piano

The Song Map

After the big opening guitar chord, John sings two verses, with Paul coming in to harmonize on a couple of lines in the middle, adding considerable energy to the mix. Paul sings the bridges on his own. The verses are very bluesy, the beginning lines a little laid back, but in contrast the bridge is very heartfelt and sentimental. There are solid rock 'n' roll breaks on both electric piano and guitar and a beautiful sparkling fade-out on guitar for the outro. Because of the contrast between the verse and bridge, and like *Can't Buy Me Love*, *A Hard Day's Night* is the very definition of Blue Notes and Sad Chords.

Personal Notes

Pizza and a Drive-In Movie
I was eight years old, and one August night my whole family went out to see *A Hard Day's Night* at a local drive-in theater. We had dinner first: the best pizza in the world (even today), at Joe's Café in Northampton, Massachusetts. I got quarters from my dad to play *A Hard Day's Night* on the brightly lit juke box. I played it over and over again. Then the movie was so great, seeing the Beatles like that, talking, joking, being themselves, and of course all the great music scenes. I always thought it was funny that they kept the footage of George falling down, then Ringo falling on him, right in the opening scene, after the big wonderful chord, when they're running down the sidewalk to get away from the crowd of crazy screaming fans.

The Details

Volumes have been written about the famous chord. It creates a great and very sudden beginning, winding things up like a sling shot, and all that energy is released when John starts in on the first verse. It's one of those chords that has a lot of extra or extended notes that aren't part of a basic three-note stack—it's really multiple chords at once. And if you listen carefully, it's not just guitar, but many other instruments too, including piano and bass.

The first lines of the verse are sung by John, his voice doubled, with a very bluesy rock 'n' roll feel. The words *dog* and *log* are sung with beautiful Lennon multi-syllable blues inflections. The energy is already upbeat, but it gets a serious boost when Paul joins in, singing in rich harmony for a few lines, the notes rising, the lyrics packed closely together with urgency. It's like they can't get the words out fast enough, they've got no time to lose. Then things calm down slightly when John sings the last lines alone again. And if you listen closely to the drums you'll hear lots of sections where Ringo is playing high-energy double-time fills throughout the verse, (listen to the turnaround at 0:22) which adds to the song's amazing energy and pace.

There's another verse, and it sounds like John sings *thing* instead of *things* at 0:29, maybe to match when he sings it again at the end of *everything* at 0:36.

Then with a major shift in feeling, Paul comes in on the bridge, his voice also double-tracked, and it's a sad plaintive pop section, no longer rock 'n' roll. Ringo helps the change here by adding in a very steady and less frantic cowbell. And Paul really bites into the second *home* at 0:51, setting things up for a feel-good resolution at the end of the bridge, where tension is again built up and released when John starts the third verse. The transition and resolution from this more emotional part back into the higher-energy rock 'n' roll verse is all very uplifting.

At 1:20, after the third verse, there's a great instrumental break, solid rock 'n' roll style, played on both guitar and electric piano, shadowing the first lines of the verse, accentuating the beat of this great driving song, and played against a full rhythmic backdrop. And like the verse, it has a little call-and-response pattern, with the notes of the call at one energy level and spacing, and the response, a much faster and densely packed set of notes.

The bridge is repeated again at 1:40, and this time around the John's *righ-ight* is two syllables. Another great part of this second time through the bridge is John's bluesy humming moan overlapping with Paul's *yeah* at 1:53.

Then there's a fourth verse, and then the outro, with two sung lines repeating the last *feel all right* of the verse, letting the energy down. Before the last *all right* is over, the beautiful fade-out on George's 12-string Rickenbacker starts, picking a repeating pattern of whirling and echoing fine-grained notes, sounding a little bit like the opening chord but a little more major-scale and happy, maybe less ominous, more pop than rock. And if the first opening chord was the start of an explosion, and the song the major blast, this fade-out is all the pieces and dust settling back down to earth.

With the famous chord, the high energy, the beautiful contrast of a driving rock 'n' roll verse and the sadder pop bridge, really great drum fills, the killer instrumental break, and the beautiful fade-out, *A Hard Day's Night* is an amazing song, and fitting as the title piece to the first, and perhaps the best, of the Beatles' movies.

Timeline

1964—March 23: John's book *In His Own Write* is published ~April 4: The Beatles have the top five spots on the Billboard Hot 100 ~June 3: Ringo has tonsillitis, drummer Jimmie Nicol fills in for him at the start of a world tour ~June 14: Ringo rejoins the band in Australia ~July 6: The film *A Hard Day's Night* premieres in London ~July 10: The Beatles are welcomed back to their home city of Liverpool with much fanfare and the album *A Hard Day's Night* is released ~

#7 *I Feel Fine*

In *I Feel Fine*, John leaned his guitar up against an amp while it was still plugged in, resulting in one of the first uses of feedback in a recorded hit song. This number also features a great Lennon guitar riff, a classic mixture of bluesy rock and pop, and beautiful three-part harmonies.

Release and Recording

UK Release: November 27, 1964
US Release: November 23, 1964
Recorded: October 18, 1964
Length: 2:25
B-side: *She's a Woman*

Charting

US: On December 26, 1964, *I Feel Fine* knocked the Supremes' *Come See about Me* out of the top slot, which had held for a single week. It stayed for 3 weeks and then *Come See About Me* came back for another week.

UK: On December 10, 1964, the song knocked the Rolling Stones' *Little Red Rooster* out of first place, which had held for a single week. It stayed for 5 weeks. It was then replaced by Georgie Fame and the Blue Flames' *Yeh Yeh*, which held for 2 weeks.

The Back Story

Legend has it that John leaned his jumbo acoustic guitar (you might think it was electric from the sound) against an amp, creating the feedback. The Kinks and the Who had done this in live shows, but this was supposedly the first time feedback ended up on a record.

The guitar riff was supposedly inspired by the 1961 Bobby Parker song *Watch Your Step*, and the drumming by Ray Charles' *What'd I Say*. The Beatles had played both of these songs in their earlier days.

I Feel Fine

0:00	Feedback and Riff

0:16	Verse

0:29	Verse

0:43	Bridge

0:53	Verse

1:07	Solo and Riff

1:25	Verse

1:39	Bridge

1:49	Verse

2:08	Outro

Fade Out

Song Map Legend

The Song Map

After the feedback and signature guitar riff, John sings the first lines of the verse alone, but then Paul and George join in to end the verse in full-bodied three-part harmony. The last line of the verse functions like a mini-refrain. The bridge is also loaded with brilliant harmony and backing vocals, and like so many other Beatles songs, uses more emotional and sentimental chords than the verse. There's a rock 'n' roll–style guitar break based on the riff and then another verse, bridge, and verse. The outro is simple, with John simply ad-libbing some very laid-back and bluesy *mms* and guitar licks. The intro riff, verses, and guitar break are all classic three-chord rock 'n' roll. In trademark Beatles style, and like *Can't Buy Me Love* and *A Hard Day's Night*, the bridge shifts emotional gears, sounding more sentimental, like high-speed doo-wop.

Personal Notes

Grand Bar Chord

When you're learning how to play the electric guitar, there's a big moment—sort of a rite of passage—when you realize you can finally make what is called a *grand bar chord*, and John's wonderful *I Feel Fine* hook is played out of one. With a grand bar chord under your belt, you can play chords all up and down the neck of the guitar. Trying to play this *I Feel Fine* riff is what led to my finally getting the grand bar chord down.

First Electric Guitar

I played my first grand bar chord on my first electric guitar, a canary yellow Epiphone Coronet. It had a single wide steel-plated pickup and the trademark E logo, like the symbol for a Euro, on a white pick-guard shaped like a miniature stretched-out bearskin. Up until this point, my guitar teacher (and the original owner of my Coronet) had been teaching me songs like Ray Charles' *What'd I Say*, and *Gloria* (actually written by Van Morrison but immortalized by the Shadows of Knight), as well as *Tom Dooley*, which had been a late 1958 Kingston Trio hit and *Louie Louie*, the 1963 hit by the Kingsmen—because they were so easy to play. He was a great teacher, and I'll never forget the way he'd bob his head up and down, lit cigarette in his mouth, eyes squinting through the smoke, while rocking away to *What'd I Say*.

The Details

The famous guitar feedback note starts with a softer bassier tone, but then gets very sharp and piercing, like a buzz-saw, until it blends into the smooth-as-glass softer, yet highly rhythmic, guitar riff. If you listen carefully you can hear some weird little rattling noises in the background. The main guitar hook is repeated four times, one for each of the classic rocker chords, 5-4-1, in descending order, with an extra one at the bottom, back in the home 1 chord. There's some great staggered drumming by Ringo, and then the lyrics to the first verse begin.

John's voice is double-tracked, there's a little delayed inflection on *hap-py* to goose the beat, and on the fourth line of the verse there's an explosion of three-part harmony, descending and echoing the guitar. The verse finishes with a drawn-out and upward-sliding *fine*, and the tail end of the guitar riff.

After going through another verse, which John ends with a bluesy multi-syllable *mmm*, the band launches into brilliant three-part harmony to start the bridge, with John then singing the lyrics again while Paul and George create a beautiful emotional backdrop of two drawn-out *oohs*.

After another verse, there's a guitar break, with George doing lots of rockabilly sounding slides and then coming back to the main riff, with both George and John playing. John then plays the main three-chord descending set of riffs (listen to Ringo's great little drumming break in at 1:21).

At 1:25 it's another verse, repeating the lyrics from the second verse of the song, and then into the bridge again. The band takes us one last time through the verse, with an extra last line of harmony at 2:03, then John lets out another couple of those bluesy wailing *mms*, against the guitar riff backdrop, and the song fades away.

The three-part harmonies are beautiful in this one, and as with so many other Beatles songs, the rock 'n' roll feeling of the verses and guitar licks drops out dramatically in the bridge, where we hear a more emotional and lovestruck-sounding set of chords along with even richer harmonies, with Paul distinctly on top. In our progression through the number 1s, this is the fullest and richest three-part harmony to date. And this is another one that features John, with several more to follow in this Lennon-dominated period.

Timeline

1964—August 11: *A Hard Day's Night* is shown in the US theaters ~August 18: The Beatles begin a twenty-five-show tour of the US and Canada ~August 28: The Beatles meet and smoke pot with Bob Dylan ~December 2: Ringo has his tonsils removed ~December 4: The album *Beatles for Sale* is released ~

#8 Eight Days a Week

A lot of songs have a fade-out at the end, but this one has a fade-in at the beginning. With bright ringing guitar chords, handclaps, and some great harmonies, this is a feel-good song, and even though John supposedly didn't like it that much, there's great upbeat energy in his voice.

Release and Recording

UK Release: Wasn't released as a single; appeared on the *Beatles for Sale* album, released December 4, 1964
US Release: February 15, 1965
Recorded: October 6 and 8, 1964
Length: 2:44
B-side: *I Don't Want to Spoil the Party*

Charting

US: On March 13, 1965, *Eight Days a Week* knocked *My Girl* by the Temptations out, which had been at the top for 1 week. It stayed 2 weeks and was then replaced by the Supremes' *Stop! In the Name of Love*, which also stayed for 2 weeks. This was the last of seven songs to hit number 1 in the US in a record-breaking single year run.

UK: No charting, as it wasn't released as a single.

The Back Story

This song is a bit unusual in that it was written primarily by Paul but the lead vocals are sung by John. And like *A Hard Day's Night*, the title supposedly comes from another one of Ringo's funny expressions. The band didn't think the song was that good, and it does sound a bit sugary compared with what came before it. Also, with this song and many to follow, they didn't have the whole thing worked out before the recording session, so they finished it when they came into the studio.

Eight Days a Week

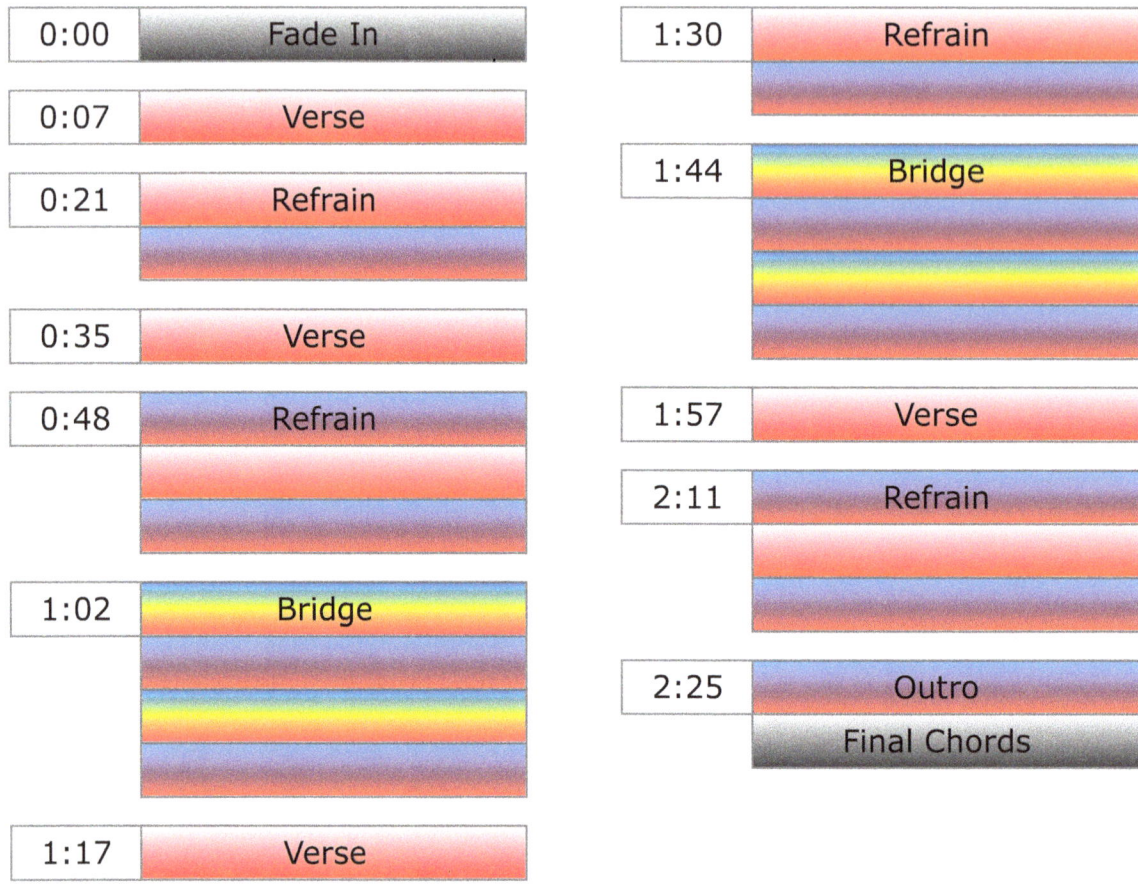

Song Map Legend

Guitar
John
John, Paul, Harmony
John, Paul, George, Harmony

The Song Map

This number features John as lead vocalist, with Paul coming in to harmonize on the refrain, and both Paul and George harmonizing on the bridge. It is much more pop than rock and blues, with plenty of sentimental chords used throughout. After the guitar fade-in, John sings the entire first verse alone. In the refrain, Paul joins in to harmonize for most of the beginning and for the title lyrics at the end. After another verse and refrain Paul and George join in to harmonize with John on the bridge and sing some very widely spaced and full-bodied harmonies. In the second half of the song, there's only one verse and refrain before the bridge. (Getting to the bridge sooner as a song progresses is a common pattern used to keep interest and build up intensity.) The outro is a simple repetition of the title lyrics in full harmony, and ends with the same chords that were used for the intro.

Personal Notes

Eight-Day Weeks
The French actually do say eight days, *huit jours*, to mean a week, and fifteen days, *quinze jours*, to mean two weeks. So maybe Ringo subconsciously picked up on this when the band was in France, and that's where the song's title came from.

This French thing is not surprising when you look at the way they put numbers together for counting above sixty. Seventy-nine is sixty-nineteen, *soixante-dix-neuf* and eighty is four-twenty, *quatre-vingt,* and so on. It's pretty amazing to think that the people who gave us Descartes, Impressionism, and Debussy have continued to count in this ancient way, not using any number words greater than the Babylonian sixty.

English Harmony
The broad droning harmonies used in the bridge in *Eight Days a Week* sound like what you might hear in an old English folk song, and are also a bit like the widely spaced harmony in *Love Me Do*. Beatle harmonies also frequently break what are considered musical rules, established back in the sixteenth and seventeenth centuries and codified in the early eighteenth century by luminaries such as Jean-Philippe Rameau (French again), in his *Treatise on Harmony,* 1722. These rules say that singers should never do things like cross voices, move in what are called parallel fourths and fifths, or get too far apart. The Beatles broke these rules all the time, and still sounded great.

The Details

This is the only number 1 hit with a fade-in, which in itself is very rare. From out of the silence, we hear the four-chord sequence rising in volume and building up the energy, starting and ending on the

1-home chord against a full drumroll backdrop, setting the stage with bright enthusiastic energy.

John starts the lyrics of the first verse as the tempo from the buildup intro shifts into to a steady, bouncy vibe with hand claps against a very solid backbeat. It's not as obvious at the start that John's voice is double-tracked on this song too. It sounds like Paul comes in for the refrain at 0:21 but the two voices together are so similar and in tight unison in the mix, it almost sounds like John is double-tracked until the two voices harmonize on the title lyrics *Eight Days a Week*. John sings another verse, then Paul comes in on the refrain again, singing harmony on the first line, adding a slight feeling of urgency with some unexpected notes, really changing the feeling. John still sings the second line alone, and then Paul comes back in to harmonize on the third line as before.

In the bridge at 1:02, they quiet things down and there's a little drop in energy, with John, Paul, and George singing in very broad droning harmony, the pitches in their voices far apart. Then there's a pause as the drumming and guitars drop out, leaving only John and Paul singing a five-syllable *lo-o-o-o-ove* against only a thumping single-note bass line in the back. At 1:09 Ringo adds in a great delayed, right-at-the-last-minute couple of beats, releasing some tension and helping to separate the bridge into two distinct parts. Then the energy builds again with deep harmonies into a climax, and lands back into the beginning of the third verse.

In the third time through the verse, we hear a classic beautiful and soulful multi-syllable Lennon *oh-oh* at 1:29. The refrain after the third verse reverts back to the simpler first version with no harmony on the first line, with John really biting into the word *ain't* at 1:37. There's another bridge and then a last refrain, which morphs into the outro. John and Paul sing the title line three times in harmony, and the song ends with a repeat of the four-chord progression that started the song, then a definite and final chord with a cymbal crash and a long sustaining bass note.

Timeline

1965—January 20: Ringo Starr proposes to Maureen Cox ~February 11: Ringo and Maureen Cox are married ~February 23: The Beatles start filming their second movie, *Help*, in the Bahamas ~March 14: The Beatles begin filming scenes for *Help* in Austria ~

#9 Ticket to Ride

This slower number is a floating mix of blues and pop. It has the Beatles' trademark alternation between unison and harmony, classic soulful Lennon *aghs*, and great guitar work, including the country-sounding licks in the outro.

Release and Recording

UK Release: April 9, 1965
US Release: April 19, 1965
Recorded: February 15, 1965
Length: 3:10
B-side: *Yes It Is*

Charting

US: On May 22, 1965, *Ticket to Ride* replaced *Mrs. Brown You've Got a Lovely Daughter*, by Herman's Hermits, which had held for 3 weeks. It stayed for 1 week and was then replaced by the Beach Boys' *Help Me, Rhonda*.

UK: On April 22, 1965, the song replaced *The Minute You're Gone* by Cliff Richard, which had been on top for 1 week. It stayed for 3 weeks and was then replaced by Roger Miller's *King of the Road*, which stayed for a single week.

The Back Story

This was supposedly a John song although there was some disagreement between John and Paul about contribution. It was included on the *Help* album and played in the movie. According to John, the song is about prostitutes in Hamburg, Germany, getting a clean-bill-of-health card, while Paul said it was named for a rail ticket to the town of Ryde on the Isle of Wight.

Ticket to Ride

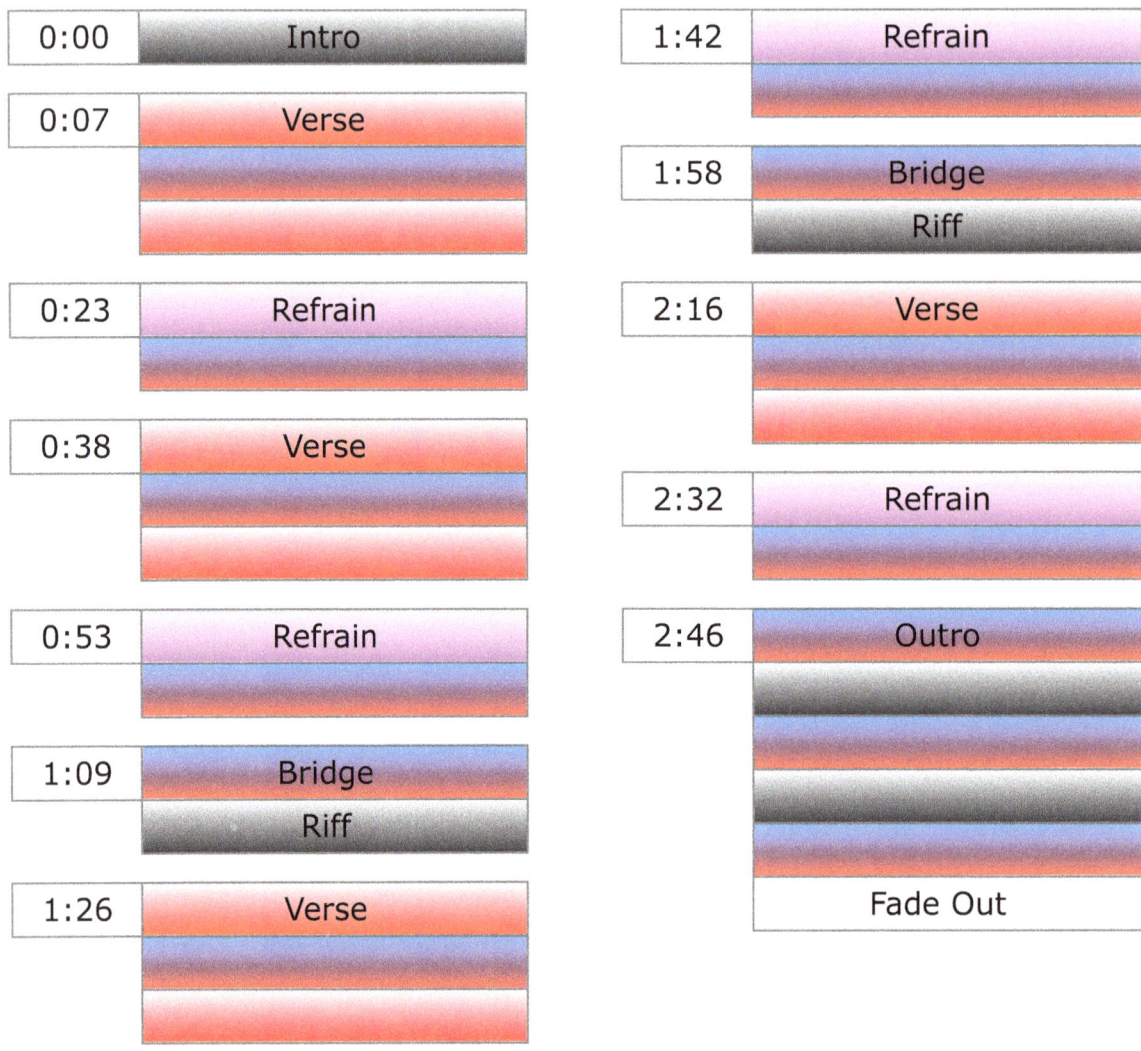

Song Map Legend

Guitar
John
John, Paul, Harmony
John, Paul, Unison

The Song Map

This one is all red, red-blue blend, and purple, with John singing lead and Paul singing in harmony or unison along with him. After the guitar intro, John begins the verse alone, with Paul coming in to harmonize in the middle, then John singing alone again for the last line. They sing the first lines of the refrain in unison but the last line is finished in harmony. The bridge has John and Paul in full harmony on every line and finishes with a strident guitar riff. The verse and refrain are a balanced blend of rock and pop chords, while the bridge is less sentimental, with a quicker pace and more energy. There's no instrumental break and a very simple outro, with John and Paul alternating between high-pitched unison and harmony, and some squawky guitar licks.

Personal Notes

John Lennon's Voice
The bluesy, sighing inflections we hear so often in John Lennon's singing are amazingly soulful and are a key aspect of what sets him, and the Beatles, apart from everybody else. Listen to the *aghs* here in *Ticket to Ride* at the beginnings of the refrains, or to the way he bites into the words in *You're Going to Lose That Girl*. It's unusual in covers, but if you listen to the Beatles' versions of Motown-style hits like the Marvelettes' 1961 *Please Mr. Postman* or Smokey Robinson and the Miracles' 1962 *You've Really Got a Hold on Me* you can hear an extra sort of energy in John Lennon's voice, a certain something that you don't even find in the originals—he just had it. I've always wished that the Beatles had recorded another early-period album with lots more girl-group or Motown covers on it. The spots in *Please Mr. Postman*, with Paul and George singing high-energy harmonized backing vocals behind John's lead, are among my all-time favorite Beatles moments.

Girl Voices
The high register *oohs* in songs like *From Me to You* and *She Loves You* were one thing, but in the *Ticket to Ride* outro, the Beatles sing in very high-pitched voices. As a young boy growing up in the 1960s, I thought this was unmanly but I also thought that for some reason, which did not apply to other male artists, it was okay for the Beatles to do.

The Details

George opens the song with a bright guitar hook on his 12-string Rickenbacker. Ringo does a roll right away then sets a lazy laid-back pace with a staggered beat along with tambourine in the mix, which gives the song a rhythmically floating and suspended feeling. John's voice is not double-tracked here in the first line of the verse. Paul jumps right in to harmonize on the end of the phrase *today yeah* with a high wailing country-western sound, and he's really laying into it.

The title words in the refrain are less bluesy and more pop-sounding, a little more urgent and with a kind of weary sadness. At the end of the refrain Paul harmonizes the last line, and then things settle back into the lazier bluesy feeling.

After another verse and refrain, the song moves into a faster, bluesy, and heavily harmonized bridge. The words are packed closely together, the harmonies are tight, and there's more of a backbeat. The bridge contains a three-line pattern sung twice, and then the tension builds up and is released at the end, with a great guitar riff, some heavy and quick low-note chords-as-beats, and drum fills.

Next, in the second half, to mix things up a bit, the band sings only a single verse and refrain before the bridge. Again, going into the bridge sooner this second time around happens in lots of songs and helps to build up emotional tension and keep things interesting. John adds a classic sad soulful descending *agh* at 1:42, and then again at 2:32 when the refrain begins again.

After the last refrain, the instruments cut out for a split second as the voices sing *my baby don't*, and then the whole band comes back in for the faster-paced outro, with a beat much like the bridge. At first, John and Paul sing in high falsetto voices, but then they zoom back down quickly into their normal vocal ranges. The guitar does a set of rockabilly riffs with lots of twangy bended notes and double strings, and then the whole thing fades away.

Timeline

1965—April 13: The Beatles are awarded a Best Performance by a Vocal Group Grammy for *A Hard Day's Night* ~April 14: Paul McCartney buys a new house in St. John's Wood, London ~ May 26: The Beatles final BBC radio session takes place ~June 12: The Beatles are named Members of the Order of the British Empire ~June 20: The Beatles begin a European tour in Paris ~June 24: John Lennon's book *A Spaniard in the Works* is published ~

#10 *Help*

Help was another hit title song for both an album and a movie, and supposedly a personal plea from John Lennon that things weren't going so well. It was the first number 1 that wasn't about romantic love. It was a new kind of song with interesting lyrics, a very elaborate vocal arrangement, unusual chords, and beautiful instrumentation.

Release and Recording

UK Release: July 23, 1965
US Release: July 19, 1965
Recorded: April 13, 1965
Length: 2:18
B-side: *I'm Down*

Charting

US: On September 4, 1965, *Help* replaced *I Got You Babe*, by Sonny and Cher, which had been at the top spot for 3 weeks. It stayed 3 weeks, and was then replaced by Barry McGuire's *Eve of Destruction*, which held for 1 week.

UK: On August 5, 1965, *Help* replaced *Mr. Tambourine Man* by the Byrds, which had been on top for 2 weeks. It stayed 3 weeks and was then replaced by *I Got You Babe*, by Sonny and Cher, which stayed for 2 weeks.

The Back Story

John said in an interview with *Playboy Magazine* that he was feeling fat and depressed and was crying out for help, struggling with the band's meteoric rise to fame and the disappearance of normal life. This song is so elaborately arranged, we can imagine it took the band a while to get it right. It's sophisticated and complex, and it's the last in a series of five early-period hits where John sings lead vocals. Among the number 1 hits, this song ends the early period of Lennon dominance. After this, most songs have Paul on lead, with John singing lead on only three more out of the seventeen that follow. It's interesting to note that this song was used to open the *Anthology* documentary film episodes, the camera starting with a shot of the four, then zooming out and away, the Beatles getting smaller and smaller.

Help

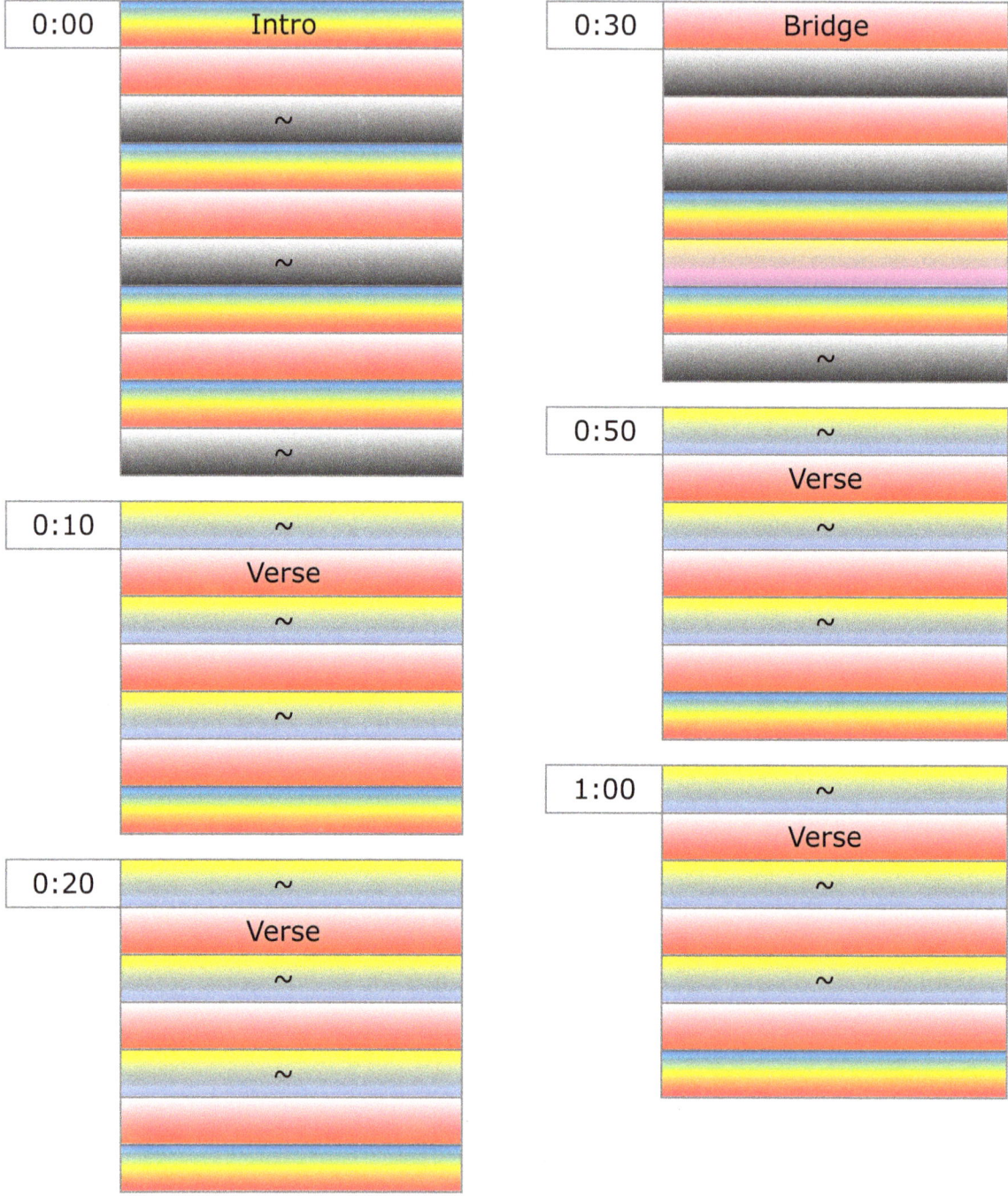

SECTION 2 : THE SONGS

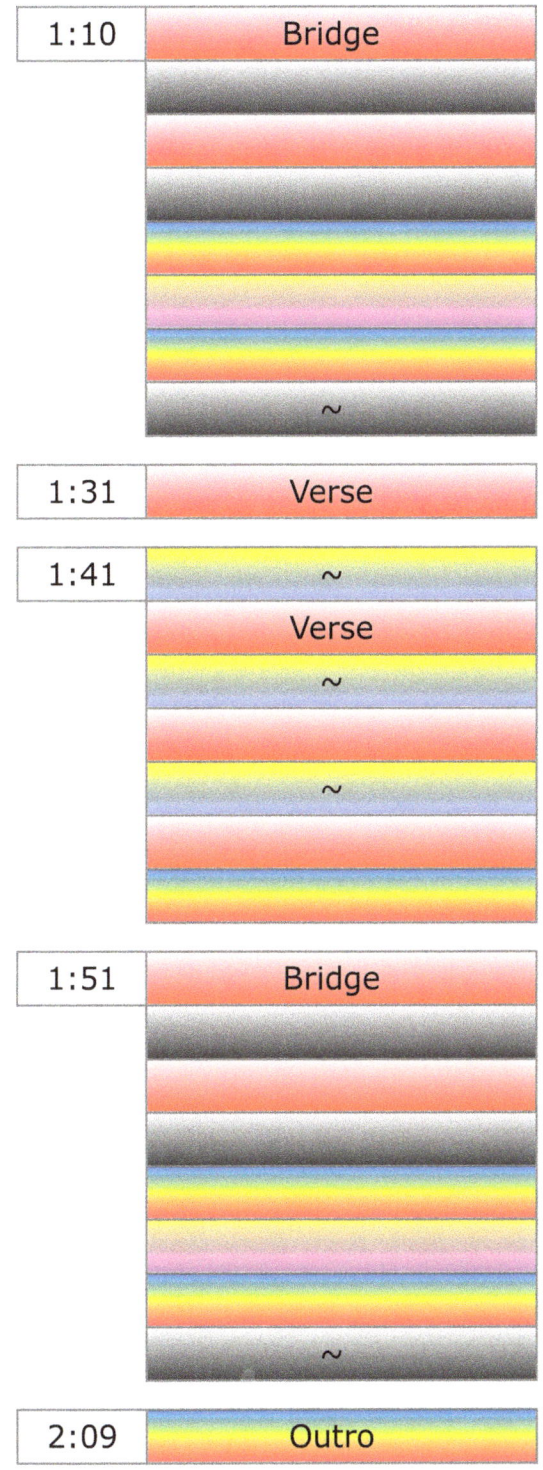

Song Map Legend

John, Paul, George, Harmony
John
Guitar
Paul, George, Harmony
John, Paul, George, Unison

The Song Map

A quick glance at the color patterns in this map shows that the song was carefully designed and planned out. Like the other songs in this Lennon-dominated period, it's chiefly red, but with lots of three-part harmony. Paul and George also do a great deal of harmonizing, in a blue-yellow fade, in the backing vocals with a staggered offset against the lead singing. The chords are primarily pop or folk-ballad sounding, not really rock or blues at all, and they come together to form a very unusual, original progression. The outro is a short and fully harmonized *help me ooh*. The rapid-fire intro and the slower refrain both use the same frantic-sounding four-chord sequence that builds up the energy and then ends unusually by settling into the song's home chord.

Personal Notes

The Second Movie

I suppose like many others, I thought that while the album was incredible, the movie *Help* just wasn't as good as *A Hard Day's Night*. There was something disjointed and maybe a little silly about it. But after all, it was the Beatles, and it still had its moments—the music scenes were great, of course. The story goes that the band had started smoking lots of pot at around this time, which doesn't seem too farfetched in some of the scenes. That said, it did look like they were having fun.

Fashion

It was right around when the album *Help* came out that the crazy 1960s changes in how kids looked really started to kick in. Teenage boys went from being shocked by the long hair of four lads from Liverpool a year before to growing their own hair long, and some of them even bought pointy black Beatle boots. Teenage girls and young women were all now wearing super short miniskirts, which were terribly shocking to parents but so wondrously distracting for a young boy. Things changed even more over the next couple years. Bell-bottom pants came into vogue. And who can forget the designs on the dresses and shirts? Wild polka-dots of all sizes, brightly glowing colors, highly detailed *paisley* patterns, named after a textile producing town in western Scotland, but originally an ornately stylized version of a fig or an almond of Persian origin. Carnaby Street in London became all the rage, setting the flamboyant styles. The way people looked would never be the same. I remember our school principal and teachers measuring the lengths of both skirts and sideburns for compliance with dress codes.

The Details

The beginning of the song is a sudden burst, with an urgent *Help* sung by John, Paul, and George in full harmony. The tension rises as they repeat *Help* three times, intermittingly sandwiching John's solo lines in a call-and-response pattern with Paul and George. John's voice is double-tracked, and he really bites into the words *I need* in the first line. As they move through the lines of the refrain, the energy rises, against a backdrop of repeated thumping bass notes, heavily slashed chords on John's jumbo acoustic guitar, and George's descending and sustained three-note guitar riffs. At the end of the refrain, the tension is released with Paul and George singing in high falsetto, and like fireworks, the descending guitar passages sparkle and float back down, setting the stage for the calmer, more personal self-reflective verse.

The verse is an elaborate interweaving of lines, actually starting with Paul and George's backing vocals, John echoing and emphasizing what they're singing, against a progression of sad pop chords. John's forlorn words float out in front of a solid backbeat, until the end, where the three singing Beatles join in harmony for *help in any way* as the short punchy guitar chords rhythmically clip the momentum to end the phrase.

Another verse is repeated and then at 0:30 there's a refrain that echoes the intro, but in a less frantic way, using a tambourine backbeat and a little more space between the words and notes. John sings the first two lines, then there's a line in three-part harmony, a quick *won't you* in unison, then three-part harmony again as the guitar arpeggios again sparkle and descend to settle things back down.

There are two more verses and another refrain, and then at 1:31, in a more intimate and personal close-up, John repeats the lines of the first verse alone. We can really hear the strings of the acoustic guitar, with the other instruments just coming in lightly on the strong beats, closer together at the end, again to solidly finish the phrase. For the last time through the verse, the interleaved backing and lead vocals pick up again.

In the last refrain, to create a more dramatic ending, there's an additional very urgent and rushed *help me help me,* with John again really biting into the words. Then it all blends into a last relieving *ooh,* fading away and leaving only the humming of the backing vocals.

Timeline

1965—July 29: The film *Help* premiers in London ~August 13: The Beatles embark on their second US tour ~August 14: The Beatles' pre-record their final live appearance on the Ed Sullivan Show ~August 15: The Beatles play to a crowd of over 50,000 at Shea Stadium in New York ~

#11 *Yesterday*

This sad, sincere first solo by a single band member has been covered 2,200 times, more than any other Beatles song. Followed by *Eleanor Rigby*, *Hey Jude*, and *Let It Be*, and set against George Martin's masterfully composed string quartet, *Yesterday* is the first in a series of timeless and strikingly beautiful McCartney hits.

Release and Recording

UK Release: Not released as a single.
US Release: September 13, 1965
Recorded: June 14, 1965
Length: 2:03
B-side: *Act Naturally*

Charting

US: On October 9, 1965, *Yesterday* replaced *Hang on Sloopy* by the McCoys, stayed for 4 weeks and was then replaced by the Rolling Stones' *Get off of My Cloud*, which held for 2 weeks.

UK: *Yesterday* wasn't released as a single.

The Back Story

In some cases, Paul came up with tunes first and then fit words to them. For the three-syllable title here, he supposedly began composing the song by singing the words *Scrambled Eggs*. He apparently wasn't sure if he had unconsciously stolen the melody from somebody else, so he played it for a number of people to make sure. And because the song is just Paul, and not a rocker or a pop song, the other three Beatles supposedly vetoed its release as a single in the UK. This may have been the beginning of some dissention in the ranks. You can find an unusual video with all of them playing an electric version of it in a 1966 Tokyo concert. We can only wonder how the other three felt when it hit number 1 in the US. It was a turning point.

Yesterday

Time	Section
0:00	Intro
0:05	Verse
0:22	Verse
0:39	Bridge
0:59	Verse
1:17	Bridge
1:36	Verse
1:54	Outro

Song Map Legend

The Song Map

The song map features blue for this very simply rendered Paul song, along with guitar and string quartet as backing. There's a short, understated intro on acoustic guitar followed by Paul coming in to sing a series of melancholy verses and bridges. The beautiful string quartet comes in on the second verse. A full palette of sad and sentimental chords is used on this one, delivered through a very sophisticated and intricate progression.

Personal Notes

Yesterday
It was Sunday, September 12, 1965, a bit after 8:00 p.m. The Beatles were on the *Ed Sullivan Show* for the fourth and final time (not counting the 1967 airing of the *Hello Goodbye* music video). For their first set they played *I Feel Fine*, *I'm Down*, and *Act Naturally*. In the second half of the show they opened with *Ticket to Ride*. After that, George, curling his lip the funny way he sometimes did when speaking, introduces the next number, saying "It's a song with ... featuring just Paul, and it's called *Yesterday*." We next see the spotlight on Paul, still standing, a lefty acoustic slung over his shoulder. He pinches a few simple chords and begins to sing. His eyes are looking around, up and back, panning around the audience in that innocent boyish way, and he sings his beautiful song. Wouldn't it be something if you could go back to that moment in your life when you first heard this song, especially with George Martin's amazing string arrangement in the background.

The Butcher Cover
It's hard to believe that a beautiful song like *Yesterday*, in one of its North American repackaging incarnations, would ever end up on an album with a cover showing the Beatles sitting together, all wearing white butcher's aprons, and covered with baby parts (broken up plastic dolls) and raw red meat. Capitol Records, the US arm of EMI, the Beatles' British record producers, often repackaged albums to better fit what they thought would go over in the US and Canada—this one was named *Yesterday and Today*. It's hard to imagine a bunch of people sitting around at a meeting saying, "Okay then, it's decided, we'll go with that photo for the cover." But they did. (Paul supposedly said it was a sort of protest against the war in Viet Nam.) The reaction was highly unfavorable, so Capitol recalled the album and re-released it with a new cover. Capitol initially just pasted the new covers over the old ones (these became highly sought-after collectors' items), but this tactic didn't last, and they ended up doing a full reprint. The album still made it up to number 1, stayed in the top spot for 5 weeks, and ended up going gold.

The Details

Yesterday starts with a few simple, alternating low bass notes and pinched fingerpicking style chords on an acoustic guitar. The notes come at a gentle pace, with just a faint bit of buzzing on the strings, giving the recording a live-performance feel. The sincere solo version of Paul's voice comes in to sing the title word, *Yesterday*, with some slight reverb; it's very simple and clear. (Remember this is the same guy who belts out Little Richard songs.) It's immediately very lonely and sad.

Up until the second verse, it sounds like an incredibly beautiful folk song, but when George Martin's string quartet comes in, things are taken to a new and different level. After this, we can still hear the soft bass notes on the guitar, but the chords get covered up a bit by the string quartet.

At about 0:52 we hear Paul's voice being doubled up for the more emotionally charged ending of the bridge. His singing is masterful, with the heartfelt multi-syllable passage *day-ay-ay-ay* contrasting with the simpler one note to one syllable style he uses in body of the song.

At about 1:25, during the second time through the bridge, we hear a passage on low strings from the quartet, which this time around, contains a beautiful blue note. This time around through the bridge, Paul's voice is not doubled as it was the first time.

For the outro there's some gentle humming, over two final sustained chords by the string quartet, and then it's over.

For such a simple and gentle sounding song, *Yesterday* has a lot of sophisticated chord changes, which is one reason the string quartet works so well. It's a sad folk song with beautiful classical music going on in the background, which is perhaps why it's been described as "Baroque Rock." It foreshadows *Eleanor Rigby* in this sense.

Timeline

1965—August 24: The Beatles take LSD with the Byrds and Peter Fonda in Los Angeles ~August 27: The Beatles meet Elvis Presley in Los Angeles ~September 13: Ringo and Maureen's baby boy Zak is born ~September 25: The Beatles cartoon show begins airing in the US ~October 26: The Beatles are awarded their Members of the Order of the British Empire medals by Queen Elizabeth ~

#12 *Day Tripper*

The first of three double-A-side singles in the set of hits, this song has another great Lennon guitar hook, beautifully elaborate and almost jazz-like *Rubber Soul* period harmonies, and a great beat.

Release and Recording

UK Release: December 3, 1965
US Release: December 6, 1965
Recorded: October 16, 1965
Length: 2:50
Double A-side: *We Can Work It Out*

Charting

US: *Day Tripper* didn't hit number 1, but did make it up to the Billboard Hot 100's number 5 spot.

UK: On December 16, 1965, along with *We Can Work It Out*, *Day Tripper* replaced *The Carnival Is Over* by the Seekers, which had held for 3 weeks. The double A-side stayed for 5 weeks and was then replaced by the Spencer Davis Group's *Keep on Running*, which held for 1 week.

The Back Story

The band supposedly needed a single for the 1965 Christmas season. John wrote most of the song and the guitar lick, with Paul helping out a good bit on the lyrics. It's great collaboration, as Paul ended up singing the first and main parts of the verses, while George played the guitar hook along with John.

Day Tripper

Time	Section
0:00	Intro Riff
0:03	Riff
0:07	Riff
0:14	Riff
0:17	Verse
0:31	Bridge
0:45	Riff
1:05	Bridge
1:20	Solo ~
1:41	Riff
1:48	Verse
2:01	Bridge
2:16	Riff
2:19	Riff

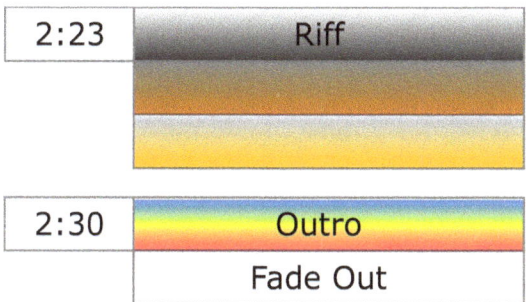

after they play the layered intro material again. The intro guitar lick and the verse are pure rock 'n' roll, but the refrain is quite different, with very colorful and more pop-sounding sequences.

Personal Notes

Ringo Starr, Drummer
The drumming is just great on *Day Tripper*, the quick fills coming in after the guitar hook and then settling into a steady and solid backbeat, creating a tight groove that holds everything together. This is definition Ringo and what he did so well. He isn't famous for virtuoso drum solos and techniques, but that's not what the Beatles were about. Some inspired drummers will point to the very creative ways Ringo expanded his drumming a bit further along in the band's career, on songs like *Rain, She Said - She Said, Strawberry Fields*, and the work on *Abbey Road*, but for my money, it's his indescribable and incredible talent for keeping that steady backbeat, framing so many of the Beatles' great songs, and helping to make them what they were. It's a little like the typically unnoticed way a great rhythm guitar player, like John Lennon, provides the glue that holds a band together.

Listen to the signature tom-tom fills that start off *She Loves You*, then the slightly staggered beats in between the title lines in the refrain, and then the air awash in cymbals for the verses. Or listen to the famously staggered beat in *Ticket to Ride*, or how the understated but steady stately beats come

Song Map Legend

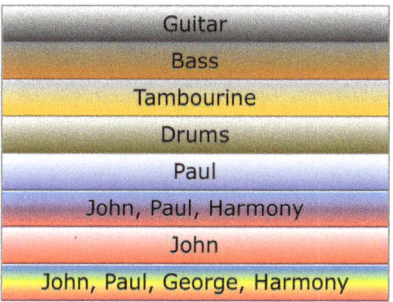

The Song Map

After the band repeats the guitar intro, successively layering in more and more instruments, shown throughout the song as a series of lengthening multi-colored bands, Paul sings the first lead lines, echoed by John's harmonies, which sound more jazz than pop. The guitar riff is a signature Beatles classic. In the bridges, John sings just a few words, then Paul and George come in on harmony, although it's hard to hear if George is really in the mix here. They use high-energy three-part harmonies at the end of the guitar solo in the middle of the song, and lots of full harmonies in the outro, in, a ways into both *Hey Jude* and *Let It Be*, or those sling-shot echoes that set up the dark and funky groove in *Come Together,* or how he fills the space between the lines in *Something*. But mostly, listen to how Ringo's simple but perfectly fitting beat just moves so many of the Beatles' songs along.

And for anybody that still has any doubt whatsoever, think about this—would the likes of John Lennon, Paul McCartney, and George Harrison (okay, throw in Rory Storm of early Liverpool stardom too) get anybody but the absolute best drummer around? It just couldn't have been any other way.

The Details

The song starts with five times through the catchy guitar hook, adding layers as it goes along. The first time it's just the guitar, the second time bass is added, the third time the tambourine comes in with some guitar chords, the fourth time nothing is added, and the fifth time there's a big pick-up fill before the drums settle down into a very catchy and solid backbeat.

Paul belts out the first and third lines of the verse, in his double-tracked, high-energy Little Richard–style voice, with John coming in to harmonize on the second and fourth lines—again more classic Beatles back-and-forth solo/harmony. This first verse has a pure rock 'n' roll sound, with the guitar riff moving up along with the chord change. But on the four-line refrain, John and Paul sing in harmony, and their voices go from rock 'n' roll into more of a pop feeling with very sophisticated jazz-like harmonies, but the guitar and bass keep it funky. The phrase *so-oo long* is extended and sustained, while *and I found out* abruptly clips things before going back to the guitar hook. The band plays the hook twice, the first time against a riled-up rattlesnake tambourine. Then there's a series of drum fills and things again settle into the solid backbeat.

They play another verse and refrain, with John really biting into the multi-syllable *sooo-oh-oh* at 1:13. In the instrumental break, the guitar hook comes in again, but this time it's moved up into a different chord, adding energy. The band repeats the hook three times, against a backdrop of big guitar chords and cymbal crashes. They then start in with a series of six fully harmonized *aghs* that foreshadow some of the full-voiced passages on *Sgt. Pepper*. The tension begins to mount against the repeated guitar notes, and while the song has been fairly medium-energy up to this point, the singing here shifts into a highly charged and harmonized *Twist and Shout*–like build up, bringing things to a frenzied climax, before settling back into the groove of the song with the steady guitar hook and the tambourine backbeat. It's a bit hard to tell whether or not George has joined in here on this harmony, but it's presented that way in the song map.

There's another time through the verse, and on the word *tried* it sounds like Paul harmonizes with himself in a double track. There's another refrain, two times through the guitar riff, and an emphasis on the *sooo-oh-oh*, but here in a high falsetto with what sounds like both John and Paul together.

At 2:16, to set things up for the outro, the band goes through the layered guitar hook again, as they did in the intro, and after four times, some drum fills, and then again into the backbeat, they repeat the title words with a very cool *yeah* thrown in every other time, and the song fades out.

Timeline

1965—December 3: The Beatles begin their final UK tour in Glasgow ~December 3: The album *Rubber Soul* is released ~1966—January 21: George Harrison and Pattie Boyd are married ~March 4: The *London Evening Standard* publishes John Lennon's remarks about the Beatles being more popular than Jesus ~

#13 *We Can Work It Out*

With an ebbing and flowing harmonium in the mix, a beautifully dark and mournful bridge, and intermittent changes in and out of waltz time, this song is clear evidence of the Beatles' growing sophistication.

Release and Recording

UK Release: December 3, 1965
US Release: December 6, 1965
Recorded: October 20 and 29, 1965
Length: 2:15
Double A-side: *Day Tripper*

Charting

US: Unlike *Day Tripper*, *We Can Work It Out* did hit number 1 in the states. On January 8, 1966, it replaced *The Sound of Silence* by Simon and Garfunkel, stayed 2 weeks, and was then replaced by *The Sound of Silence* again, which stayed for another week. On January 29, it made it back up for another week at the top—an example of an unusual little battle between two hit songs.

UK: On December 16, 1965, along with *Day Tripper*, *We Can Work It Out* replaced *The Carnival Is Over* by the Seekers, which had held for 3 weeks. The double A-side stayed for 5 weeks and was then replaced by the Spencer Davis Group's *Keep on Running*, which held for 1 week.

The Back Story

For the other side of the double-A with *Day Tripper*, Paul wrote the verses, and together with John, the bridge. The darker bridge is more Lennon than McCartney and there's no rock 'n' roll feel to it at all, but it doesn't quite sound like what you'd call a pop song either. It was supposedly George's idea to add the waltz time sections in, and he may have been influenced by the switching out of and back into waltz time that happens in the Beatles' earlier cover of *A Taste of Honey*, a track on their second album, *With the Beatles*.

We Can Work It Out

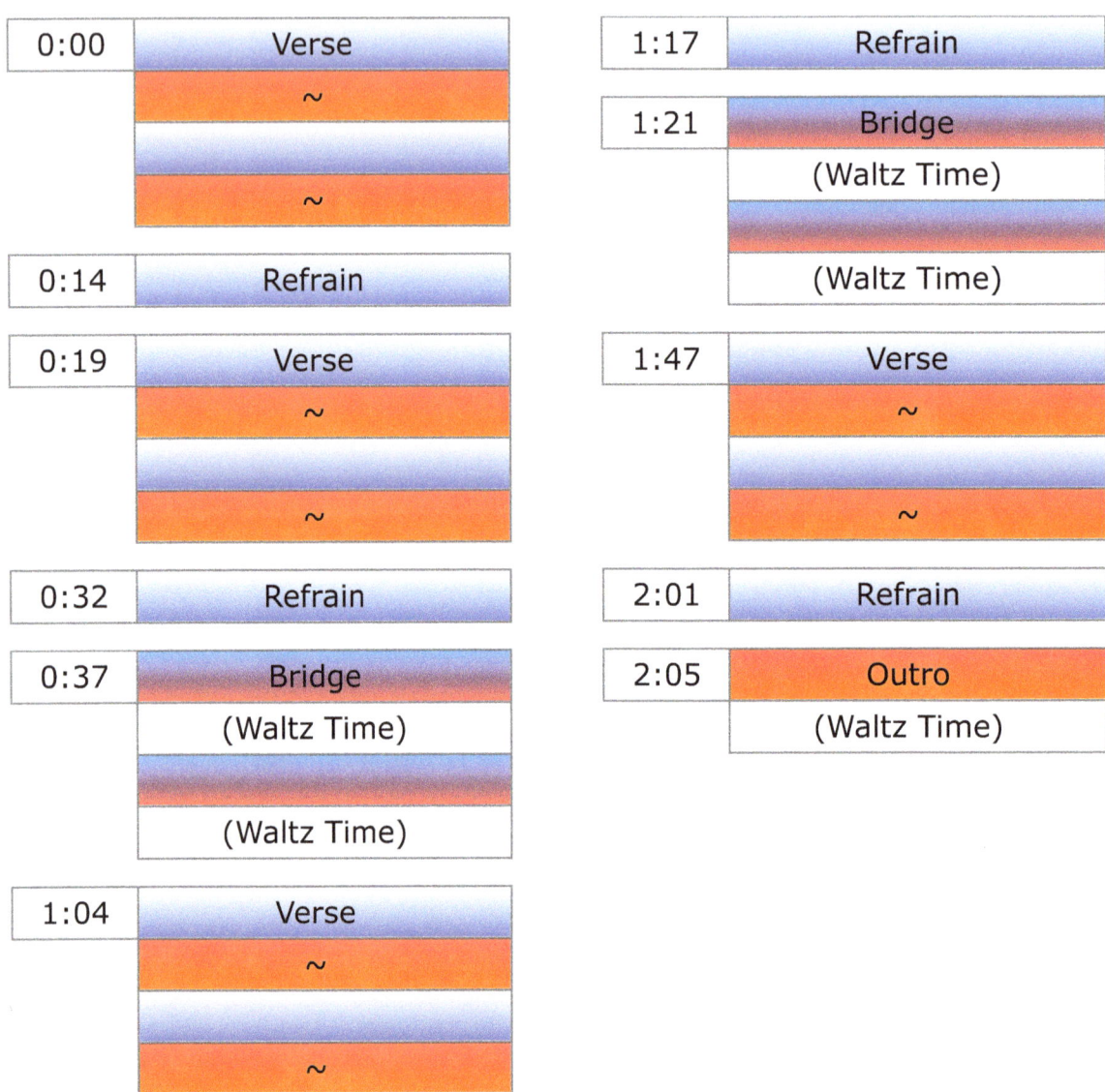

Song Map Legend

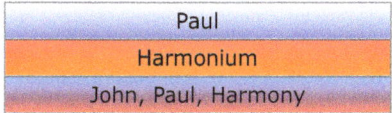

The Song Map

There's no intro, and lots of blue with Paul singing the verses and refrains. The exotically colored harmonium behind Paul adds a beautiful texture to the song. John joins in to harmonize on the bridges, when they switch in and out of waltz time. The difference between Paul's matter-of-fact verse and refrain, with almost no chord changes, and the plaintive and melancholy bridge, is another example of classic Beatles high contrast in mood and feeling between different parts of the same song.

Personal Notes

A Change in the Air
The swelling breathing sound of the harmonium and the changes in and out of waltz time in *We Can Work It Out* sounded so exotic. The Beatles were constantly changing over the course of their seven years in the world's spotlight. It's not always easy to divide the singles and the albums into separate periods but I distinctly remember noticing, right around the time that *We Can Work It Out* and *Day Tripper* came out, how much the Beatles' music had changed, and was still changing—it's the *Rubber Soul* period. If you were really tuned into the Beatles, as so many of us were, you could really feel it. The energy was different, turned down a few notches; the lyrics were not as simple; and the chord changes, vocal arrangements, and mix of instruments were all getting much more sophisticated. The Beatles had no doubt learned much from George Martin and were interested in trying new things in the studio, and of course they were just evolving. In any case, by late 1965, the frantically energetic and sentimental teenage pop songs like *She Loves You* and *I Want to Hold Your Hand*, the songs that had catapulted them into stardom, were a thing of the past.

The Details

This is another number that starts with a burst—there's a big chord, bass note, tambourine, and Paul starting to sing, all at once. It's heavier, slower, and more brooding than the other hits to date. Paul sings the words *keep on talking* against the first swelling and breathing harmonium chords, which gives the song a suspended and pensive feeling. Paul's voice is double-tracked here, but it's turned down in the mix and less obvious.

In the short refrain, Paul repeats the title words twice, snapping the words *We Can* together quickly, and then goes back to the verse.

After the second verse, there's another refrain, and then the song moves into the beautifully harmonized bridge, with much darker and forlorn thoughts about life, and in vivid contrast to the simply stated verses. In the middle of the bridge, there is a surprising and unusual switch into waltz time, but only for just a few bars. This is accompanied by some big cymbal crashes and a very richly harmonized and sustained five-syllable *ti-i-i-i-ime*. Then the waltzing stops and the song snaps back into the regular groove, with a feeling of settling down and getting back on track. This alternating pattern between regular and waltz time repeats again. During this waltz part, we can hear texture and feeling foreshadowing *Being for the Benefit of Mr. Kite* that will appear on the *Sgt. Pepper* album a few years from now.

The band takes us another two times through the single verse, refrain, and bridge, with a steady medium energy and momentum. As in many other songs, the second and third times through, they play only one verse and refrain before going back into the bridge, which compresses things and adds to the emotional intensity. If you listen carefully, right around 1:09, there are some perfectly placed rhythmic variations of acoustic guitar strumming, with some quick snaps and extra strums, and a few less noticeable ones that follow.

For the somewhat sudden outro, the song switches back into waltz time, and we hear a three-chord pattern on the harmonium which is very much like what you might hear in a church at the end of a hymn. This is a common element in Western religious music, referred to as a "plagal" or "amen" cadence. Here it serves to provide a feeling of relief and lasting resolution after the somewhat heavy mood of the song—it's a bit like "the mass is ended, go in peace".

Timeline

1965—December 3: The Beatles begin their final UK tour in Glasgow ~December 3: The album *Rubber Soul* is released ~1966—January 21: George Harrison and Pattie Boyd are married ~March 4: The *London Evening Standard* publishes John Lennon's remarks about the Beatles being more popular than Jesus ~

#14 Paperback Writer

This song, in the form of a letter, has one of the best electric guitar riffs of all time, brilliant multi-part harmonies, heavy echo effects, and some of Paul's best bass playing ever. It also has John and George singing the French nursery rhyme *Frère Jacques* in high falsetto in the background.

Release and Recording

UK Release: June 10, 1966
US Release: May 30, 1966
Recorded: April 13 and 14, 1966
Length: 2:18
B-side: *Rain*

Charting

US: On June 25, 1966, *Paperback Writer* replaced *Paint It Black* by the Rolling Stones, which had been on top for 2 weeks. It held for 2 weeks and was then replaced by *Strangers in the Night* by Frank Sinatra, which stayed for 1 week.

UK: On June 23, *Paperback Writer* replaced *Strangers in the Night*, which had been on top for 3 weeks, stayed for 2 weeks and was then replaced by the Kinks' *Sunny Afternoon*, which held for 2 weeks.

The Back Story

This song was next to impossible to perform live, as films of some Beatles concerts show. It's not easy to get this level of sophisticated harmonizing in a live setting. This song is not about love, and neither are any of the hits that follow, except for *Something*. Like parts of *P.S. I Love You* and *From Me to You*, *Paperback Writer* is a letter, but unlike most other Beatles songs, it stays in one chord for nearly the whole time. The UK single was promoted with the crazy butcher cover photo, showing the Beatles covered with meat and ripped-apart plastic doll parts.

Paperback Writer

Time	Section
0:00	Refrain ~
0:06	Riff
0:12	Verse
0:30	Verse
0:49	Refrain ~
0:55	Riff
1:01	Verse ~ ~ ~
1:19	Verse ~ ~ ~
1:38	Refrain ~
1:44	Riff
1:50	~ Outro ~ ~ ~
	Fade Out

Song Map Legend

The Song Map

This is a very colorful song map because of all the three-part harmony. It opens with John, Paul, and George singing the title, a cappella, with a complex set of harmonized tracks and slightly staggered lyrics (which are simplified in the map) and then the killer guitar riff. Paul's bass really dances all over in this one, with lots of variation. Paul sings most of the first two verses alone, with John and George coming in briefly at the ends. In the middle of the song, the backing vocals in the verses have John and George harmonizing, singing *Frère Jacques* in very high voices. After every two verses we hear the refrain and guitar. The ending is a set of alternating very high multi-voice lines interspersed with lower three-part harmony, and a fade-out.

Personal Notes

Paul McCartney, Musician
The lead guitar riff in *Paperback Writer*, supposedly played by Paul and not George, is amazing and so loaded with sling-shot energy, at first blasting off, rising up high, leaping an octave in four notes, then crashing down hard and bluesy, with a heavy driving rhythm, and all this in such contrast to the floaty and highly harmonized a cappella vocals in the refrain. Paul also played other notable guitar parts, like the fractured and chaotic mish-mash on *Taxman*, or the main riffs on *Drive My Car*. And then there's his fingerpicking. We first hear it, simply, on songs like *Yesterday*, but listen to how elaborately beautiful it has become in *Michelle* or *Blackbird*. Paul is known, of course, for his bass playing. From the solid backbeat patterns he plays in the early part of the catalog, to the unbelievably creative, melodic, and always varying backdrops like the one here in *Paperback Writer*—it's just masterful. He also plays piano, including a wide variety of rock, or rollicking saloon, or jazz-age music hall, but most especially the soft and comforting chord progressions behind *Hey Jude* and *Let It Be*. And then there's the drumming ...

British Guitar Players Rule
You have to admit that nearly all of the really best rock guitar players of the 60s were British: Jimmy Page, Eric Clapton, Jeff Beck, Pete Townshend, Alvin Lee (one of my really favorite and slightly unsung guitar heroes), and many others. But then there was Jimi Hendrix, who nobody could really touch, and these other guitarists would be the first to say so.

The Details

The song opens with a voices-only hook, singing the title words *Paperback Writer*, led by Paul with John and George singing background harmonies. John and George's lines are slightly offset and delayed, coming after Paul's, and the word *Writer* is echoed twice. The voices trail off, there's a quick snap on the drums, and then we hear the piercing tones of an amazingly tight and rhythmic rocker-style electric guitar riff, which is also played twice, against a solid backbeat on the drums. The sharp fuzz-tone of the upwardly leaping and then descending guitar riff is in stark contrast to the high floating voices that preceded it. Then there's a quick fill on the drums, a drum-fill-like set of notes and downward slide on the bass, and the first verse starts, with Paul's voice double-tracked.

One interesting thing about this song is that it's just about all played in one chord (Paul did say that he was trying to write a song with just one chord). Perhaps because of this, Paul seems to have made a special effort to make the bass interesting and, unlike most bass parts, it varies continually throughout the song. All through the verse, the bass rhythmically pulses and dances around behind the lyrics, and the chord stays in the home key up until 0:25. Here there are energetic chord changes for just a few seconds, a flourish of high voices, drums, and heavier electric guitar, and then things come back down for the beginning of the second verse.

At the end of the second verse, the full choir of Beatle voices stops and echoes off, warbling a little as it goes, but just for an instant, before they sing the vocal hook and play that mean guitar riff again.

In the third verse, John and George join in singing as background vocals the French nursery rhyme *Frère Jacques* in a high falsetto and tight harmony (how crazy is that?). The first three syllables rise, the fourth comes back down to home, which also helps to make the mostly one-chord verse interesting. And this time, between verses, they don't stop and do the vocal hook or guitar riff, but just sing *Paperback Writer* once.

In the outro, it's actually John and George's backing vocals we hear first, singing again in the high falsetto, with Paul following after a slight delay, and then they fade out.

Timeline

1966—May 1: The last UK Beatles concert takes place at Wembley ~May 19: The Beatles film the music videos for *Paperback Writer* and *Rain* ~June 1: George Harrison attends a Ravi Shankar concert in London ~June 17: Paul McCartney buys High Park Farm in Kintyre, Scotland ~June 20: The album *Yesterday and Today* featuring the butcher cover is released in the US ~

#15 *Yellow Submarine*

Ringo's upbeat number is the title song for the brilliantly animated 1968 film of the same name. Another double A-side with *Eleanor Rigby*, *Yellow Submarine* is like a children's song, with crazy sound effects and comical voice-overs, but there's still a little Beatle harmony buried in the mix.

Release and Recording

UK/US Releases: August 5, 1966
Recorded: May 26 and June 1, 1966
Length: 2:38
Double A-side: *Eleanor Rigby*

Charting

US: Neither of the two A-sides charted in the states. *Yellow Submarine* did make it up to number 2, while the Supremes were on top with *You Can't Hurry Love*, which held for 2 weeks.

UK: On August 18, 1966, the double A-side replaced *With a Girl Like You* by the Troggs, which had been on top for 2 weeks. It stayed for 4 weeks and was then replaced by the Small Faces' *All or Nothing*, which stayed for 1 week. This was the Beatles' record-setting eleventh number 1 hit in the UK.

The Back Story

Paul wrote *Yellow Submarine* for Ringo to sing. The song was also track number six on the first side of *Revolver*, which was released on the same day in August 1966, a couple of years before the film. Scottish singer-songwriter and Beatles' friend Donovan supposedly added the line about the blue sky and the green sea. George Martin's experience with sound effects for comedy TV like *The Goon Show* is in evidence here, with various gadgets being put to use, including chains, a bath tub, a cash register, bells, and whistles. The brass band foreshadows *Sgt. Pepper*.

Yellow Submarine

Time	Section
0:00	Verse / ~ / / ~ / ~
0:17	Verse / (Waves)
0:36	Refrain
0:52	Verse / Voices / Noises
1:05	Solo
1:10	Refrain
1:27	Submarine Noises / Voices / ~ / ~
1:45	Verse / ~ / / ~ / / ~ / / ~ / / ~
2:03	Refrain
2:20	Refrain / Fade Out

Song Map Legend

The Song Map

Ringo's singing is the color of the *Sea of Green* from the film, his color in the song maps picked especially for this number, his one featured song in the set. The refrains use the four-way color blend for the four Beatles in harmony, but there was a much larger cast of characters singing backing vocals and making noises, including Mal Evans, George Martin, Geoff Emerick, Neil Aspinall, Alf Bicknell, Pattie Boyd, Marianne Faithfull, Brian Jones, and Brian Epstein. The break, featuring submarine noises and nautical shouts, is rendered using the submarine's ochre yellow. There's a longer alternating section at 1:45, showing Paul's shout out echoes in blue, interleaved with Ringo's singing.

Personal Notes

Yellow Submarine, the Movie

"Once upon a time, or maybe twice," ... as described in the opening lines of the movie, 80,000 leagues beneath the sea is a great distance, it's more than 250,000 miles, so *Pepperland* was very far away.

I remember first seeing *Yellow Submarine* at the Calvin Theatre in Northampton, Massachusetts, shortly after its US release in November 1968, and two years after the song was released. Like many theaters, the Calvin, which still stands today, has huge spaces, vaulted ceilings covered with gaudy baroque ornamentation and paintings of classical characters with flowing beards and muscular figures, surrounded by angels and cherubs, and all enveloped in swirling clouds and stars. In the flickering lights, popcorn in your lap, you sat in these old scratchy corduroy seats that you didn't really want to lean your neck back onto.

The film was unbelievably imaginative, with its vivid multi-colored scenes and characters popping out of the screen, lighting up the old dark theater to the sounds of Beatle songs or George Martin's swirly orchestral score. The cast of characters included Old Fred and the Lord Mayor, with their shaky ancient voices, and the alter-ego Beatles as the brass *Pepperland* band, all the characters with large exaggerated legs and feet and tiny little heads, a little like R. Crumb meets Peter Max. Then there was the chief Blue Meanie with his creepy drawling high-pitched voice and his trusted assistant, weird little Max. There were the Apple Bonkers, Butterfly Stompers, Snapping Turtle Turks, Jeremy the strange little squeaky voiced Nowhere Man, and of course, the dreaded Flying Glove. It was indeed all too much. I especially liked the *Eleanor Rigby* number, which features a white bulldog wearing the Union Jack, as well as the Yellow Submarine floating silently and slowly around the old dark buildings, the big clock, the very clever scenes, and the repeating jerky motions of the characters.

The Beatles at first had supposedly wanted to keep the project at arm's length. It had started with the *Beatles* cartoon show that aired in the US from 1965 to 1969, each episode featuring a song. The voices weren't the Beatles' or even English, let alone from Liverpool. The Beatles were apparently not too keen on the TV show, but thanks to a very gifted and tireless animation team, the results were brilliant (they did end up getting real English voices). Due to contract obligations, the Beatles were supposed to provide four new songs for the sound track, but because of their initially lukewarm attitude toward the whole thing, the songs were maybe not their best (except for *Hey Bulldog*, which is a masterpiece and ironically didn't get included in the first version of the US film). But after seeing the final product, the Beatles changed their minds, and at the end of the film you see them doing a silly little skit, John with a telescope, saying there've been sightings of Blue Meanies in the vicinity of your theater, and ending with the goofy *All Together Now*.

You Can't Hurry Love
I got my first transistor radio in September 1966, about a month after the double A-sides *Eleanor Rigby* and *Yellow Submarine* came out. It was a General Electric model. It had a round dial, which lit up at night, to select stations, a thin red needle, and that swirly GE logo that looks a little like a couple of music score G-clefs back to back, inside a little silver square on the bottom left. *You Can't Hurry Love*, my favorite-ever hit by the Supremes, was at number 1, and stations played it over and over, which didn't bother me at all. With its great happy-sad-happy chord progression and the soulful-but-sweet Diana Ross in her prime, you just can't listen to a song like that too much. At night I used to get under the covers and listen to that little glowing radio into the wee hours of the morning, with the volume down very low so I wouldn't wake anybody up.

The Details

The song starts out very simply, like a folk number, with some sparse but solidly rhythmic strums on an acoustic guitar, faint bass guitar in the background, and something that sounds like a tambourine on the backbeats. Ringo's voice is simple and clear, not double-tracked. At about 0:10 we hear some heavy bass drum foot stomps come in.

When the second verse starts, the rhythm shifts and the feeling gets a little more fluid and swinging, with more acoustic guitar strums filled in. We hear the sound of ocean waves.

Everybody joins in on the refrain. There's some harmony going on here, but there are lots of voices and it's not the typical highly chiseled Beatles harmony. The waves continue to wash around us.

In the third verse we hear some sound effects and speaking voices. There's metal or glass clinking and banging, bird sounds, random noises—it sounds like a party. Ringo announces the brass band, which starts up and plays a bouncy march for just a few seconds, then there's another refrain and the sound effects and voices drop out. At 1:27 the submarine and crew come in for their break. They're all having fun, mimicking what they imagine it sounds like to be on a submarine, and making all sorts of noise.

For the next verse at 1:45, the background voices and noises drop out, but a call-and-response starts up with what sounds like Paul repeating the last words in the lines in a comic falsetto, which he finishes up with a wild cowboy laugh. Then there's a repeat of the refrain lines and a fade-out.

Timeline

1966—July 1 and 2: The Beatles perform at Nippon Budokan Hall in Tokyo ~July 4: The Beatles perform in Manila, Philippines, and get into hot water by snubbing first lady Imelda Marcos ~July 6: The Beatles take their first trip to India ~July 29: The US magazine *Datebook* republishes John Lennon's comments about Christianity ~August 5: The album *Revolver* is released ~August 11: The Beatles embark on their last tour in the US ~August 29: The Beatles perform their last live concert in San Francisco ~

#16 *Eleanor Rigby*

Eleanor Rigby is described by some as Baroque Pop, but does that really fit? This incredibly creative hybrid, featuring George Martin's amazing string quartet, defies classification. It's not pop or rock—it's a one-of-a-kind blend of masterfully chiseled classical music superimposed over a sad and hauntingly beautiful Paul McCartney song.

Release and Recording

UK/US Releases: August 5, 1966
Recorded: April 28 and 29 and June 6, 1966
Length: 2:08
Double A-side: *Yellow Submarine*

Charting

US: Neither of the two A-sides charted in the states. *Eleanor Rigby* only made it to number 11.

UK: On August 18, 1966, the double A-side replaced *With a Girl Like You* by the Troggs, which had been on top for 2 weeks. It stayed for 4 weeks and was then replaced by the Small Faces' *All or Nothing*, which stayed for 1 week. This was the Beatles' record-setting eleventh number 1 hit in the UK.

The Back Story

Although there is a grave marked with the name Eleanor Rigby in St. Peter's Church, Liverpool, Paul, who wrote the song, claims that's not where the song's name came from, although he didn't provide too many details.

George Martin's contribution here cannot be overstated. *Eleanor Rigby* is unlike any other Beatles song. This is an unprecedented collaboration between two musical geniuses. Yes, the strings on *Yesterday* were beautiful, but with *Eleanor Rigby*, they attained a totally new level of musical expression and beauty.

Despite the elaborate and beautifully crafted string quartet, there are really only two chords in the song, and this is the only number 1 hit when there are no Beatles playing instruments.

Some have wondered whether John and George are actually doing backing vocals during the first refrain. It is hard to tell, but if you're really curious, you can use OOPS (see the Sidebar) to cancel out the stereo in the middle. With this method, you can hear that John and George are singing backup vocals, especially in certain spots like around 1:27 on the word *lonely*.

Eleanor Rigby

0:00	Refrain

0:14	Verse

0:31	Refrain 2

0:45	Verse

1:03	Refrain 2

1:16	Refrain

1:30	Verse

1:48	Refrain 2

Song Map Legend

John, Paul, George, Harmony
String Quartet
Paul
Paul, Paul, Harmony

The Song Map

This song has no intro or outro; it's a simple set of verses with two different refrains. George Martin's string quartet can't be fully portrayed using our song map technique, so it's only suggested here in the first refrain, in deep red, and then as backing throughout the rest of the song. Besides the Paul, John, and George three-part harmony in one of the two refrains, it's all Paul blue. The harmonies at the end are actually Paul harmonizing with himself, so a new blue is used for that.

Personal Notes

Eleanor Rigby, Poem

In the fall of 1966, I was in the sixth grade. For a homework assignment, our English teacher asked that each student copy out a poem they liked. I handed in *Eleanor Rigby*, which does read like a poem, and got an A.

Song Map Limitations

The song map technique used in this book to portray vocal arrangements and harmony doesn't lend itself well to rendering instrumental music, like George Martin's string quartet in *Eleanor Rigby*. I tried to come up with a way to do it, but for now haven't figured it out. I did study lots of very creative ways people are trying to visualize music, but none of them seemed to fit. However, if you watch and listen to David Barlow's wonderful YouTube video (http://y2u.be/7z0h5Zxdff8) where he presents the musical score to *Eleanor Rigby*, you'll see at the beginning a beautifully multi-colored track map that provides a simple portrayal of the string quartet.

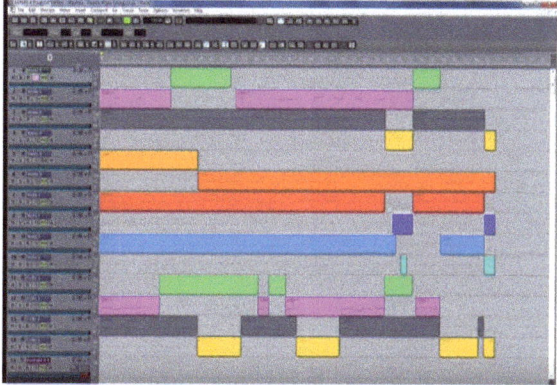

David Barlow's Colorful Mix

George Martin, Composer

George Martin's contribution to the Beatles' success was crucial. He gave them their first real break, providing them the opportunity to make records at EMI. He helped them discover their best sounds, finding just the right balance between guidance and letting them do their own thing. He scored musical pieces, many based on their songs, for the movie soundtracks in *Help* and *Yellow Submarine*. He even ended up playing on their records, like the keyboard solo in *In My Life*. (He played piano or organ on many of other songs, too.) And then there are the full-blown compositions he created for some songs. There's the quartet in *Yesterday*, the orchestration in *All You Need Is Love* or *Penny Lane*, the help with the crazy ideas for *A Day in the Life*, and, most especially, this double quartet in *Eleanor Rigby*. This piece, devised to enhance Paul McCartney's one-of-a-kind classical-music folk song, has emerged as a masterful musical composition in its own right, with the quartet-instruments-only track featured on both the *Anthology* and *Love* albums. It's an amazing piece of music. There's always been a lot of discussion about who was the fifth Beatle—for me, it will always be George Martin.

The Details

Like many other Paul McCartney songs, this one has no intro, no build up—very suddenly out of the silence the refrain bursts out in full brilliant force. Paul's double-tracked voice sings the first line, with John and George singing beautiful harmonies in the backing vocals. From the beginning, the song sets a starkly sad and brooding tone, with the strident pulsing strings of George Martin's masterful quartet filling in the spaces after each line. There is an interesting interplay between the sung lines, with a call that at first lifts us up just a little, but then in the strings, answering in a response that brings us back down, the words and music each delivered with equally tragic and poignant energy.

In the first verse, Paul's voice is single-tracked, oddly enough except for the very first word, *Eleanor*, and he begins the telling of a sad lonely story in just a few simple scenes. The strings are sparse for the first three-line section of the verse, but the second time around they play in double time, adding an increased urgency to the song's ebb and flow.

The second time through the refrain we only hear Paul, this time against a flowing and less urgent backdrop of four slowly descending, brooding cello notes. The two lines are repeated twice, and after the words are over, the strings echo the notes of the second more final and emphasized *where do they all belong*.

There's another verse, and this time in the second part, the strings don't play with the same tragic pulse as they did the first time. Instead there's a finely crafted counter melody, which rises and falls along with the words in a slower and gentler way.

At 1:16 the more energetic main refrain that the song started with is repeated.

In the second part of the third verse at 1:40, the energy increases significantly, with the again strident and striking strings playing double time, describing Father McKenzie's actions after he's dug Eleanor's grave, and the tragic notes of the sung words are doubled exactly in the lonely single cello line.

There's a last second refrain, and again, things are more filled in and flowing here, because we also hear Paul, in backing vocals to himself, blending and interleaving lines from both refrains together. After these words, there's a last descending series of notes played by the string quartet, and on a very final and funerary chord, it's over.

Timeline

1966—July 1 and 2: The Beatles perform at Nippon Budokan Hall in Tokyo ~July 4: The Beatles perform in Manila, Philippines, and get into hot water by snubbing first lady Imelda Marcos ~July 6: The Beatles take their first trip to India ~July 29: The US magazine *Datebook* republishes John Lennon's comments about Christianity ~August 5: The album *Revolver* is released ~August 11: The Beatles embark on their last tour in the US ~August 29: The Beatles perform their last live concert in San Francisco ~

#17 *Penny Lane*

Another double A, and the flip side of John Lennon's *Strawberry Fields Forever*, this song is Paul's upbeat trip down memory lane, evoking the sights and sounds of his boyhood haunts. He delivers nostalgia for a past Liverpool here through a set of dramatic, mostly upbeat, and unusual chord changes. Also featured is an instrumental solo performed by virtuoso English piccolo trumpet player David Mason.

Release and Recording

US Release: February 13, 1967
UK Release: February 17, 1967
Recorded: December 29, 1966—January 17, 1967
Double A-side: *Strawberry Fields Forever*
Length: 3:03

Charting

US: On March 18, 1967, *Penny Lane* replaced *Love Is Here and Now You're Gone* by the Supremes, which had held for 1 week. It stayed 1 week and was then replaced by the Turtles' *Happy Together*, which stayed for 3 weeks.

UK: This was the first time since *Love Me Do* that a single didn't chart in the UK, but it did make it up to the number 2 spot.

The Back Story

Penny Lane is the name of a street and a busy intersection in Liverpool, and like *Strawberry Fields Forever*, is a boyhood haunt—a spot where John and Paul would get the bus. Although released as a double A-side, *Strawberry Fields Forever* never made it into the number 1 set, only making it up to number 8 in the US. Penny Lane, the street, is supposedly named after James Penny, an eighteenth-century Liverpool merchant and slave-ship owner. The promotional video shots of the Beatles walking and on horseback were actually shot in London, not Liverpool.

Penny Lane

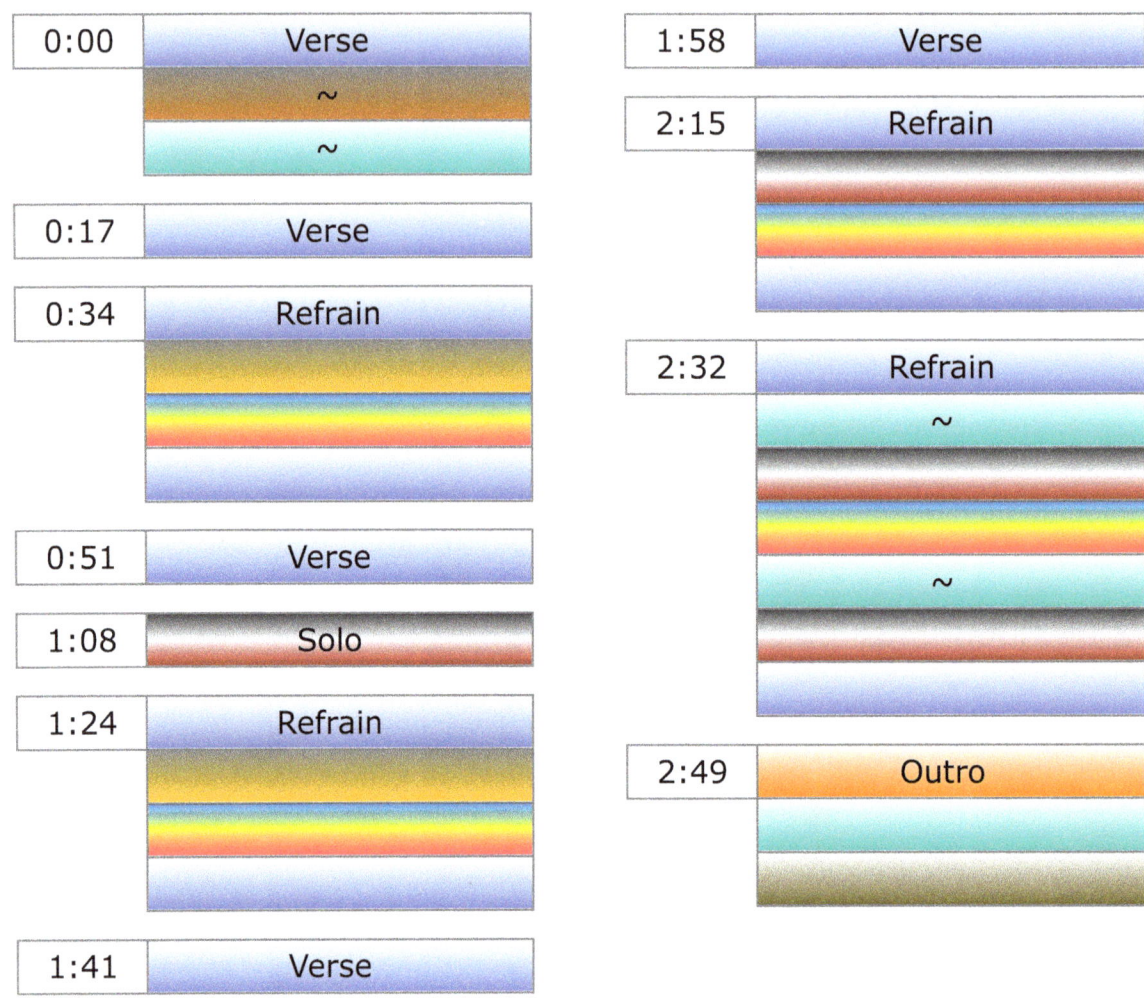

Song Map Legend

Paul
Bass
Fife
Brass Band
John, Paul, George, Harmony
Piccolo Trumpet
Piano
Cymbal

The Song Map

The lyrics are mostly blue with Paul singing the verses and refrains. There's lots of golden brass mixed in with both a full ensemble, and a featured solo on high-pitched piccolo trumpet, along with what sounds like a fife at the beginning and end, shown in light blue. The refrains have a splash of brightly colored three-part harmony and the ending just sort of stops, with a cymbal crash. There's a very unusual happy-to-dark chord change in the verse, some other unusual key changes, and a nostalgic, sentimental chord progression in the refrain. The refrain is repeated a second time at the end, the home chord shifting up a notch (modulating), which results in a very uplifting feeling.

Personal Notes

Pairs of John and Paul Songs

There are so many times when Beatles songs seemed to come out together as John and Paul pairs, released around the same time or even as flip sides of the same forty-five. Early on there were the love songs *If I Fell* and *And I Love Her*. There are the sad pasts evoked in *Yesterday* and *In My Life*. There's the silly, upbeat nonsense in *Hello, Goodbye* and the dark brooding atmosphere in *I Am the Walrus*. There's nostalgic boyhood reminiscing in both *Penny Lane* and *Strawberry Fields Forever*. And there's even the case where two songs get merged together in *A Day in the Life*. These pairs of songs form binary sets, a yin and a yang, each half always very different from the other, but complementary and still seeming like two sides of the same coin—you couldn't have one without the other. There's a lack of classic collaborative harmony in these songs; they were separate and individual efforts. Song map–wise, more distinctly red and blue than blended or purple, they reflect an essential duality at the Beatles' core.

The Beginnings of Music Videos

How crazy was the video for *Strawberry Fields Forever*? It was like the Marx Brothers on acid. Set in the English countryside, it had the Beatles walking forward and then in reverse, and an old ghostly keyboard instrument attached to a tree with thin spider web–like strings. It was clear that another major Beatles transformation was taking place. It was also the first time a single didn't hit the top spot in the UK, so Beatlemania was over. The band was wearing brightly colored *Sgt. Pepper*-style clothing, running toward the viewer in a slow-motion, floaty way. It looked like Ringo, and then George, were riding in circles around the others on bicycles. At one point, Paul at the keyboard took a few odd steps back and then flew backward up into the tree. There was a red-light ball and something silvery up in the tree. It was day and then night. Together with the films *A*

Hard Day's Night and *Help*, the Beatles' music videos like this one are the ancestors of MTV.

The Details

The intro to *Penny Lane* is only a few high sweet notes on the bass. Paul's double-tracked voice comes in right away, the notes descending happily against a backdrop of percussive piano chords and a very prominent, bubbly bass line. At 0:07 the upbeat sing-song feeling gets a bit moodier and dramatic, with a classic McCartney old-music-hall chord change, along with a sustained note on a flute, some cymbals, and some other instrument that's hard to identify. At 0:13 there's a little turn-around riff played on a woodwind, the drums start up, and then the song settles into its easy-going groove.

The first verse is about the barber, and the second, the banker. At 0:34 there's a major emotional shift from the more matter-of-fact and somewhat silly verses to a more heartfelt and nostalgic refrain, and a dramatic uptick in emotional energy. Paul sings the first line, then there's a flourish from the brass band, and next comes a line of high-pitched voices as John and George join in with full harmonies. Paul calms things down with a last solo line before going back to the verse, as John and George's last harmonized word, *skies*, blends in with the beginning of Paul's next line.

In the third verse, which is about the fireman, at 0:58 and 1:02 the flute adds sets of three-note echoes to the lyrics, and in a buildup, we hear the brass come in and some clanging to evoke the fire station.

The instrumental solo is a virtuoso performance on piccolo trumpet along with some intermittent woodwinds that almost sound like a high-voiced music-hall chorus, a bit like what will be heard later in *Lady Madonna* or *Your Mother Should Know*. This instrumental break again provides more tension and buildup before another blissful refrain.

There are another two verses, and in the fourth verse Paul varies things just a little by singing a multi-syllable *pla-ay-ay-ay* at 1:52, followed by a sustained brass note at 1:55, then he sings a fifth verse.

The next time through the refrain there's more going on, with the piccolo trumpet playing a happily rising and uplifting line against a backdrop of some lower rhythmic chords by the brass band. At the end of this refrain there are some heavy drum beats and what sounds like a hand running down a good stretch of piano keys. The band then launches into the refrain one last time, but this time on a new, higher chord, to really build up the energy for the song's climax and ending. Paul is really singing his heart out here and this time the notes he's singing are doubled by what sounds like a high-pitched fife. There's another flourish on the piccolo trumpet, then the fife again playing behind the voices, but this time in harmony, matching what John and George sing. After a few more notes on the piccolo trumpet, Paul sings a final *Penny Lane* before an unusual instrumental ending consisting of a big echoing piano chord with an ethereal morph into a very high-pitched note and a tightly packed cymbal roll, almost sounding a little Eastern, and then it's over.

Timeline

1967—January 11: Paul McCartney and Ringo Starr see Jimi Hendrix perform in London ~January 18: Paul McCartney talks about the counterculture on the *Scene Special* TV show ~January 24: Paul McCartney and Brian Epstein discuss the Beatles' next film with playwright Joe Orton; it will become *Magical Mystery Tour* ~January 30 and 31: The Beatles film the music video for *Strawberry Fields Forever* ~

#18 *All You Need Is Love*

Another one-of-a-kind song, *All You Need Is Love* opens with a brass orchestra playing *La Marseillaise*, the French national anthem. The Beatles played this song on the first live, international satellite broadcast of a TV program, *Our World*; they invited a rich cast of characters including the Rolling Stones, Eric Clapton, and Keith Moon to help them close the show. It was seen and heard live by over 400 million people around the world.

Release and Recording

UK/US Release: July 7, 1967
Recorded: June 14 and 19-25, 1967
Length: 3:57
B-side: *Baby, You're a Rich Man*

Charting

US: On August 19, 1967, *All You Need Is Love* replaced *Light My Fire* by the Doors, which had been on top for 3 weeks, held for 1 week and was then replaced by *Ode to Billie Joe* by Bobbie Gentry, which stayed for 4 weeks.

UK: On July 19, 1967, it replaced *A Whiter Shade of Pale* by Procol Harum (the band's name is an area on the map of the moon) which had been on top for 6 weeks, stayed for 3 weeks and was then replaced by Scott McKenzie's *San Francisco*, which stayed for 4 weeks.

The Back Story

The Beatles were commissioned by the BBC to write a song for the UK's contribution to the *Our World* show, which had a total of nineteen different countries participating. In keeping with what was happening in the world in the summer of 1967, the central theme of John's quickly worked out song was *love*. (In the segment broadcast in the US, just before the song, we saw a house where Lyndon Johnson and Soviet Premier Alexei Kosygin were meeting.) George Martin once again arranged masterful orchestra strings and brass scores, although he was supposedly nervous about the whole thing coming off without a hitch because of the technical complexities involved, with each country handing the production off to another via satellite.

All You Need Is Love

0:00	La Marseillaise / ~ Military Drums ~

0:08	Refrain

0:27	Verse

0:44	Verse

1:01	Refrain

1:19	Solo

1:36	Refrain

1:53	Verse

2:10	Refrain

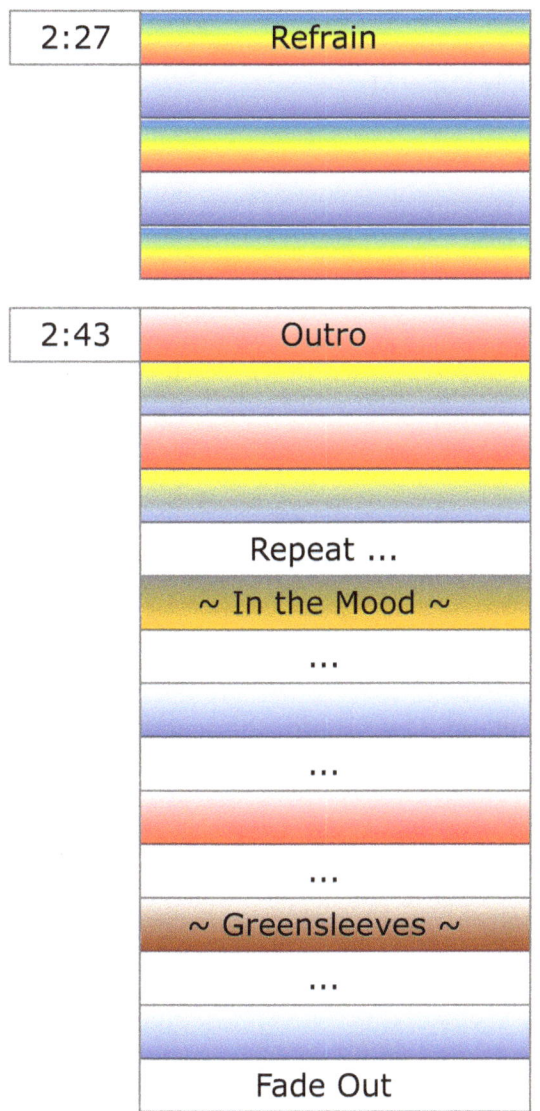

Song Map Legend

Brass Band
Drums
John, Paul, George, Harmony
String Quartet
John
Paul, George, Harmony
Guitar
Orchestra
Paul

The Song Map

The first colors show the brass orchestra playing the French national anthem, along with a military sounding drum roll. The harmonized parts use two-color blends, one for John, Paul, and George singing in three-part harmony, and the other where Paul and George provide harmonized backing vocals behind John's lead. However, many other people were actually singing backup vocals, including Mick Jagger, Keith Richards, Keith Moon, Graham Nash, Eric Clapton, Marianne Faithfull, Mike McGear, Jane Asher, and Pattie Boyd. Throughout the song, John's voice is interspersed between other voices and instruments, including a *Pepperland*-sounding brass section, a cello, and other orchestra strings. There's a guitar break about halfway through against a fully harmonized choir. The ending is long and drawn-out, with Paul interjecting whoops and hollers and at one point singing the refrain from *She Loves*

You. There are also horns playing parts of Glenn Miller's big-band hit *In the Mood* and the string section playing the melody to the old English folk song *Greensleeves*.

Personal Notes

The Our World Show

It was 1967 and the Summer of Love. *Sgt. Pepper* had been released just a month earlier, in June. I saw the live broadcast of *All You Need Is Love* on the *Our World* first-ever-satellite-TV show, and one of the things I remember was that John was chewing gum, and maybe Paul was too. The Beatles were all wearing headphones, which helps musicians to stay in-tune and in-time when there's a lot of sound going on around them. John wasn't playing an instrument; he was holding a single headphone up to his right ear and keeping time with his left hand. The Beatles were wearing *Pepperland*-like clothing, and while the original broadcast was in black and white, you can see on videos of it today how very colorful it all was. Paul, wearing a little heart near his left ear, wasn't playing his famous Hofner violin bass, but the Rickenbacker, the one that looks like part of it is made of a giant piece of melted gum, one like he played on the *I Am the Walrus* video. George was wearing bright red pants. Somebody else was drumming to the left of Ringo, twirling the drumsticks and brushes. Watching that video today is a bit like looking at all the things on the *Sgt. Pepper* album cover; there's lots to see—colored balloons, flowers, giant puppets, posters, lots of famous people. It's an encapsulated version of the Summer of Love.

Rolling Stone Magazine

The first issue of *Rolling Stone* magazine came out after the Summer of Love, in November 1967. Founded in San Francisco by Jann Wenner and Ralph Gleason, it featured stories about all the great music and musicians of the day, along with a healthy dose of counterculture politics. The first issue, with John Lennon as his *How I Won the War* film character on the cover, cost only 35 cents and looked like a little tabloid newspaper, a format the magazine used up until 1973. It was an amazing and welcome thing—a newspaper dedicated to rock music! Yeah Man. *Rolling Stone* started to get more focused on politics in the 70s, featuring writers like gonzo-journalist Hunter S. Thompson. The magazine published many, many famous interviews, like John Lennon's in 1968 about the *Two Virgins* album. With all the famous people on each issue's cover, *Rolling Stone* was like *Time* magazine for hippies.

Rolling Stone has been criticized for focusing too much on the 60s and 70s, and that's probably true, but like many, I do think the music we were listening to then was the best ever. It was such an extraordinary time, like no other musical time before or after.

Maybe because of the too-60s-and-70s criticism, the magazine started to cast a wider net in the 80s and 90s, including rap and hip-hop, creating kind of a strange mix if you're a 60s music nut. (I always thought they should have split it out into two separate magazines.) In any case, *Rolling*

Stone is still going strong today, more than fifty years later, still putting out an issue every two weeks. It's grown into quite an empire, publishing books of interviews and lots of lists, like the 100 or 500 greatest albums, songs, guitar players, or songwriters of all time, which is always a slippery slope, but it's still interesting to see what they come up with. Today you can actually buy a full set of CDs that contains the magazine's entire content from the first 40 years, which is really fun to look through.

The Details

All You Need Is Love begins with the stately opening notes of *La Marseillaise*, played by a harmonizing brass ensemble, and complete with a military parade drum roll. The Beatles' high-pitched voices, with John's out front, begin to slowly and calmly repeat the descending three-word chant *love love love*, set against a simple backdrop of rhythmic keyboard and drums. A long and descending harmonized cello line comes in at 0:17 and sets things up for the first verse.

John starts the verse in a relaxed and matter-of-fact way, against the repeating three high-pitched *ah ah ah*s in the backing vocals, which echo the *love love love* heard at the beginning, and the bass comes in now too, with some nice and simple resonating notes played on the heavy beats. The cello comes in again at 0:37. The lyrics are in the form of slightly nonsensical but innocent statements, very Lennon-esque, which continue throughout the song.

In the second verse, John's singing starts to sound much more heartfelt and emotional—his inflections are more sincere and even a little melancholy. This feeling is heightened as the orchestra's string section comes in.

The refrain is delivered as a call-and-response, with John's lines answered by a descending, almost comedic big-band horn section. And as he sings the title words, almost all on one note, there's a nice contrasting upbeat and harmonized three-note passage on the woodwinds. When John sings the last line of the refrain in a calmer and more matter-of-fact way, there's a release of tension.

At 1:19 a strident electric guitar wails into the mix, bending strings and working off the descending three-note theme that's so much a part of the song, but then at 1:27 the guitar just stops when you think there might be a few more notes coming. The high-pitched backing vocals continue and then the orchestra's string section starts to build up the energy, first with a swirling passage, then transitioning into a very rhythmic and choppier section.

There's another refrain, John singing the simple words with the orchestra strings and electric bass in the background, and this time through there's what sounds like a little yell from Paul at 1:40. The next time through the verse, the string section starts playing a newer rising, higher, and more uplifting melody.

At 2:10, and another time through the refrain, there are more voices and harmonizing as John holds a single note while the other musical lines all change around him. And then, in a buildup of emotional energy, the refrain is repeated, with Paul interjecting some easygoing come-all-ye lines.

At 2:43 the whole feeling changes—things become faster and more energetic as John repeats and is answered by the harmonized lines and endlessly repeated line. The ending is a crazy drawn-out minute-long hodgepodge, with bits of Glenn Miller's *In the Mood*, the English folk song *Greensleeves*, and maybe John singing the song titles *Yesterday* and Paul, *She Loves You*. It's engineered cacophony.

Timeline

1967—June 1: The album *Sgt. Pepper's Lonely Hearts Club Band* is released ~June 4: Only a few days after its release, Paul McCartney hears Jimi Hendrix play the title song to *Sgt. Pepper*, at a show in London's Saville Theatre ~June 19: Paul McCartney repeats on TV that he has taken LSD ~August 27: Brian Epstein is found dead from a drug overdose ~

#19 Hello, Goodbye

In this upbeat, lighter-fare song, we clearly hear the beginnings of the style that would become a hallmark of Paul McCartney's post-Beatles career. Shown as a video on the Ed Sullivan Show, where we see the Beatles go from black and white into color, *Hello, Goodbye* has a long crazy ending, and surprisingly enough, enjoyed the longest run of any number 1 hit in the UK charts.

Release and Recording

UK/US Release: November 24, 1967
Recorded: October 2—November 2, 1967
Length 3:27
B-side: *I Am the Walrus*

Charting

US: On December 30, 1967, *Hello, Goodbye* replaced the Monkees' *Daydream Believer*, which had held for 4 weeks, stayed for 3 weeks and was then replaced by *Judy in Disguise*, by John Fred and His Playboy Band, which held for 2 weeks.

UK: On December 6, 1967, *Hello, Goodbye* replaced *Let the Heartaches Begin* by Long John Baldry, which had been on top for 2 weeks, stayed 7 weeks and was then replaced by Georgie Fame's *The Ballad of Bonnie and Clyde*, which held for 1 week.

The Back Story

Hello, Goodbye was another Paul song and the first single to be released after the death of Brian Epstein. It's very creative McCartney pop and forms a striking contrast against the B-side, *I Am the Walrus*, which John wanted for the A-side. *Hello, Goodbye* supposedly originated from word-play based on opposites, between Paul and Alistair Taylor, who had originally been manager Brian Epstein's personal assistant (he later went on to become an executive at the Beatles' company, Apple Corps).

Hello, Goodbye

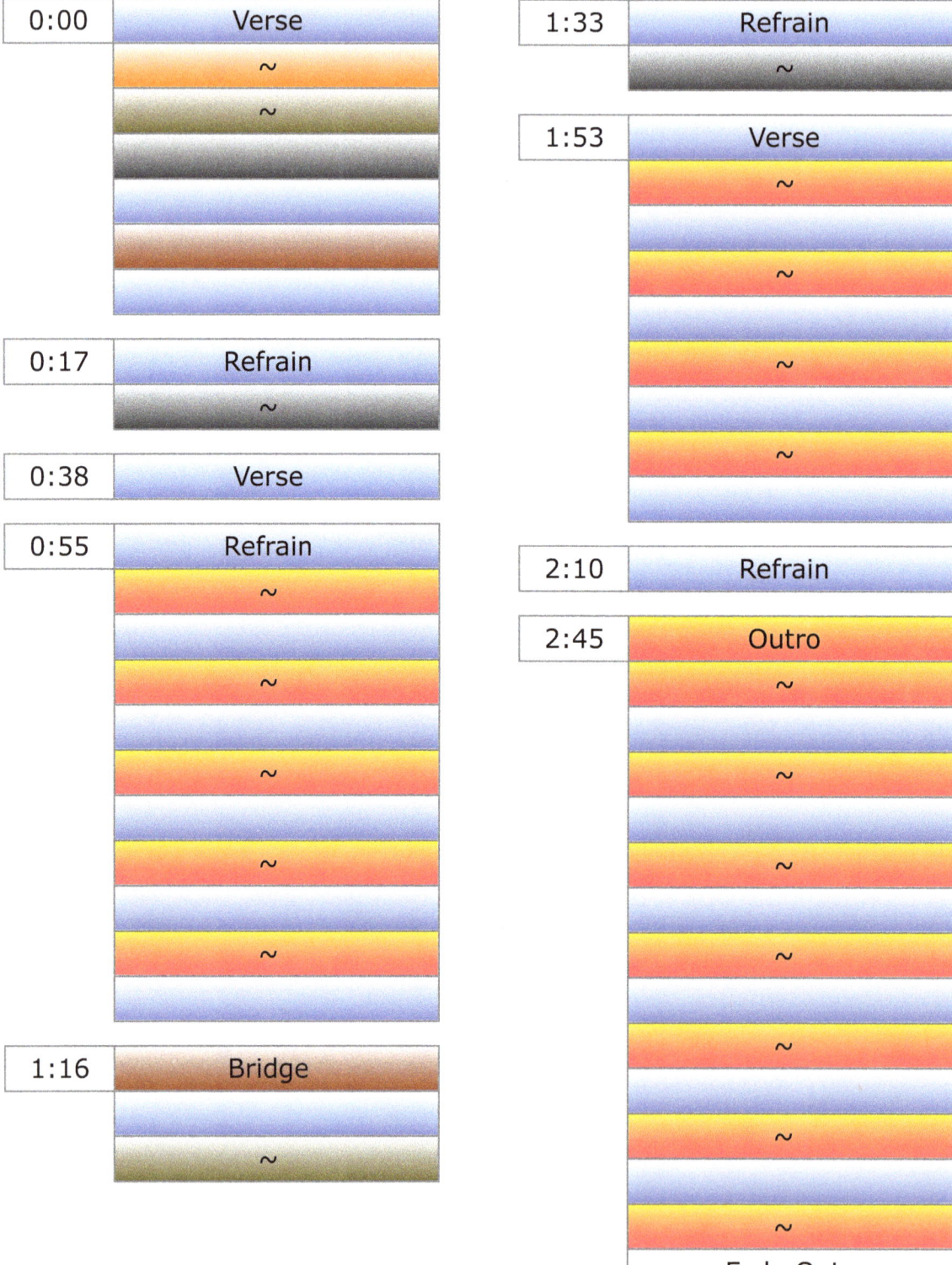

Song Map Legend

The Song Map

Like so many other hits in the second half of the Beatles' career, this one has lots of McCartney blue. There are a few spots where instruments, including piano, drums, the piercing guitar, and the orchestra are shown coming in. John and George sing call-and-answer style harmonized backing vocals the second time through the refrain, and then come in again for the long crazy outro, where their nonsensical *hela heba helloa*s are interspersed with Paul's hooting and hollering.

Personal Notes

Paul McCartney's Music-Hall Sound

This is one of the first songs where you can really hear Paul starting to morph into what will become his sound for his very long and successful post-Beatles career. There are many aspects to this transition, but one key element of it involves an old stage-show music-hall feel, which had always played a role in his musical interests. It's prominent in *When I'm Sixty-Four*, which he wrote in his pre-Beatle days on the piano at home (he was influenced by his dad, who had played in a jazz band in the 1920s). This old-music-hall feeling shows up in several McCartney numbers, such as the unusual chord here at the end of the verse in *Hello, Goodbye* or in the backing vocals in *Lady Madonna*. You can also hear it clearly in *Your Mother Should Know* and *Honey Pie*. There are many sides to Paul McCartney. There really is something very special and beautiful about these music-hall songs, adding even more to such a rich musical mixture. Remember, this is the same guy who wrote *Yesterday, Eleanor Rigby, Hey Jude,* and *Let It Be*, and the same guy who used to belt out high-energy rock 'n' roll songs in Little Richard style, like *Long Tall Sally* and *I'm Down*.

And for something so totally different, and a huge Lennon-McCartney contrast, consider the B-side to *Hello, Goodbye, I Am the Walrus*. Maybe it's just a crazy coincidence, but I always wondered if the ACDE chord progression in the verse did suggest the slang for LSD.

Four Years Later

I remember seeing the video for *Hello, Goodbye* on Ed Sullivan. It aired on Sunday, November 26, 1967. It was just about four years after the Beatles first appeared on the show in 1964. A lot had happened, and the Beatles had undergone quite a transformation. And this time they weren't even really there—they showed a little movie of them instead. The scenes changed from black and white into color, and at one point John slung his acoustic guitar over his neck, looking like Elvis. There were girls in grass skirts and a long goofy ending.

This was all a part of the *Magical Mystery Tour* project, which ended up being fifty-two incoherent minutes of randomly strung together scenes and musical numbers. The film first aired in the UK on the BBC channel on Boxing Day (the day after Christmas), 1967. Although it did show in a few places in the US in 1968, most Americans didn't see it until 1974, when it was released for theaters. The band had decided not to distribute it widely because it was so badly received in the UK. It's probably one of the only times that pretty much everyone would agree the Beatles fucked up.

The Details

As with many other songs, the very first thing we hear breaking the silence is Paul's voice. The song doesn't have an intro; it starts right in on the first verse. Paul's voice sounds double-tracked, but it's very smooth and blended, so the double-tracking may be a little less obvious. There are a lot of different instruments playing. The maracas are shaking away, there are orchestra strings, piano, and lots of bass lines walking up and down. At 0:07 we hear a long descending run down the scale of nine almost comical bass notes, like someone coming down a ladder in a cartoon. When the bass hits bottom, the drums start in with a great solid beat that feels like it's keeping things slowed down just a bit, using a sort of sustained backbeat. Before Paul sings *oh no*, there's a prominent, squawking downward slide on the guitar.

In the refrain, just after Paul sings the first line, the sharp-toned lead guitar moves in an opposite direction from the verse, and climbs back up the ladder with a very happy sounding *do-re-mi-fa-so-la-ti-do*. At the end of the refrain, we hear a somewhat unusual ragtime-like music hall chord, a little darker and dramatic than the bubbly material that leads up to it, and contrasting with the otherwise upbeat feeling.

For the second run through the verse, the string section is still backing Paul's voice, but it's a little different from the preceding time, to keep things interesting. Then at 0:46, the strings mimic the long descending line that the bass handled in an earlier section.

In the second time through the refrain, John and George come in with backing vocals, repeating the song's title words, with George's whispery high-pitched voice a little out front.

In the bridge, if you listen carefully, there are a couple of funny little clicks just before the string section plays a wavering, wandering little melody, accompanied by lots of drumming on the snare, sounding a little circus-like. Then Paul sings a repeating set of *why*s that echo off into a reverb-laden distance, and he does this again with a set of *bye*s a little later.

The next time through the verse at 1:53, the backing vocals get busier and begin to have their own side conversation in a call-and-response with Paul's main lyrics. At 2:05 Paul's high-pitched multi-syllable *oh-oh* sounds ironically alarmed and panicky.

The refrain is repeated twice more, this time finishing the last *hello* with a long string of more dramatic rising and falling *oh*s, all against some very heavy descending chords on guitars and bass. Then there's a final *he lo oh* along with a sustained chord on the piano, and it sounds like the song is over.

But it's a false ending and a setup for the long, crazy outro. The pace quickens, there's lots of tambourine, everybody is singing in harmony together, the voices are higher. The singers endlessly repeat the nonsense syllables *hela heba helloa*, with Paul ad-libbing some syncopated *cha chas* on the off-beats and then some whoops and hollers, like it's a Western, and it's all one chord and crazy as hell.

Timeline

1967—November 22: The BBC bans *I Am the Walrus* because of the phrases *pornographic priestess* and *knickers down* ~November 27: The album *Magical Mystery Tour* is released ~November: George Harrison begins recording the soundtrack for the film *Wonderwall* ~November 27: The album *Magical Mystery Tour* is released in the US ~December 26: The BBC broadcasts the film *Magical Mystery Tour* ~

#20 Lady Madonna

This song is a funny mixture of jump blues, boogie-woogie, and early twentieth-century jazz. It's got Paul's very different-sounding Fats Domino voice (Fats did actually cover the song later in the year). It features famous London Soho club owner and sax player Ronnie Scott in the break. Recorded before the Beatles left for India, *Lady Madonna* was their last release on the Parlophone/Capitol labels—everything after this was on their own Apple label.

Release and Recording

UK/US Release: March 15, 1968
Recorded: February 3 and 6, 1968
Length: 2:16
B-side: *The Inner Light*

Charting

US: *Lady Madonna* only made it up to number 4 on the Billboard Hot 100.

UK: On March 27, 1968, *Lady Madonna* replaced *The Legend of Xanadu* by Dave Dee, Dozy, Beaky, Mick & Tich, which had been on top for 1 week. It stayed for 2 weeks and was then replaced by Cliff Richard's *Congratulations*, which held for 2 weeks.

The Back Story

This was the Beatles' last Parlophone label release in the UK, and Capitol label release in the US—after this everything by the Beatles was released on the bright green Apple label. *See how they run*, the last line in the bridge, is also found in the lyrics to *I Am the Walrus*, which was released some four months earlier. The sax solo is performed by Ronnie Scott, a jazz musician and the owner of the famous Jazz Club bearing his name in Soho, London. Supposedly, Scott didn't think his part was loud enough in the mix, so Paul brought it out more in subsequent versions that can be heard on the *Anthology* and *Love* albums. Note that Saturday is missing from the description of the struggling single mother's days.

Lady Madonna

0:00	Intro
0:09	Verse
0:18	Verse
0:26	Bridge
0:44	Verse / ~
0:53	Sax / ~ Guitar ~ / ~ Handclaps ~
1:01	Bridge / Sax Break / ~ / ~ / ~ / ~ / ~ / ~
1:19	Verse
1:28	Sax / ~ Guitar ~ / ~ Handclaps ~
1:37	Bridge / ~ / ~ / ~ / ~ / ~
1:54	Verse
2:06	Outro / Cymbal Crash

Song Map Legend

Piano
Paul
John, Paul, George, Harmony
Guitar
Sax
Handclaps
John, George, Harmony
Cymbal

The Song Map

The song opens with a lively barrelhouse piano intro, feeling like vintage rock 'n' roll but with some heavier and more modern-sounding rock chords thrown in. There's lots of blue as Paul goes through the verses and bridges, singing from the back of his throat and not sounding like his usual self. There are two spots in the verses where the sax steps out to make a quick statement against a backdrop of guitar and handclaps, and there's a very jazzy break on sax accompanied by some roaring-twenties-sounding backing vocals, rendered in high falsetto, and shown here in John and George's harmonizing red-yellow fade. The last time through the bridge, instead of the sax, Paul's singing is interspersed with the backing vocals, before the last verse in blue.

Personal Notes

The White Album

Even though it was recorded and released months before, I always thought that *Lady Madonna* had a *White Album* feel to it, a hint of what was coming. Maybe it's because Paul has that crazy new sound in his voice, the sound that would morph into the way he ends up singing *Why Don't We Do It in the Road* or *Get Back*.

The *White Album* came out in November 1968, and I'll never forget hearing it for the first time. I think it was the last week of the month, a few days after the official release date of November 22. All day, the DJs had been really building it up on the radio station I listened to: WDRC, 102.9 FM in Hartford, Connecticut. They started playing it at about 11:00 p.m. and they played the whole thing. It was a school night; I was thirteen and in the eighth grade, but I stayed up to hear it, all thirty songs, all ninety-three-plus minutes. I was off in a remote upstairs room of our house, sitting in an old cloth-covered rocking chair, where I used to listen to music for hours and hours on this great old antique radio and sneak cigarettes. The radio gave off this dimly glowing golden light, creating quite an atmosphere for listening to music.

The *White Album* songs were *so* different, unlike anything we'd ever heard from the Beatles before. Sure, it's a surprise that some of the songs actually made it out of George Martin's studio, but so many of the tracks were just totally amazing, with such incredible variety in the lot, such opposites, and such a full spectrum of feelings and sounds in between. There's the rocker opener, *Back in the USSR*, which starts with the landing airplane noises and then uses Beach Boys overtones in the bridge, followed by John's gentle *Dear Prudence*. There's the acerbic and jarring *Glass Onion* and the goofy *Ob-La-Di, Ob-La-Da*. There's George Harrison's masterful *While My Guitar Gently Weeps*, with Eric Clapton's incredible playing (before finding out it was Clapton I remember thinking that George had something new in his playing). There's Paul's beautiful *Blackbird* and the folksy *Rocky Raccoon* (the band wrote many of these songs in India, where Donovan supposedly got them started fingerpicking). But the first time I heard *Why Don't We Do It in the Road* and then *Helter Skelter*, I remember just thinking *what the fuck*? But then there's the calming *I Will*, the tenderly heartfelt and soothing *Julia*, the incredibly sad *Long, Long, Long*, and so many others. It all ends with Ringo's *Good Night,* which sounds like the end of some weird and wonderful movie soundtrack.

I love the part in the *Anthology* film, when they're talking about how some of the songs may not have been fit for an album, where Paul just says, "It's the Beatles' bloody White Album." That says it all.

The Details

The beginning is a few bars of rollicking boogie-woogie piano and some swishy brushes. Paul sings the title words to start the first verse. His voice is different. He's singing in an unusual falsetto. It's not his Little Richard voice, but it's still much sharper and harder than usual, no sincere angelic choir boy sound here. There's a hard backdrop of thundering bass notes and very heavy drum beats.

For the first two verses, the song is more or less a rocker, although it does have an unusual-sounding chord that's not in the 3 chord set of classic rock 'n' roll or blues. At the bridge, there's a major gear shift, evoking a kind of roaring twenties music hall. At the second line in the bridge, there's a long line of descending bass notes, going down and down, until they change direction and come back up a little. In the last line, in sharp contrast to Paul's crazy falsetto, there's a beautiful burst of multi-part harmony.

The third time through the verse, a sharp electric guitar comes in, exactly matching the rising phrases in the bass line. Paul ends this verse with a high multi-syllable *re-est*. After this there's a short solo break featuring the sax, matching the bass and electric guitar lines, and playing the same few bars that were used for the intro.

On the second pass through the bridge, there's both a high falsetto 1920s refrain and a very jazzy sax solo, although the sax seems to be more in the background with the voices out front and prominent. At the end of this solo, we again hear the fully harmonized last line, and this time there's a sharp, downward cascading run on the electric guitar to change things up a little.

There's another verse, a little instrumental break, and the bridge again, this time with the high voice falsetto *pa pa pa pas* as a backdrop to Paul's singing.

There's one last verse, with Paul singing the last multi-syllable *mee-eet* way up high, as he did in a previous verse, and then a very short outro, with just piano, bass, some nice staggered drumming, and a little cymbal crash and last piano note to finish things up.

Timeline

1968—January 25: The Beatles film their little scene for the end of the movie *Yellow Submarine* ~February 6: Ringo Starr appears on Cilla Black's TV show ~February 15: The Lennons and the Harrisons arrive in Rishikesh, India. Paul McCartney, Jane Asher, and the Starrs arrive a few days later ~March 1: Ringo and Maureen Starr leave India ~May 14: John Lennon and Paul McCartney appear on *The Tonight Show* and announce their new production company, Apple Corps. ~

#21 Hey Jude

Lasting for more than seven minutes, Paul's comforting and uniquely beautiful song *Hey Jude*, written to cheer up Julian Lennon after his parents split up, is the longest of all the hit singles. Another McCartney song that defies classification, it somewhat foreshadows *Let It Be*. And in case there's any doubt, *Hey Jude* assures the world in the summer of 1968 that the Beatles are still as amazing as ever.

Release and Recording

UK/US Release: August 26, 1968
Recorded: July 31—August 1, 1968
Length: 7:10
B-side: *Revolution*

Charting

US: On September 28, 1968, *Hey Jude* replaced *Harper Valley PTA*, by Jeannie C. Riley, which had filled the top spot for a week. *Hey Jude* stayed on top for a whopping 9 weeks and was then replaced by Diana Ross and the Supremes' *Love Child*, which held for 1 week. This was the longest run at number 1 for any Beatles song, and tied with Bobby Darin's 1959 hit, *Mack the Knife*, which had also been on top for 9 weeks.

UK: On September 11, 1968, *Hey Jude* replaced the Bee Gees' *I've Gotta Get a Message to You*, which had been on top for 1 week. It stayed 2 weeks and was then replaced by Mary Hopkin's cover of the translated Russian song *Those Were the Days* (also arranged and produced by Paul McCartney), which stayed an impressive 6 weeks.

The Back Story

Originally called *Hey Jules*, this was Paul's song to comfort Julian Lennon after John and Cynthia split and John got involved with Yoko Ono. It was the band's first single on their new green Apple label. And even though it was written with Julian in mind, John supposedly thought it was Paul's way of saying that his being with Yoko Ono was okay.

Hey Jude

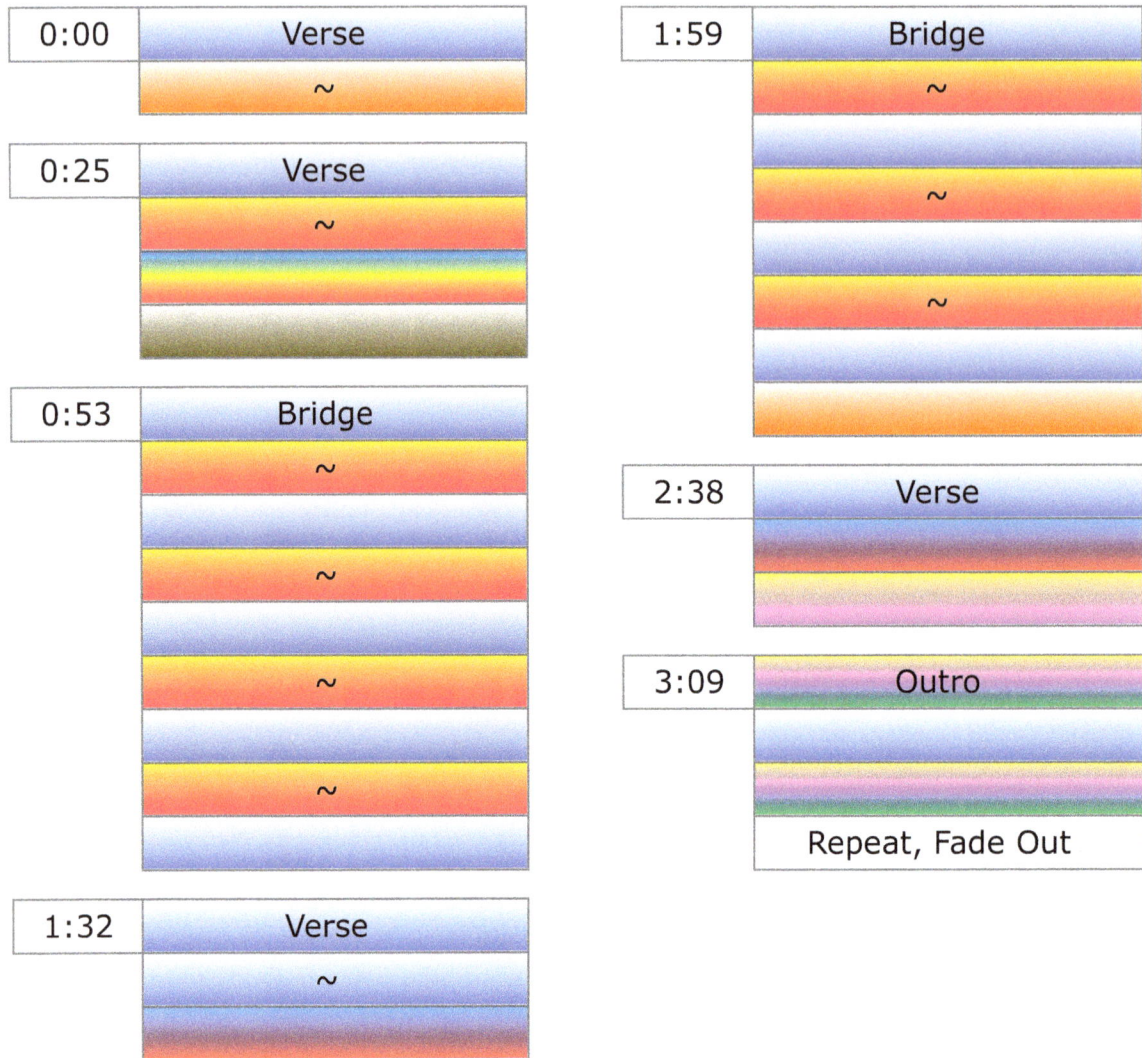

Song Map Legend

The Song Map

Hey Jude features another all-blue Paul beginning, his singing measured and sincere against the piano. John and George join in with some harmony for the end of the second verse and again in the bridge. In the third verse, there's an unusual little section where Paul is singing background vocals behind his own lead vocals, then John comes in to harmonize with him. After another bridge with John and George still harmonizing, John comes in to harmonize for most of the final verse. The song ends with a long drawn-out mantra-chanting outro, shown as all four Beatles in unison.

Personal Notes

The Beatles in 1968

Before *Hey Jude* came out at the end of the summer in 1968, I remember thinking that maybe the Beatles were slipping out of the scene. *Sgt. Pepper* had come out well over a year before, and their previous single, *Lady Madonna*, released over five months earlier, had failed to hit the top spot in the US. The album *Magical Mystery Tour* had done very well in the US, but the TV film of the same name had been panned in the UK. The *White Album* was still four months away.

There was also just so much other great music coming out. The Stones had released *Jumpin' Jack Flash*, one of their best hits ever, back in May, and *Street Fighting Man* had just hit the airwaves. There were top albums by Cream, the Doors, Hendrix, Big Brother and the Holding Company, and many others. And the Beatles were just so different now. A lot had changed after the album *Revolver* came out in 1966, and with *Eleanor Rigby*, a song which arguably cuts the Beatles' set of hits into two very different halves. The band had stopped touring, Brian Epstein had died, the number of singles had slowed down, and while they continued to score top hits, they generally didn't stay at the top of the charts for as long.

Then *Hey Jude* came out.

A month after its release, *Hey Jude* hit number 1 in the US and stayed for a total of 9 weeks, the longest any of the Beatles' singles would ever stay at the top spot. It was clearly more of a Paul song than a Beatles song, if the distinction can be made, but it had a universal appeal. In the UK it stayed at number 1 for only 2 weeks. It's hard to say why it did so much better in the US. Maybe it has something to do with how soothing the song is and how much everything seemed to be unraveling in 1968, with the Tet Offensive in Vietnam, President Johnson announcing that he wouldn't run again, the assassinations of Martin Luther King Jr. and Robert Kennedy, the rioting and violence at the Chicago Democratic Convention.

It's also interesting to note that the other two sincere, sentimental Paul McCartney numbers, *Yesterday* and *Let It Be*, along with George Harrison's *Something*, didn't hit number 1 in the UK either.

The Details

The song starts with Paul singing the title words very calmly and clearly, using a more sustained and rising note for the word *Hey*, and then coming down solidly on the first beat with *Jude*. The piano chords are gentle and graceful, the chord progression is calm, the simple words comforting.

In the second verse, an acoustic guitar comes in with very simple strumming, while the tambourine adds to a sparse but stately beat. This time around we hear John and George add in harmonized *agh*s to back up the third and fourth lines, along with a beautifully harmonized *better* as the last word. At the end, Ringo adds in some great slightly staggered drumming, taking a full trip around his kit to bring up the energy a little for the transition into the bridge.

The bass comes in as the bridge starts, playing a slow descending line, and what started out as simple voice and piano has been built up, by gradually adding more and more layers, into a very full sound. John and George continue to sing the drawn-out, descending harmonized *agh*s behind Paul's now slightly more energy charged lyrics. The bridge ends with Paul singing a string of *nah nah*s and then a bluesy piano chord, echoing the notes of the last few *nah*s that preceded it, which leaves us waiting with a bit of anticipation for the next verse to start.

The third time through the verse at 1:32, the tambourine is now playing double time and filling in more space, adding energy. This time through the verse, to change things up, Paul adds in a few of his own ad-libbed backing vocals, which blends in with John joining in to harmonize on the last two lines, and we hear another little *Hey Jude* from Paul, again faintly in the back.

On the second bridge we can hear what sounds like an organ coming in to play a few chords around 2:13, after which Paul gets more soulful and bluesy, really biting into some of the words. Then we hear the quizzical line containing the word *shoulder* (supposedly John's idea to keep in the song), before another string of *nah nah nah*s and finishing with a bluesy but understated *yeah* from Paul.

Paul sings a longer and more heartfelt multi-syllable *Hey Ju-uh-uh-uh-de* at 2:38, and then John joins in to harmonize with him for this entire last verse. If you listen carefully you can hear someone yell *oh* around 2:56, supposedly John, and then at about 2:58 it sounds like someone saying *fucking hell*, supposedly Paul, for making a mistake on the piano. At the end of the verse, the harmony ends and we hear a high-energy string of rising *better better better*s. And just like that, this gentle stately song transitions into a long, drawn-out series of seemingly endless chanting—*nah nah nah nah nah nah nah* *nahhhh,* with Paul ad-libbing various *yeah yeah yeah*s, some howling, some high-energy *Judey Judey Judey* parts, and an assortment of other rantings and ravings. At 3:48, a full 36-piece orchestra joins in on the fun with long drawn-out notes, and it just goes on and on. This ending, which lasts for about four minutes, is actually longer than the main part of the song.

Timeline

1968—July 17: The film *Yellow Submarine* premiers in London ~July 31: The Apple Boutique store in London closes its doors ~August 22: Ringo Starr walks out of the *White Album* recording sessions ~September 3: Ringo rejoins the Beatles ~November 22: The *White Album* is released in the UK and US ~

#22 Get Back

With tinges of country-western set to a steady galloping groove and lots of instrumental breaks, *Get Back* showcases yet another version of Paul McCartney's voice, along with Billy Preston on electric piano. John's lead guitar licks are super slick, and the lyrics tell a funny little story about Jojo and Loretta Martin, who turns out to be a man.

Release and Recording

UK/US Release: April 11, 1969
Recorded: January 27–28, 1969
B-side: *Don't Let Me Down*
Length 3:14

Charting

US: On May 24, 1969, *Get Back* replaced *Aquarius/Let the Sunshine In* by the 5th Dimension, which had held for 6 weeks, stayed 5 weeks and was then replaced by Henry Mancini's *Love Theme from Romeo and Juliet*, which stayed for 2 weeks. This was the Beatles' seventeenth US number 1, surpassing Elvis, who had had sixteen.

UK: On April 23, 1969, *Get Back* replaced *Israelites*, by Jamaican reggae Desmond Dekker & The Aces, which had held for 1 week, stayed for 6 weeks and was then replaced by Tommy Roe's *Dizzy*, which held for a single week.

The Back Story

Another Paul song, the *Get Back* single was officially credited to "The Beatles with Billy Preston," which was a first, as no other artist's name had ever been included on a release. It was also the first stereo release of a Beatles single in the US, although it was still released in mono in the UK. Some of the main lyrics were supposedly inspired by George Harrison's song *Sour Milk Sea*, which included the line *get back to the place you should be*, and for which Paul had played bass on Jackie Lomax's recording some months earlier. An earlier version of the song had been morphed into a satire about racism in the UK and US, with references to Pakistanis and Puerto Ricans.

Get Back

0:00	Intro / ~
0:08	Verse
0:23	Refrain
0:39	Solo
0:54	Refrain
1:12	Solo
1:28	Verse
1:43	Refrain
1:59	Solo
2:14	Refrain / False Ending
2:34	Reprise / Ad-libbing
2:51	Refrain / Fade Out

Song Map Legend

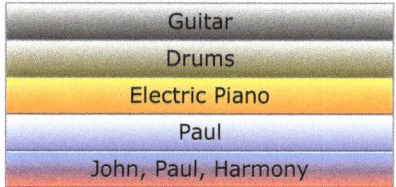

The Song Map

Again, lots of blue with Paul singing most of the parts on his own. The intro is tight, driving band work featuring guitar and drums, and tailing off with just a little electric piano in the mix. There are plenty of slippery country-sounding guitar licks, courtesy of John Lennon. John only comes in to harmonize with Paul the second time through the refrain. There's lots of funky Billy Preston electric piano in the mix as well as for the solo. We hear John's smooth guitar work throughout. At 2:34 before the outro, there's a little drum and guitar moment to set up for some McCartney ad-libbing.

Personal Notes

John Lennon, Guitar Player

John played the great rockabilly guitar licks that we hear in *Get Back*. He also wrote and played the catchy and classic guitar hooks in *Day Tripper* and *I Feel Fine,* the great bluesy riffs in *You Can't Do That,* the dark haunting break in *Come Together,* and the main riffs in *Revolution*. While he was officially the band's rhythm guitar player, he clearly ended up playing some very memorable lead guitar parts.

Rhythm guitar players are the unsung heroes of rock 'n' roll. John Lennon once said in an interview, talking about his guitar playing, that he knew how to move the band along, and that he surely did. Rhythm guitar players provide a major part of the beat and the harmonic foundation for a song. Look at Chuck Berry's amazing rhythm guitar playing, or what Peter Townshend did in the Who with his crazy windmill strumming. And while he did take lead breaks in many Rolling Stones songs, Keith Richards was still the essential driving rhythmic force in the band, playing killer guitar parts, as did Jimmy Page in Led Zeppelin. People might think it's easier to play rhythm than lead, but there's a special indescribable quality to good rhythm playing, a bit more like drumming or bass playing, and it's a rare skill.

The Nomads

When I was in junior high school, we had the best local band ever. They called themselves *The Nomads*. Their first name was *Non, C'est Fou,* which means "No, it's crazy" in French, because there are so many families of French Canadian ancestry in the part of rural western Massachusetts I grew up in.

This band of six guys, with a lead singer, rhythm, lead, and bass guitars, keyboards, and drums, was unbelievably good. They used to win all the *Battle of the Bands* contests, and they played at all the high school dances. Their set list included all the great hits of the day—*Light My Fire, Purple Haze, 96 Tears, The Midnight Hour, The Letter, For Your Love,* and so many other great songs (the lead guitar player could even play the blazing guitar licks from the Monkees' number *Valeri*), but their best number was a cover of the Vanilla Fudge's version of the Supremes' *You Keep Me Hangin' On*. They'd set the mood with that swirly organ intro. The lead singer would be solemn, staring down at the floor, his hand raised in the air, just waiting mysteriously under a spot light, his face in darkness, then the drums would loudly hammer in, the tension would build, and you'd be hit with the opening lyrics. It was unforgettable—they were the best.

I'll also never forget the rhythm guitar player (my idol at the time, and still my friend today) lending me his beautiful yellow-to-red-sunburst Rickenbacker semi-hollow-body guitar for a weekend when I was in the eighth grade—I was in guitar heaven, and I still think those are the most beautiful guitars ever made.

The Details

Get Back starts with an energetic buildup on guitar, bass, and drums, the bass thumping away on a single driving note. The snare drum is almost military, going along at a good clip and progressively getting louder. The feeling is tight, almost restrained, until the end, when we hear a couple of simple bluesy notes on Billy Preston's electric piano and a big release in pressure through a quick couple of chord changes and cymbal crashes, and then the first verse starts. This steady-driving-then-release pattern is used throughout the entire song, in all the refrains and instrumental breaks.

Paul's voice is different here again—he seems to be singing from the back of his throat and restricting his normally full toned voice, resulting in a tight and slightly clamped sound. After every two lines in the verse, John plays some great country-western-sounding guitar licks, filling things in with a rising then falling passage, almost sounding like a slide guitar.

In the refrain, each of the lines starts with the title words *Get Back*, with Paul's voice now higher and floating a little, but still in the crazy tight-throated falsetto. All the while, the drums are galloping along like a horse, in the same steady beat. In the second half of the refrain, the dropping chord changes and cymbal crashing get louder and more dramatic, changing things up, and serving to break up what might otherwise become a little monotonous from the constant steady drive.

After the refrain, John steps out front with a slick but laid-back guitar solo, smoothly sliding into and bending the notes, repeating the pattern of the intro. He plays some especially cool licks at around 0:53, filling in more space between the notes and building up energy before finishing up just after Paul's funny little *go home* at 0:49.

Instead of another verse after the guitar break, John comes in to harmonize with Paul for another refrain. Their voices together are now lower than what's been heard so far, with Paul singing an octave below this time, and the feeling changes, getting a little darker. This refrain contains the only vocal harmony in the song. Billy Preston's electric piano is also now answering the singers' calls to *Get Back* with some simple between-the-lines blue notes.

This time at the end of the refrain, there's a descending set of electric piano notes, slowing things down to a short pause, almost creating a false ending. Paul comes in with a quick *get back Jo*, and then it's Billy Preston's turn for a break. He plays a very bouncy, upbeat solo with quick snappy notes and chords, echoing the steady and tight groove of the song. For this break, Ringo has altered the drumming, no longer playing the galloping snare but instead just hitting backbeats, to leave a little more space for Billy Preston's riffs.

There's another verse at 1:28, matching the first, Paul now singing about a new character with some quizzical transgender lines, and no obvious connection with the first verse's Jojo.

On the next refrain, Paul changes his voice, biting into the first *Get* and then floating his tone up a little on the *Back*. He adds an extra ad-libbed and punctuated *get back Loretta* at the end, with a funny little squeak and a hoot at around 2:00.

John takes another guitar break, much like the first, but he varies it just enough so that it doesn't sound repetitive. Paul then sings another refrain, and he's letting loose more now, building up the energy. At the end of this refrain, there are more descending notes on the electric piano, a high-pitched, drawn-out *oooh* from Paul, and a more pronounced false ending.

There's a great pick-up fill from Ringo before the song slides back into a rock 'n' roll groove, transitioning into the outro refrain with Paul ad-libbing some comical lines, initially more spoken than sung, his voice all over the place. Then it starts to fade away, as we hear a last little *Jojo* from Paul, and the snare drum galloping away into the distance.

Timeline

1969—January 13: The *Yellow Submarine* soundtrack album is released in the US ~January 30: The Beatles perform together for the last time on Apple's London rooftop ~March 12: Paul McCartney marries Linda Eastman in London ~March 20: John Lennon marries Yoko Ono in Gibraltar ~March 25: John Lennon and Yoko Ono stage a bed-in in Amsterdam ~April 22: John Lennon changes his middle name to Ono ~

#23 The Ballad of John and Yoko

The Ballad of John and Yoko takes place in Southampton, Paris, Gibraltar, Vienna, Amsterdam, and London. John sings about the hassles he and Yoko faced getting married and holding their bed-ins. The song is bouncy with a straight rock 'n' roll chord progression, heavy bass, and squawky electric guitar licks. *Christ* and *crucifixion* are continually mentioned in the refrain, and the ending has a mariachi-band feel.

Release and Recording

UK/US Release: May 30, 1969
Recorded: April 14, 1969
Length: 2:59
B-Side: *Old Brown Shoe*

Charting

US: *The Ballad of John and Yoko* made it up to number 8 in the US charts.

UK: On June 11, 1969, it replaced *Dizzy* by Tommy Roe, which had been at number 1 for a single week. It stayed at the top spot for 3 weeks and was then replaced by Thunderclap Newman's *Something in the Air*, which held for 3 weeks. It was, sadly, the Beatles' last UK number 1 single.

The Back Story

John wrote this song while he and Yoko were on their honeymoon in Paris, detailing the events they had to go through to get married. He also recounts their follow-up Amsterdam bed-in and other adventures. Only John and Paul perform on the recording, with Paul on drums. George and Ringo were away and there was a hurry to get the song done. Because the lyrics include the words *Christ* and *crucify*, some radio stations in the US refused to give the song any air time. This was the first Beatles release of a stereo single in the UK.

The Ballad of John and Yoko

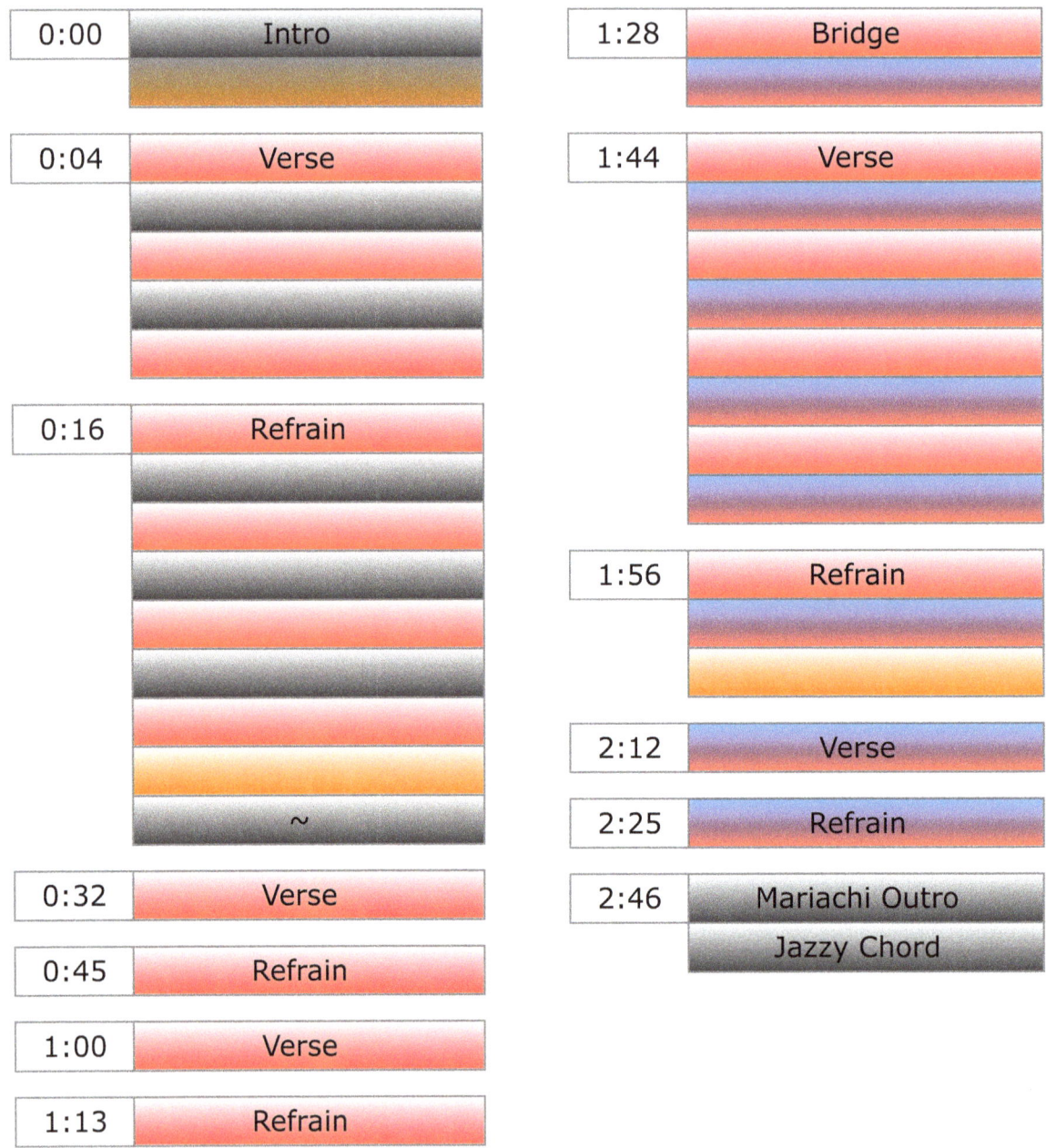

Song Map Legend

Guitar
Bass
John
Piano
John, Paul, Harmony

The Song Map

The first four sets of verse and refrain are all in John Lennon red, with lots of guitar work used in a call-and-answer pattern, and a little piano, highlighted in the first part of the map. About halfway through the song, we see the red-blue blend, when Paul comes in to harmonize, his voice sounding comedic and even sarcastic. He intersperses some echoed words in a verse and continues to harmonize for the rest of the song. A piano comes in after the second-last refrain playing a repeated boogie-type backdrop to lift the energy up for the end. The outro sounds a bit like a mariachi band.

A Personal Note

Two John Lennons

The world saw multiple versions of each Beatle over the years. At first, they all look alike: clean-cut mop-tops in black and white, all wearing the same stylish, collarless Pierre Cardin suits and Beatle boots, saying quirky things, bowing after each performance, all their songs about adolescent love sung with incredible energy. While their individual personalities came through, they were each a part of a more important whole. Then things changed, and along came the wildly colored clothing, mustaches and beards, their individuality showing more. The music and the lyrics changed a lot too; we started to hear sitars and orchestras in the mix. But more than any other Beatle, over the brief seven years of their spotlight on the world stage, we saw two very different and distinct John Lennons.

It's hard to say exactly where the dividing line is, when the changes occurred. It's safe to say that a major transformation occurred in 1966, the year the album *Revolver* was released and the Beatles had stopped touring. Earlier in the year John had made the comment about being more popular than Jesus, then he sort of apologized months later when there was such a visceral reaction, especially in the southern US where they burned Beatles records. Then there's of course the whole story with Yoko. There's also his crazy off-the-wall stuff, like the 1968 *Two Virgins* album showing John and Yoko naked on the album cover, bagism, the bed-ins, all the anti-war events, the song *Give Peace a Chance*.

There were lots of changes in his music, too. He went from a soulful rhythm-and-blues rock 'n' roller to a much more sentimental and emotional songwriter, penning beautiful numbers like *In My Life*, *Julia*, *Across the Universe*, all wonderful songs. It's just hard to believe that the John we see traipsing across the screen in the white suit and sneakers, when he and Yoko are going to Gibraltar to get married, is the same guy we saw standing brazenly front and center, his legs wide apart, rocking the world and singing *Twist and Shout* only a few years earlier.

The Details

This song starts with a simple intro, just a few bars of one chord, and a solid backbeat, with the bass playing a classic rock 'n' roll line like the one you can hear in Larry William's 1958 hit *Slow Down* (which the Beatles covered in 1964) and some other early rockers. John's voice is single-tracked, and there are some funny little rockabilly guitar squeaks and squawks that follow his lines.

In the refrain, which starts with references to Christ, John's singing is interspersed with country-style guitar licks, this time as call-and-answer sets of descending short chords. At 0:29 we hear simple and rapidly repeated boogie notes come in on the piano, but only for a few seconds.

John goes through the verse and refrain a few more times, and then just before the bridge there's a flourish on the piano, with more pronounced 1950s style rock 'n' roll twinkling and descending high notes.

Paul joins in to harmonize with John for the second half of the bridge. There's a conspicuous little pause at the end of the bridge, followed by a few pick-up beats on the drums to transition back into the next verse.

In the next verse, Paul joins in to harmonize on the last words of each of John's lines.

Paul harmonizes on the last part of the next refrain, and he stays in to sing along with John for the rest of the song. The piano notes are now in full time, making things a little more frantic, and there are some quick, sharp slides on the guitar.

The last two lines of the refrain are repeated for the outro. There is a relatively short mariachi-sounding run on the guitar, and then the song ends on a jazzy chord.

Timeline

1969—May 4: John Lennon and Yoko Ono buy the Tittenhurst Park estate ~May 8: Manager Allen Klein signs a three-year contract with three of the Beatles; Paul McCartney does not sign ~June 1: John Lennon and Yoko Ono record *Give Peace a Chance* with many others in Montreal ~July 4: *Give Peace a Chance* is released by the Plastic Ono Band in the UK ~

#24 Something

George Harrison's unique contribution to the set of Beatles hits is a beautifully crafted love ballad. A double A-side with John Lennon's *Come Together*, *Something* has turned out to be the second most covered Beatles song of all time, after *Yesterday*. It's no wonder that Frank Sinatra sang it too, declaring it to be "the greatest love song of the past fifty years."

Release and Recording

UK/US Release: October 6, 1969
Recorded: May 2 and 5, July 16, and August 15, 1969
Length: 2:59
Double A-side: *Come Together*

Charting

US: On November 29, 1969, the *Something* double-A with *Come Together* replaced *Wedding Bell Blues* by the 5th Dimension, which had been at the number 1 spot for 3 weeks. The double-A stayed for a week and was then replaced by *Na Na Hey Hey Kiss Him Goodbye* by Steam, which stayed for 2 weeks. (It was at this point in time that Billboard changed the practice of counting sales and airplay separately.) This was the Beatles' eighteenth number 1 hit single in the US, again breaking Elvis's record, which was now seventeen.

UK: The double A-side didn't hit the top spot, but it did make it up to number 4.

The Back Story

Whether inspired by the Hindu deity Krishna, wife Pattie Boyd, or both, George's first A-side has been covered by Elvis, Frank Sinatra, Ray Charles, James Taylor, and many others. A music video of the song was made with each band member shown with his wife (the Beatles were not actually together for the shoot). George had been working on *Something* earlier in 1968, during the *White Album* recording sessions. The opening lyrics are based on a James Taylor song, *Something in the Way She Moves*. (Taylor got his start on the Beatles' Apple record label.)

Something

Time	Section
0:00	Intro
0:05	Verse
	~
	~
0:27	Refrain
	Riff
	~
0:38	Verse
1:00	Refrain
	Riff
1:15	Bridge
1:42	Solo
2:13	Verse
2:35	Refrain
	Riff
2:43	Outro

Song Map Legend

The Song Map

In *Something*, George's one song in the set of hits, his pale yellow is prominent. This color was chosen for his voice in the song maps so that it would blend to show harmonies and unison singing with John's red to make orange and Paul's blue to make green. This song of course has lots of masterful Harrison guitar, using his signature strident electric rock licks, in contrast with the gentle flow of the song, and still fitting in perfectly. Paul comes in to harmonize, at first in the bridge, played only once, and then again for the entire last verse. There's an expectedly amazing and generally longer guitar solo, covering the material from both the verse and refrain. George sings the last refrain alone, and then the outro is a mix of guitar and orchestra. This song map has some unusual blends of color to try to capture combinations of drums, bass, guitar, and orchestra.

Personal Notes

George Harrison, Songwriter

When *Something* hit the top of the charts in the US, it was obvious to everyone that George Harrison had developed into an amazing songwriter. There was clear indication of this a year before as well, with *While My Guitar Gently Weeps* standing out as one of the best numbers on the *White Album*.

While John and Paul wrote and sang most of the lead vocals to the band's songs, George always had a track or two on every album. In the beginning these were covers, like *Chains*, *Roll Over Beethoven*, and *Devil in Her Heart*, or songs penned by John and Paul, like *Do You Want to Know a Secret?* or *I'm Happy Just to Dance with You*. Then with his early and somewhat dark *Don't Bother Me*, George started to write his own songs, and followed with the floaty wah-wah-laden *I Need You*, then the strident and jarring *Taxman*.

George developed a strong interest in Indian music. He first heard the sitar on the set of *Help* in early 1965. Later that year he bought one for himself, which we first heard on *Norwegian Wood*. He went on to take lessons from virtuoso sitar player Ravi Shankar. This Indian influence shows up in full force on *Revolver's Love You To* and then on *Sgt. Pepper's Within You Without You*. The Indian sounds added a new and unusual flavor to the music. You have to wonder what the other Beatles must have thought at first, as it was pretty far out, even for the 60s, but they went along with it just the same.

It must have been hard for George at times, probably feeling overshadowed by John and Paul, but in the end, he really did come into his own. And he was so much a part of it all anyway, playing those fractured early rocker-style guitar breaks, adding the jazzy extended chords at the ends of so many songs, filling in on so many backing vocals in wonderful slightly whispery mid-range harmony with John, Paul, or both. You just can't imagine the Beatles without him.

The Details

Something starts with Ringo's fill - quick, deeply resonating beats, landing on a last cymbal at the same time as Paul hits a sustained note on bass. George plays the song's signature seven-note guitar riff, slightly piercing with just a little distortion. There's a smooth magic-trick sounding wash of cymbal that fills the air just as George comes in to start the first verse.

In contrast to the lead guitar, George's voice is soft and sincere. There's a lot of space between the words, and the instruments work together in an interesting way with simple warm notes on bass behind mildly distorted guitar chords and drum fills. At the end of this first verse the energy picks up a little, the chord changes introduce a little tension, George sings a multi-syllable *woo-ooh-oohs me* as the bass dances around, adding in more notes (which happens a lot in this song), and the energy comes up a notch.

George's voice is doubled for the refrain, and the feeling in the words and music is not quite as gentle as it was in the verse; here he's getting a message out. Billy Preston's organ starts up with a simple pulsing in the background, the bass and guitar still in, but sparse. Then the orchestra comes in, ever so gradually, ending up with a very full sound, and again we hear the shimmering wash of the cymbal wrapping around all the other sounds.

George sings a second verse, his voice back to a single track. The orchestra and violin section are swirling away in the background and now filling in all the space between the lines. In this verse, at the same place where he sang the *woo-ooh-oohs* last time around, George sings, with a rise and fall, a very heartfelt *tha-at shows me*.

At the end of the next refrain there's another major change and rise in the energy. The strings in the orchestra are louder, playing a long sustained and rising passage alongside the guitar riff. This all blends together into a new urgent chord, providing a dramatic transition into the bridge. George, now double-tracked, sings the first words alone, and then Paul comes in, and together they really belt it out. There's a staggered and descending passage of notes, very low and pronounced, with the organ a little out front at the end. They sing the refrain again, but this time Paul comes in with higher and more energetic harmonizing, sounding a little like parts of *Lucy in the Sky with Diamonds* on steroids.

The bridge is loaded with energy. Paul comes in to sing along with George in harmony as Ringo plays a cascading set of rolls in a trip around his kit, the orchestra's string section playing some beautiful melody lines underneath. As there is an unexpected chord to change things up and create tension to go into the bridge, there is another masterfully placed change to come *out* of it. And again, we hear a set of staggered descending notes, which serves to calm things down and set up for the guitar solo.

As befits a number 1 George Harrison song, the guitar solo, at a bit over half a minute, is longer than most, and it covers the material found in both the verse and the refrain. It's delivered in Harrison's slightly fractured and piercing style, with lots of note-bending and some unusually wobbly passages repeated a few times at around 2:03. All in all, it's sweet, understated, and emotional.

For the third and final verse Paul harmonizes with George, their voices blending smoothly together. If you listen carefully through these passages, you can hear some really great rhythmic and slightly more energetic strumming on electric guitar, especially around 2:33.

There's another refrain, and then for the outro, outro, George simply plays the song's guitar riff, hits the same dramatic chord that he played just before the bridge, and then repeats the riff in unaltered form. This blends into a long, sustained last sweet chord played by the orchestra, and it's over.

This song really stands out as unique in the set, George's style markedly different from all the Lennon-McCartney numbers. The construction and use of interesting and unexpected chords, the continual buildup of energy throughout, the wonderful drumming and bass work, and of course George's guitar playing, all work together to make this a truly remarkable song.

Timeline

1969—August 28: Mary McCartney is born in London ~September 13: The Plastic Ono Band plays at the *Toronto Rock 'n' Roll Revival* ~September 17: An article entitled "Is Beatle Paul McCartney Dead?" appears in Iowa's Drake University student newspaper ~September 20: The Beatles sign a new contract with Allen Klein and John announces that he is leaving the band ~September 26: The album *Abbey Road* is released ~Nov: 25: John Lennon returns his Member of the Order of the British Empire medal ~

#25 Come Together

This dark and moody Lennon number started life as the intended campaign song for Timothy Leary's run for governor of California against Ronald Reagan, but Leary ended up getting arrested for possession of marijuana and that was that. Loaded with funky hippie street jive and lots of bluesy and atmospheric instrumental sections, *Come Together* was chosen as the opening track on *Abbey Road*.

Release and Recording

UK Release: October 31, 1969
US Release: October 6, 1969
Recorded: July 21–30, 1969
Length 4:18
Double A-side: *Something*

Charting

US: On November 29, 1969, the double-A with *Something* replaced *Wedding Bell Blues* by the 5th Dimension, which had been in the number 1 spot for 3 weeks. The double-A stayed for a week and was then replaced by *Na Na Hey Hey Kiss Him Goodbye* by Steam, which stayed for 2 weeks. (It was at this point in time that Billboard changed the practice of counting sales and airplay separately.) This was the Beatle's eighteenth number 1 hit single in the US, breaking Elvis's record, which was now seventeen.

UK: The double A-side didn't hit the top spot, but did make it up to number 4.

The Back Story

With *Something* on the flip side, this John song was the third and last Beatles double-A. It supposedly started life as a campaign song for Timothy Leary's bid for governor of California, but the candidate was arrested for possession of marijuana, putting an end to his political aspirations.

In 1973 Chuck Berry sued John Lennon, charging that the lyrics *here come ole flat-top* were lifted from his 1956 single *You Can't Catch Me*. The case was settled out of court.

Come Together

Time	Section
0:00	Intro
0:12	Verse
0:35	Intro
0:46	Verse
1:09	Refrain
1:15	Intro
1:27	Verse
1:49	Refrain
1:56	Intro
2:01	Solo / Slide Riffs / ~
2:31	Verse

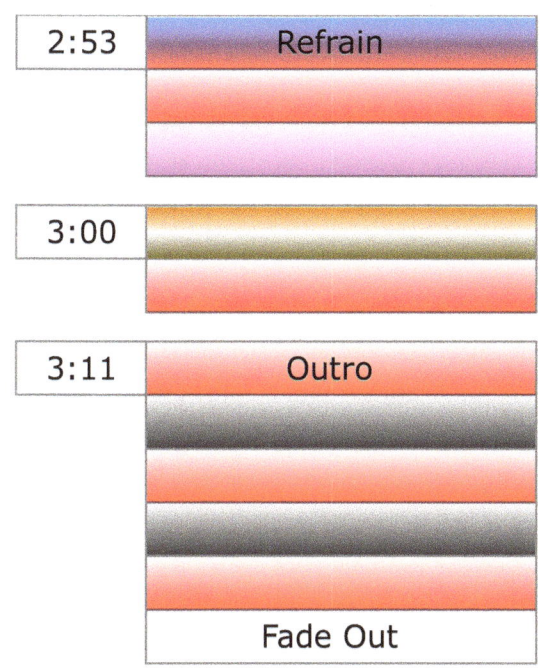

Song Map Legend

The Song Map

The song map shows John in red for the intro and first verse, and a special blend for the prominent bass and drum parts. The material from the intro serves as a theme that's repeated throughout the rest of the song. The feeling from beginning to end is dark and atmospheric. Paul comes in to harmonize on the second verse and for most of the rest of the song. Paul's voice adds a strange tension, a little like the almost sarcastic harmony we hear in *The Ballad of John and Yoko*, but it's moodier here. There's a great instrumental break featuring Billy Preston on electric piano, along with some low-down and lazy slide guitar. After a last time through the theme the song fades out, with more slide guitar. As funky as this song sounds, some slightly sentimental chords are used in the short refrain, in yet another perfect example how the Beatles evoked multiple moods and feelings in the same song.

Personal Notes

Sex, Drugs, and Rock 'n' Roll

In the fall of 1969, when I was just turning 14, and right around the time *Come Together* came out, my family moved from a small rural hill town in western Massachusetts to Northampton, a much larger and bustling college town. It was a big change, and there was a lot going on. There were long-haired hippies everywhere and the counter culture was in full swing. It was quite an awakening for a boy my age. Teenage culture had radically morphed from black-and-white, cigarette-smoking, short-haired, motor-head, frequently racist, fighting-and-drinking patriotism to brightly colored, joint-smoking, long-haired, sex-drugs-and-rock-'n'-roll-infused civil disobedience and anti-war sentiment. The distinction between *jocks* and *freaks* was coming into being.

Drugs were everywhere, and there were many different kinds. Kids of all ages were smoking grass and hash; taking speed, either as pills or shooting it into their veins; dropping tabs of acid with names like Orange Sunshine, Chocolate Chip, and Cherry Dome; and taking mescaline, peyote, or psilocybin. Some kids were even sniffing glue and gasoline. And while most young people seemed to get through this insane period relatively unscathed, a small percentage just went totally off the deep end, ruining themselves and their lives. If you were alive at this time you probably knew people like this. They self-destructed, becoming dark, hollow burnt-out shells of who they had been. It's like the Blue Meanies had sucked all the color out of them, leaving them gray, lifeless statues. I love the song *Come Together*, but with its vivid and bizarre depiction of a crazy street cat, its dark and moody atmosphere, and the timing of its release, it has always conjured up for me images of these people and their broken lives.

Joe Cocker and Across the Universe

Who can forget the great musical scenes from Woodstock, with Richie Havens, Alvin Lee and Ten Years After (his scalding licks on *I'm Going Home* some of the truly best guitar playing of all time), the Who, Santana, Country Joe and the Fish, Hendrix and his *Star-Spangled Banner*, so many others ... and, of course, Joe Cocker singing *I Get By with a Little Help from My Friends*. Wearing his tie-dyed shirt, gesticulating wildly, playing the air guitar, his gravelly soulful voice at first singing the words calmly and sincerely and then amping it all up into a such a soulful and frenzied performance.

Fast forward 38 years to 2007, and we find Joe Cocker again, this time on the set of the film *Across the Universe* singing *Come Together*, and he nails it again, his voice and crazy character spanning the decades, bringing it all back.

The soundtrack to *Across the Universe* is an incredibly beautiful reminder of just how great the Beatles were, how much they tugged on our heartstrings, how much they energized us, how they were such a part of the crazy 60s. From the opening scene with a forlorn Jim Sturgess as Jude singing *Girl* on the beach, to a lovely and love-struck Evan Rachel Wood as Lucy singing *If I Fell* in the old deserted waterfront building, to a hard-crushing T.V. Carpio as Prudence singing *I Want to Hold Your Hand* on the football field, the beautifully arranged songs bring the Beatles' music back with such simple and heartfelt clarity. I'm usually not a big fan of Beatles covers, but the music in this film is just amazing. And it probably wasn't easy to try to patch all those Beatles songs and 1960s themes and events into a cohesive story, but they just did. Hats off.

The Details

It sounds like just *shh* at first, but if you listen carefully, especially the third time around, it does sound like John is saying *shoot me*, which is pretty creepy and foreboding to say the least. Along with the bass, Ringo's drums are prominent, with sets of fills that seem to echo each other and move all around in the mix. There's just a faint hint of electric piano and guitar in the background.

John's lyrics are crazy and puzzling from the very start. The bass and drums are very thumpy, moving through a repeated pattern consisting of a louder and lower solid note and then rising up a little. It's very sparse and bluesy, with John alternating between very suddenly clipped words and longer drawn-out syllables. The whole first half of each verse stays in one chord, making things more rhythmic and chant-like than melodic. (If you listen carefully you can hear a funny little whistle after the last word *please* in this verse, at about 0:34).

The intro is repeated in its entirety between the first and second verses.

In the second verse Paul comes in to harmonize on every other line. The harmony is certainly not what you'd call sweet or tight Everly Brothers style. There's something ominous about it, with Paul holding the same notes for long stretches, using an almost *Lady Madonna*–like voice, which underlines the dark and moody feeling in the song. Again, this unusual and somewhat unsettling harmony is also a little bit like what we hear on *The Ballad of John and Yoko*. The lyrics continue to describe a very colorful character. John sings the last two lines of the verse alone, single-tracked this time around.

At 1:09 we hear the very short refrain. The guitar barges in with a very driving and percussive riff that stops as suddenly as it started. Paul harmonizes on only the title words *Come Together*. Each time through the refrain in this song, they vary the voice mix. The whole feeling of the song changes in the refrain—whereas the verses and repeated intros all use straight rock and blues chords, the refrain adds an unexpected, upbeat, if not short-lived, release from the otherwise dark and brooding tension of the song, with a slightly pop-sounding sad-to-uplifting-energy chord change. While fleeting, this is another classic instance of Blue Notes and Sad Chords.

The band takes us yet again through the intro material and then another verse. The words just keep getting crazier. There's a quick half-intro after the next refrain, a nice staggered pick-up fill on the drums, John letting out a relatively higher-energy *right* as things transition into the solo.

As in the single-chord intro and first part of the verses, Billy Preston's electric piano solo is more rhythmic than melodic, repeating the same passage four times. There's a panting sound in the background (it's hard to tell if it's an instrument or a human voice) while the guitar plays solid rock and blues licks. At the chord change, Preston drops out and we hear a very bright, high-pitched slide guitar, in high contrast to the material that preceded it. The slide guitar plays through a simple riff a few times, changing it and descending the second time through, and then ends on a very high wavering note that sounds like a musical saw. And all the while John has been whispering the word *come* hauntingly in the background. The electric piano comes back in and out front, all the other instruments dropping out, to end the solo, playing a lingering atmospheric passage, which slows everything down and brings the energy way back down.

After the solo, the band goes through a last verse. Paul again harmonizes on every other line. At the end of this verse, it sounds like there's a slight variation in the voice mix, with John and Paul possibly singing the last two lines in unison.

There's a last short refrain, and more great staggered drumming by Ringo to transition into the outro.

The outro, like many song endings in the second half of the Beatles' career (*Hello Goodbye, All You Need Is Love, Hey Jude*), is long and drawn-out. This one lasts for a whole minute, and it stays in a single chord the whole time, like much of the song proper. John repeats the title words of the song along with some funky and delayed *yeah*s that get longer and higher as things progress. His sparse lyrics are interspersed with sets of slinky, understated blues guitar licks, sounding like a slide with lots of bended notes, and, echoing John's *yeah*s, as things get higher and more intense in a few spots. All of this is set to a steady pulse of bass and drums with lots of washy cymbals and masterfully placed fills in the mix. At the end, it all fades away into the background.

Timeline

1969—August 28: Mary McCartney is born in London ~September 13: The Plastic Ono Band plays at the *Toronto Rock 'n' Roll Revival* ~September 16: *Abbey Road*, the Beatles' last album, is released ~September 17: An article entitled "Is Beatle Paul McCartney Dead?" appears in Iowa's Drake University student newspaper ~September 20: The Beatles sign a new contract with Allen Klein and John announces that he is leaving the band ~September 26: The album *Abbey Road* is released ~Nov: 25: John Lennon returns his Member of the Order of the British Empire medal ~

#26 Let It Be

With the heavenly organ and angelic choir, *Let It Be* has an almost church-like feel. Paul McCartney's last great number as a Beatle is based on a comforting dream he had about his mother Mary (not the Virgin Mary), who died when he was just fourteen. In the dream, she comes to him to tell him everything is going to be okay, to let it be. He had the dream in 1968, which was a troubling time, when the Beatles had started to unravel.

Release and Recording

UK/US Release: March 6, 1970
Recorded: January 31 and April 30, 1969, and January 4, 1970
Length: 3:50
B-side: *You Know My Name (Look Up the Number)*

Charting

US: On April 11, 1970, *Let It Be* replaced *Bridge Over Troubled Water* (a song with a similar message), which had held for 5 weeks, stayed 2 weeks and was then replaced by the Jackson 5's *ABC*, which held for 2 weeks.

UK: *Let It Be* didn't make it to number 1 in the UK, which is hard to believe.

The Back Story

This is the title track to the album, things unraveling for the band at this point. Interestingly, John played a 6-string bass in this song, and Linda McCartney joined in on the choir. The song, featured in the documentary film of the same name, won a 1970 Academy Award for Best Original Song Score.

Some music critics have suggested that *Let It Be* was just a remake of *Hey Jude*. One music critic even went as far as to say that song "catered to the lowest common denominator emotional stasis of its listeners." Nothing could be further from the truth. Yes, the songs have similar textures, with Paul McCartney's sincere sentimentality and gentle piano playing. But *Hey Jude*, which primarily uses upbeat happy chords and has a long crazy ending with a prominent blue chord, was written to cheer up a sad child. *Let It Be*, on the other hand, features more pathos infused vocals, a softer and more poignant chord progression, church-like organ and choir, and a rocker guitar break—and the song is about universal acceptance, which is at the heart of many religions and philosophies. Anybody thinking that *Let It Be* is just a rehash of *Hey Jude* has the musical sensibility of a turnip.

Let It Be

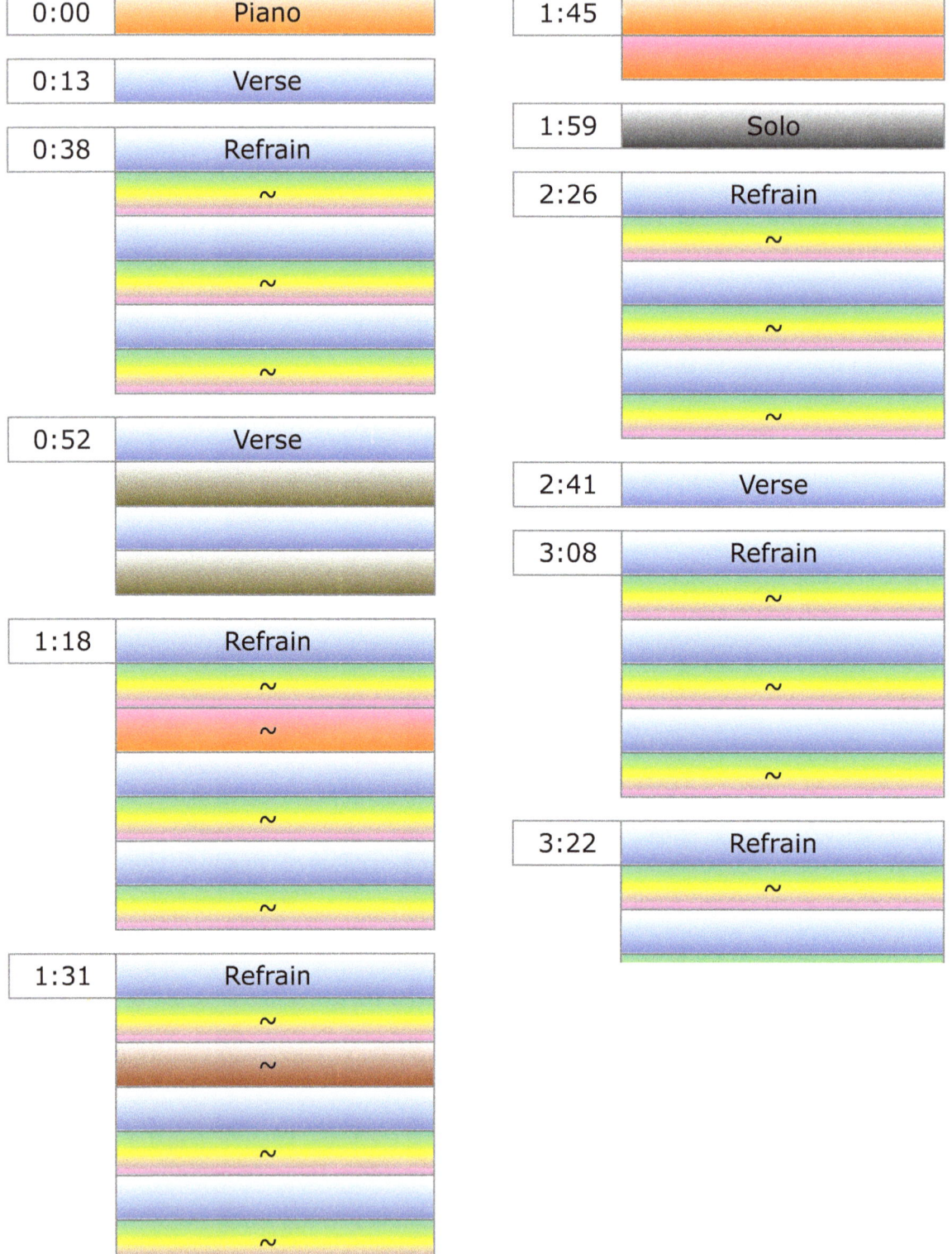

Song Map Legend

The Song Map

Paul sings lead here, so we see blue throughout the song but with lots of other colors mixed in from harmony and instruments. A heavenly choir, consisting of Paul, John, George, and Linda McCartney, comes in on the first refrain and is shown here as a fade of purple, yellow, and green. Sounding like church, the organ comes in for the second refrain, and then a full orchestra the next time through. There's a mini instrumental passage on piano which is then echoed by the organ before George's great uplifting guitar solo. Paul sings another verse and a couple of refrains with the choir still in the back, and then there's a gentle descending finish on piano.

Personal Notes

The End of the 60s
The Beatles broke up in 1970, serving to emphasize that the 60s had really come to an end. Maybe it was inevitable that they would go their separate ways. They had never stayed still; they were always changing, going from one incredibly creative phase to the next, getting more and more sophisticated with their recordings, the band's output driven more and more by solo work. In just eight years they had gone from local Liverpool scruffs to the most successful and popular music act the world had ever seen.

Like so many other things in the 60s, the Beatles had gone through a fundamental, volatile transformation. The Black Panthers grew out of the Civil Rights movement, the SDS morphed into the Weather Underground. The contrasts between good and evil at the end of the decade were glaring: the Summer of Love and the assassinations a year later, Woodstock then Altamont, the Human Be-In and the My Lai Massacre, Timothy Leary and Charles Manson. While the analogy between the times and the Beatles shouldn't be exaggerated, it did feel like things were falling apart.

I remember seeing the movie *Let It Be* in the early summer of 1970, which was after the Beatles had broken up. It was very different from either *Help* or *A Hard Day's Night*. There was no story, just an inside look at a band before they broke up. It was still the Beatles, and some of the music was great, but there was clearly something that didn't feel right, an underlying edginess. But I did love the album, especially the title song and John's *Across the Universe*.

One of the songs, *One After 909*, has always struck me as a musical clue indicating that the Beatles were broken. If you're a fan, you may have the double CD of the early 60s BBC recordings. This great set of music is loaded with classic rockers and covers, performed with trademark Beatles energy and gusto, along with some originals, like John's *One After 909*. The contrast between that early version of this song, from 1963, and the one on the *Let It Be* album, couldn't be more striking. The energy is *so* much lower in the *Let It Be* version, so lackluster compared to the earlier high-energy, tight, and hard-as-nails rock 'n' roll song. That contrast says it all.

With *Let It Be*, the Beatles left the world with a deeply comforting swan song. Who but the Beatles would let us down so gently, with a musical version of the *Serenity Prayer*, to face a difficult but inevitable end to something so cherished.

Crazy B-Sides

How does a song like *You Know My Name (Look Up the Number)* end up as the B-side to a song like *Let It Be*? Maybe it's another clear indication that the boat was sinking, that things were just falling apart. It doesn't really sound like a Beatles song. It starts out with a late-1950s-style sentimental rock 'n' roll chord progression, then there are bizarre voice-overs and lounge noises, and it keeps shifting into ever sillier music and lyrics. Like a few of the songs on the *White Album*, it's hard to believe that it ever got out the door, that George Martin went along with it.

There are many other examples of crazy filler songs that ended up on major artists' records. Maybe *Dirty Maggie May*, on the *Let It Be* album, is in the same vein, but consider *Mother's Lament*, the last track on Cream's 1967 masterpiece album, *Disraeli Gears*. This is one of my favorite albums of all time, but I always wished they had picked something else to end it with.

The Details

At the beginning of *Let It Be*, we hear a simple set of piano chords, the same that are used for the verse. The piano intro ends with a very gentle and peaceful change and a short passage of stately descending notes, which serves as a theme for the entire song and the ending of each part. As mentioned in the write-up for *We Can Work It Out*, this type of chord change is called a *plagal cadence* and is often heard in Christian church services. It's the chord change we sometimes hear when a congregation sings one of those long and drawn-out *amen*s all together.

The first verse starts with Paul's voice clear, single-tracked, deeply sincere, and at the same time relaxed. The piano is the only thing in the background for the whole verse. The words are comforting, the verse is two repeated sections, each ending with the title lyrics, *Let It Be*.

For the refrain, which consists mainly of the title lyrics repeated, a choir comes into the background singing a set of extended *ooh*s that descend along with the piano, imparting a feeling of coming to rest. The refrain has a sadder set of chords in its first section, but it ends using the same descending and comforting chord sequence as the verse.

For the second time through the verse, at 0:52, Ringo comes in with some understated hits on his hi-hat cymbals. Paul sings through the verse and then at the end there's a big lift in energy as Ringo plays a louder and fuller set of fills to help transition into the next refrain. Paul earnestly emphasizes and half-speaks some of the words. If you listen closely you can hear a funny little sound like somebody whispering at around 1:07.

For the next refrain at 1:18, in addition to the choir backdrop, the organ is added in as a new layer, the sound getting fuller and more emotionally charged. Paul's voice is changing here—it sounds a little like his *Lady Madonna* voice for the just the first *Let It Be*. The refrain ends with the same music and uplifting lyrics as the preceding verse, but this time around, Paul throws in a quick little *yeah* before the last lines.

There's another refrain and here the orchestra, with brass out front, comes in as yet another layer. Then before transitioning into the guitar solo, there's a simple pass through the song's descending come-to-rest theme, first on piano with some higher-energy drum fills, and then louder and very church-like on Billy Preston's organ—at this spot you can practically see the doves flying around up in the rafters.

The guitar solo has George playing against the verse's chord progression. It's interestingly sharp and slightly distorted, starting down in a lower register. It sounds just the faintest bit out-of-tune, but still wonderful, reaching up to hit some higher and more emotional notes at the end.

The rest of the song is another refrain, one more verse, then two more times through the refrain. (Overall in the song, there are three verses, or four if you count the guitar solo, and six refrains.) For these refrains, Paul slides his voice up a full octave to sing the ending title words way up high. And in the verse, we hear Ringo mix things up for the just the first few lines with what sounds like maracas. There's a noticeable buildup of energy through all this, with the choir getting louder, more drum fills, some guitar licks thrown in here and there, and Paul changing his vocal inflections.

The outro finishes the song with the descending come-to-rest theme, although at this stage there's a lot more energy and feeling poured into it. It all ends on a last majestic chord. If you listen closely at the end you can hear the bass, played by John here, doing a funny and slightly accelerated ascending scale.

Timeline

1970—March 8 and 11: Ringo Starr records *It Don't Come Easy* ~March 27: Ringo Starr's solo album *Sentimental Journey* album is released ~March 29: Ringo Starr appears on David Frost's TV show ~April 10: In a press release for the solo album *McCartney*, Paul announces that he has left the Beatles ~

#27 The Long and Winding Road

This is the last one in the set, so it's fitting that it's on the sad side. With no vocal harmonies or guitar, and with Phil Spector's overbearing and sickly-sweet orchestra in the back, *The Long and Winding Road* features only Paul singing to an indeed long and winding chord progression on piano.

Release and Recording

UK/US Release: May 11, 1970
Recorded: January 26, 1969
Length 3:40
B-side: *For You Blue*

Charting

US: On June 13, 1970, *The Long and Winding Road* knocked *Everything Is Beautiful* by Ray Stevens out, which had held for 2 weeks. It stayed for 2 weeks, and was then replaced by the Jackson 5's *The Love You Save*, which also stayed for 2 weeks. It was the Beatles' twentieth and last number 1 in the US.

UK: This song never made it to the top spot in the UK.

The Back Story

The Long and Winding Road also shows up on the *Let It Be* album, most of which was recorded in early 1969, well before *Abbey Road*, but not released until spring 1970. Much to Paul McCartney's chagrin, Phil Spector was called in to finish off the album's production. Spector added wall-of-sound overdubs with harp, orchestra, horns, and a women's choir to the song *Let It Be*. He also did this to the songs *Across the Universe* and *I Me Mine*. A short while after Paul heard Spector's overdubs, he formally broke with the band. It was one of the reasons cited in the legal proceedings for dissolving the Beatles. (If you want to hear the unadulterated version of these songs, listen to the album *Let It Be... Naked*, released in 2003)

The Long and Winding Road

0:00	Verse
	~

0:43	Verse
	~

1:27	Bridge
	~

1:42	Verse
	~

2:25	Break

2:39	Verse
	~

3:24	Outro
	~

Song Map Legend

| Paul |
| Piano |
| Orchestra |

The Song Map

This song map features blue, with just Paul singing. The piano which is actually played for the entire song, is only shown in the beginning, as it is really gets drowned out by Phil Spector's orchestra, which takes a solo break toward the end. In many spots, the swirling orchestra and the wondrous choir give the song a sort of a Star Trek vibe. We can only imagine how irate Paul was to have his piano playing smothered in this last number.

Personal Notes

The Year the Music Died

On Friday, September 18, in 1970, Jimi Hendrix, 27 years old, died from an overdose of sleeping pills in London. Just a little over two weeks later, on Saturday, October 4, Janis Joplin, also 27 years old, died from a heroin overdose in Los Angeles. The deaths of Hendrix, who had released the album *Band of Gypsys* at the beginning of the year with the amazing track *Machine Gun*, and Joplin, who had recently formed the new Full Tilt Boogie Band and had been recording the album *Pearl*, were terribly sad shocks to the music world. Along with that, the Beatles had broken up earlier in the year, adding to the feeling that 1970 was indeed the end of something.

If the charts are any indication, people's tastes had changed. It's hard to believe, but the bubblegum pop song *Sugar, Sugar*, by the fictional cartoon band the Archies, had actually been named the number 1 single of 1969 by *Billboard Magazine*. There was, of course, still some great music coming out; Led Zeppelin had released *Whole Lotta Love* in late 1969, and in September 1970 the Rolling Stones released the live album *Get Yer Ya-Ya's Out!* and Santana came out with *Abraxas*. But if you scan the US and UK chart toppers for 1970, both singles and albums, you can see that it was a different sort of mix, with a different feel, and I remember thinking that the golden era of 60s rock music was coming to an end.

But all was not lost. The likes of Jimi Hendrix, Eric Clapton, Jimmy Page, Alvin Lee, Duane Allman, and others had ushered in a new era of amazing blues guitar playing, and along with it, a re-discovery and new appreciation for the black American blues artists that had inspired so many. I bought all the albums I could find—Muddy Waters, Junior Wells, Howlin' Wolf, BB King, John Lee Hooker, Buddy Guy, Sony Terry and Brownie McGhee, Son House, and so many others.

Paul McCartney, Ex-Beatle

Creating the song map and listening closely to *The Long and Winding Road* wasn't nearly as much fun as working on the other twenty-six songs in this set. This song feels much more like a post-Beatles McCartney song, so different from the bluesy and harmony-rich opener, *Love Me Do*, at the beginning of the set.

The Details

Paul starts the first verse with the title lyrics, just a light sprinkling of piano in the background. But this doesn't last long as we immediately hear the orchestra blast in with some very percussive and pronounced notes before it all morphs into a swirling Muzak-laden wall of sound. Paul's voice is very sincere, and very British sounding on *disappear* as well as later when he sings the multi-syllable *here*s. At around 0:30 we hear a choir of voices come in for just a few bars, sounding a little like those wondrous galactic melodies you sometimes hear on an episode of Star Trek, and this continues throughout the song.

After another verse, we come to the bridge. Paul's voice gets a little more matter-of-fact and narrative, a little less emotional, but as the bridge finishes the orchestra, again, really ramps up—more Star Trek.

After another verse, the orchestra takes the break with a series of ascending passages played by the string section. Higher and higher they go, getting more and more emotional.

There's another verse and then the outro, which is a last major swirling blast from the orchestra along with some very unexpected and bluesy ad-libbing *yeah yeah*s from Paul.

Timeline

1970—May 8: The album *Let It Be* is released in the UK ~May 18: The album *Let It Be* is released in the US ~May 20: The film *Let It Be* premieres in the UK; no Beatles attend ~November 27: George Harrison's triple solo album *All Things Must Pass* is released ~December 31: Paul McCartney files a lawsuit to dissolve the Beatles ~

SONG MAP PATTERNS OVER TIME

In the following pages you'll see all twenty-seven song maps in a simplified and reduced format, without any words or time ticks. They are followed by a full legend of all voice and instrument colors. If you visually scan the full set of maps as a series, a few patterns should become apparent. First, at the beginning there's lots of red-blue fades and purple. The first four songs, *Love Me Do*, *From Me to You*, *She Loves You*, and *I Want to Hold Your Hand*, all feature John and Paul in close collaboration, singing in note-on-note harmony. Then we see the first case of an all-blue McCartney song, *Can't Buy Me Love*. Other McCartney-only songs will follow later in the set—*Yesterday* and *The Long and Winding Road*. But first, there's a five-song Lennon-dominated period, from *A Hard Day's Night* to *Help*. There's a bit more harmony in *Day Tripper* and *We Can Work It Out*, and then things change. The entire second half of the set is dominated by McCartney songs, with a total of nine, plus three for John, and one for each of Ringo and George.

You can also see how elaborate some songs are, like *Help* and *All You Need Is Love*, and how some unusual instrument passages stand out, like the harmonium in *We Can Work It Out* or the sax and roaring twenties backing vocals in *Lady Madonna*. There are also similarities between *Yesterday* and *Eleanor Rigby*, featuring Paul's blue voice and the string quartets.

While we have to be careful about using only these number 1s to describe the Beatles' trajectory, we can generally see a period of intense collaboration at the start, a shorter Lennon period, then the longer McCartney one, with less harmony, more of a mix in styles, and more elaborate instrumentation.

BLUE NOTES AND SAD CHORDS

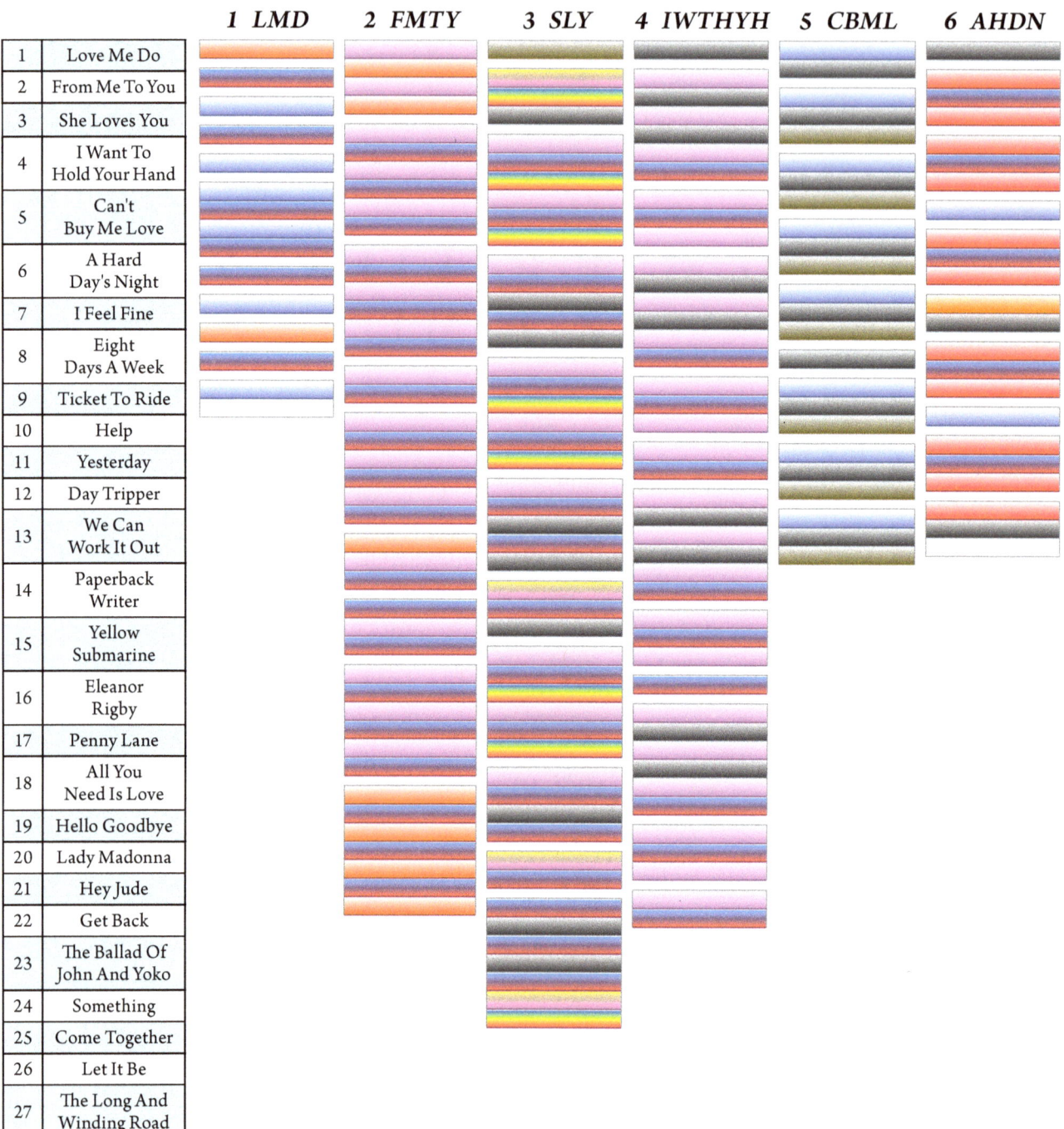

SECTION 2 : SONG MAP PATTERNS OVER TIME

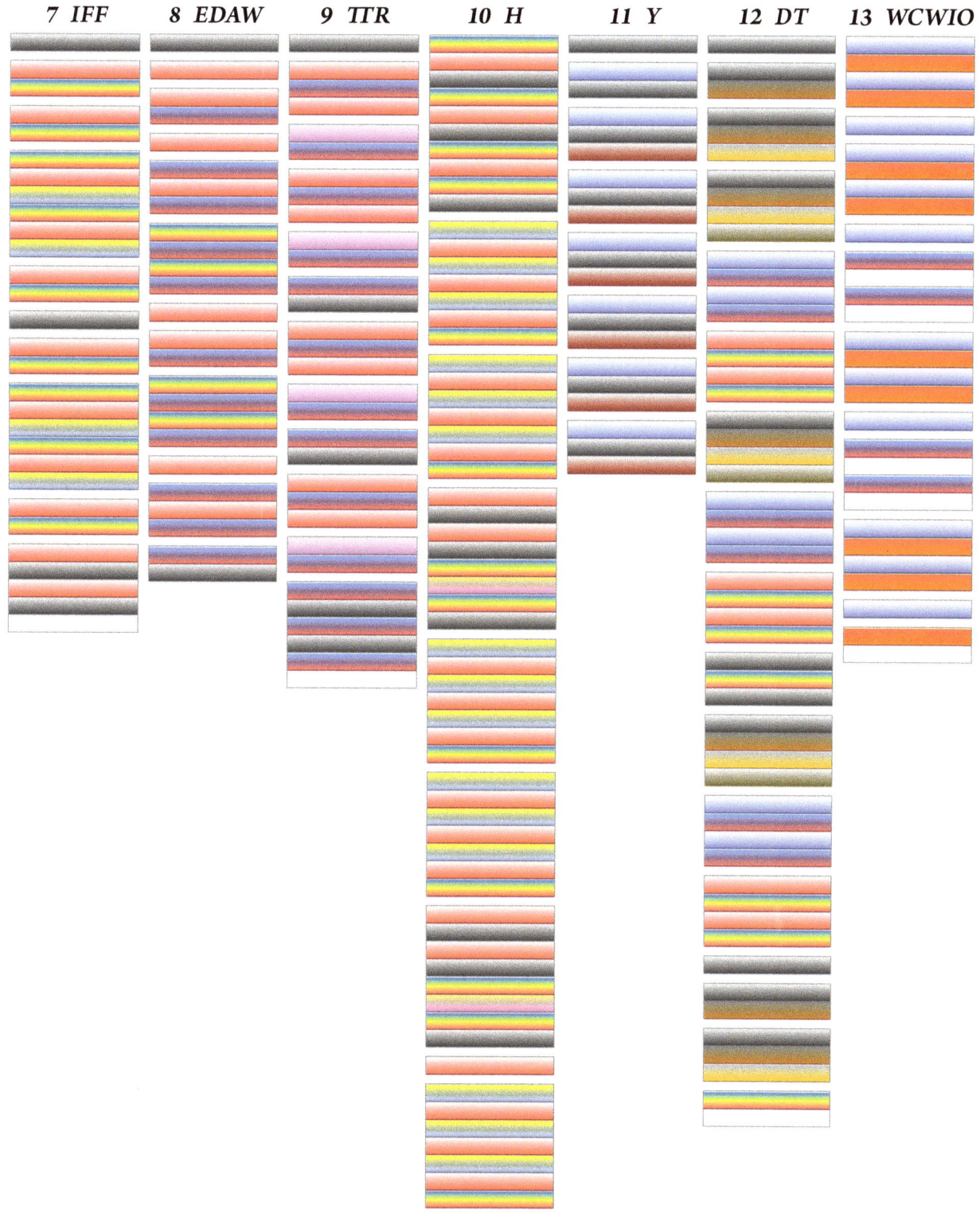

BLUE NOTES AND SAD CHORDS

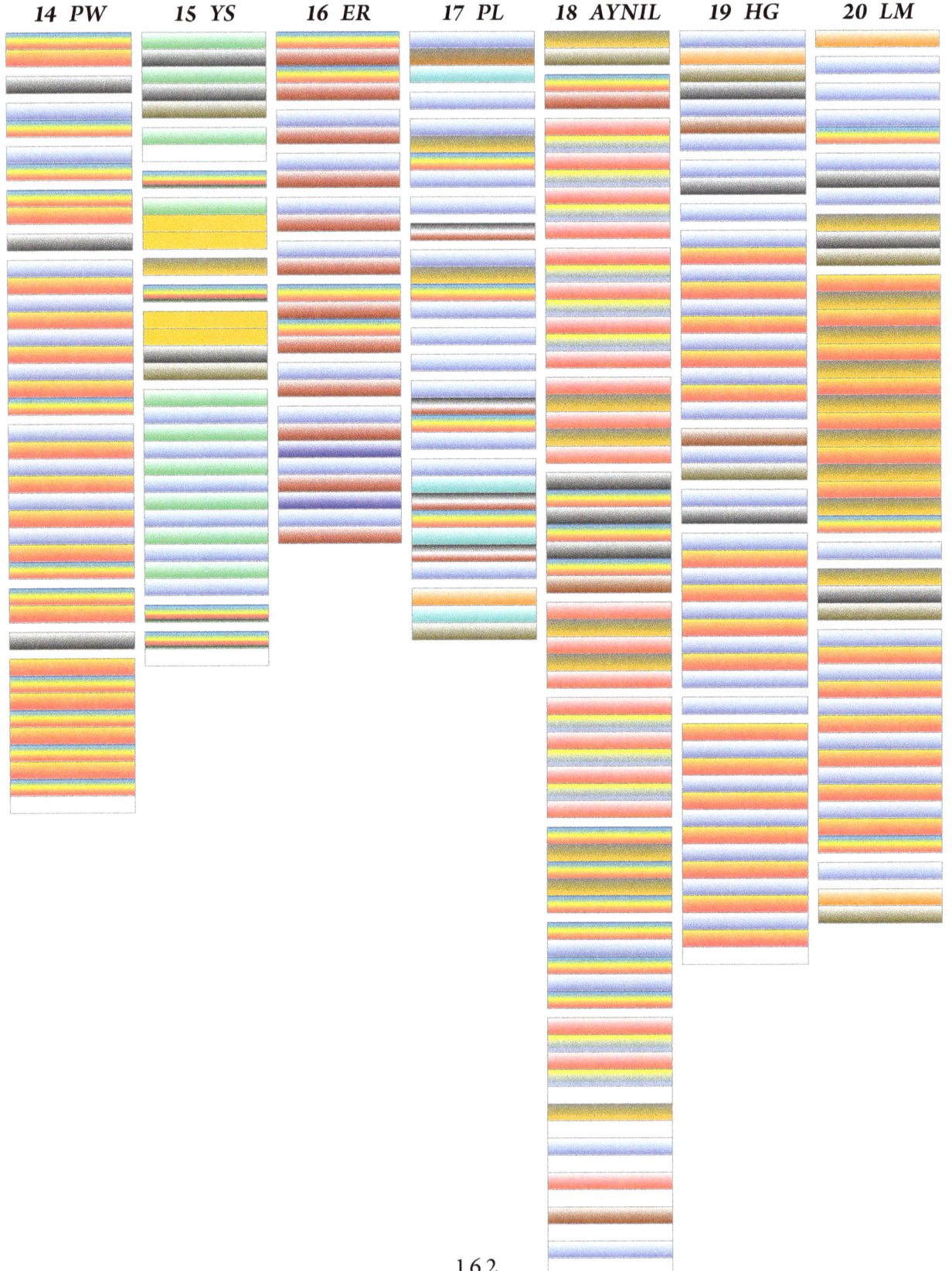

SECTION 2 : SONG MAP PATTERNS OVER TIME

Song Map Legend

John	Bass
Paul	Bass, Drums
George	
Ringo	Guitar, Drums
	Guitar, Orchestra
John, Paul, Harmony	
John, George, Harmony	Piano
Paul, George, Harmony	Electric Piano
Paul, Paul, Harmony	Harmonium
	Organ
John, Paul, George, Harmony	
All Four Beatles, Harmony	String Quartet
	Orchestra
John, Paul, Unison	Brass Band or Sax
Paul, George, Unison	
John, Paul, George, Unison	Piccolo Trumpet
All Four Beatles, Unison	
	Woodwinds
Guitar	
Drums, Cymbal, Handclaps	Choir
Tambourine	
Harmonica	Submarine Noises
	~ Backing Vocals/Instruments

SIDEBAR
OUT OF PHASE STEREO (OOPS)

If you're a die-hard fan, you'll get hours and hours of enjoyment listening to the Beatles' songs in what's known as *out of phase stereo*, or OOPS. OOPS allows you to hear new details in many of the instruments playing in the background, and in some cases backing vocals. If you are a hard-core fan, you simply *have to* try this.

OOPS involves cancelling out the middle portion of a stereo recording and hearing only what's left on the "edges" of the stereo image. Because most recordings have vocals up front and in the center, in many cases listening in OOPS will allow you to hear instruments in more detail. This includes guitar riffs, chord strumming, bass, drums, and in the case of the Beatles, piano, organ, string quartets, brass bands, and orchestras. In a way, it's like enhancing a photograph to get details to appear at the edges that weren't visible in the original.

OOPS can be set up to work on stereo equipment by rearranging how speaker wires are connected to the amp, but it's much easier to do with a computer program like Audacity, which is free and can be downloaded from http://www.audacityteam.org/download/

OOPS only works with stereo recordings, so depending on which incarnation of a given single or album recording you have, you may not be able to use it on some early Beatles tracks. Many of these early numbers are however now available in stereo in some of the more recent packaged sets.

Here's how to listen to songs in OOPS with Audacity version 2.1.1:

1. If you have your Beatles music on CD, for example the remastered *1* CD that was released in 2011, you'll need to convert the CD tracks into MP3 or WAV files, using a simple software tool like Express Ripper.
2. Open the MP3 or WAV file with Audacity. (You can easily just drag and drop the file into Audacity if it's already open.)
3. In the main menu, select *Effect > Vocal Reduction and Isolation*.
4. In the dialog box that appears, under *Action*, select *Remove Center* and then click *OK*. The appearance of the waveforms in each stereo channel will change.

5. From the upper left corner of the waveform display, click the pulldown arrow and select *Split Stereo Track*.
6. Now play the song. Experiment by alternatively muting the left and right tracks.

For example, if you listen to only the instrumental edges of the stereo image in *I Want to Hold Your Hand*, you'll hear George Harrison's guitar work in much clearer detail, which involves some very cool bluesy licks as well as some other notes that are otherwise buried in the standard recording. (Look at the Appendix to see how OOPS was used to determine what a specific chord is in *I Want to Hold Your Hand*.)

Hearing things in OOPS, which also little distortion, can make you feel like you have privileged and private access to sounds that you'd otherwise never hear. It can also give some passages in a song a more primitive, raw, and intimate sound, and even uncover some imperfections.

A few other things to listen for in the number 1s using OOPS:

SONG	LEFT	RIGHT
A Hard Day's Night	rhythm guitar	lead guitar and piano
I Feel Fine	drums	guitar
Eight Days a Week	drums	hand claps and backing vocals
Ticket to Ride	drums	
Help	electric guitar, drums, bass	acoustic guitar
Yesterday	string quartet	acoustic guitar
Day Tripper	rhythm guitar and drums	lead guitar, tambourine, backing vocals
We Can Work It Out	guitar, tambourine, and bass	harmonium
Penny Lane	piano and brass	high woodwinds
All You Need Is Love		backing vocals and orchestra
Hello Goodbye	piano, maracas, piano in outro	violins, lead guitar, and backing vocals
Lady Madonna	piano	bass and drums
Hey Jude	acoustic guitar	piano
Get Back	lead guitar	
Something	electric guitar and organ	bass and orchestra strings
Let It Be	guitar solo	

You can also use Audacity to cancel out the stereo edges and hear only what's in the center, using the similar *Isolate Center* command. This can give you a more detailed close-up of whatever is in the center of the stereo image, which is typically the vocals.

One early album to try OOPS on is *With the Beatles* in its stereo reincarnation. There are also many websites that go into more detail and call out particularly interesting Beatle songs to try it on—to find these, just do a Google search of Beatles and OOPS.

The best way to discover hundreds of wonderful musical details that you've never heard in your favorite Beatles songs is just to try it yourself. Some of songs on the *1* CD are good candidates, but there are many other non-hit singles that provide amazing results when heard this way, too.

SECTION 3

BLUE NOTES AND SAD CHORDS

MUSIC 201

MAPPING COLORS TO CHORDS

In this section, we use a different color mapping system to visually portray an essential and distinguishing characteristic of how the Beatles wrote their songs. The general idea here is to show how the Beatles used different sets of chords, like the different sets of colors on an artist's palette, to evoke the many different moods we hear and feel in their music. Using this technique to look at the twenty-seven number 1 hits will help you further appreciate just how creative the Beatles were in structuring their songs. We'll use colored chord diagrams to show how the Beatles uniquely mixed different musical genres, especially hard-driving rock 'n' roll and sentimental pop music, within the same songs.

The twenty-seven song maps that make up the main body of this book use a simple color scheme to show which Beatles sing the different parts of each song, whether they're singing lead or backing vocals, whether two or more Beatles are singing in unison or in two or three-part harmony, and when instruments come in. Most people can hear the difference between solo, unison, and harmony singing; harmony creates a special kind of resonating musical energy that's very pleasing to the ear. On the other hand, picking out which chords are being used in the different parts of a song isn't quite as easy, even if you're a musician, but this too can be communicated using color. And to emphasize the analogy with the painter's palette, we'll call these graphic depictions of the chords used in a song *chord palettes*.

While we will go into some detail, using colors to describe the different feelings associated with various chords, you don't really have to be able to identify individual chords by their sound (although many musicians can). Just knowing that some chords are generally bright and happy, some dark and sad, and still others bluesy or different in some other way, is all you really need to get the gist of the chord palettes.

HAPPY AND SAD CHORDS CONTINUED

Earlier in the book we saw that chords, in their simplest form, are stacks of three notes that sound good together, and that you can build a chord on any of the seven notes in the scale. You also learned that three of the seven chords, the 1, 4, and 5, are happier sounding, three others, the 2, 3, and 6, are sadder sounding, and one, the 7, was a strange-sounding oddball that's neither happy or sad. As a reminder, below is a diagram of the seven basic chord stacks, this time with the main note colored.

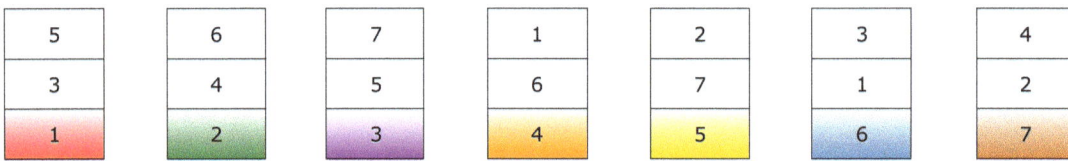

The Seven Basic Chord Stacks with the Main Root Note Colored

The reason that chords sound happy or sad to us is a bit of a mystery. Some people think it's cultural and that chords sound to us the way they do because of where we are born and in what time we live. Others think it's because of the basic characteristics of the vibrating frequencies in related notes and in the distances between them, which is essentially a physical reason. In fact, using the full set of black and white keys on a piano, the number of notes in between the bottom and top of each chord stack is always six (except in the oddball 7 chord, which is why it sounds so strange). But, because of the uneven spacing of the seven scale notes within the full set of twelve, as seen in the inconsistent spacing between the white and the black keys on a piano, the middle notes in the happy chord stacks are one note higher than the middle notes in the sad chord stacks. In other words, there are three piano keys in between the bottom and middle notes in the happy chords, but only two in the sad chords. So, it's the note in the middle of the stack that determines whether the chord sounds happy or sad—or, in musical terms, *major* or *minor*.

Each simple chord is called a triad because it has three notes, or *tones*. And each note in the set of seven that make up the major scale participates in three chords. In this way, each note contributes to the overall sound and feeling evoked by the chord. While the main note, or the *root*, gives a chord its prominent sound, the middle and top notes in the stack, called the third and the fifth, regardless of which note the chord is built on, complete the overall sound. The root and the fifth give a chord its overall structure, and the third determines whether it's a happy major or a sad minor.

Rock or pop songs don't usually use all seven chords in the scale. Instead, they use a smaller subset, with a song generally starting on the 1 chord, progressing through a series of different chords, and then landing back on the 1. Because each individual chord has a different feeling to it, happy or sad, the set of the chords used, and how they change back and forth, is one of the main factors determining a song's overall mood or feeling. For example, a song that uses only the happy major chords (as many vintage rock 'n' roll songs do, like *Roll Over Beethoven*), will tend to sound more positive and upbeat, whereas a song that also includes sad minor chords will often sound more emotional and sentimental, like *From Me to You*. Songs that *only* use minor chords can sound really sad, or even dark, like *And I Love Her*.

In addition to just sounding happy or sad, and very much like the seven dwarves in the tale of *Snow White* (which I like to think is not just a coincidence) each chord evokes a specific character and feeling. In the section that follows, we show four different chord groups. Each chord in a group is shown with its chord number, assigned a color, and described in terms of the feelings it's associated with. The happy major chords are assigned brighter warmer colors and the sad minor chords, darker cooler colors. The oddball 7 is given an in-between color. The descriptions of the feelings evoked by a given chord suggested here are certainly subjective, but you'd be surprised at how many musicians would generally agree with them.

The concept that combinations of notes that make up a chord give it a certain feeling is a little bit like the way that different sub-groups of three people, from a larger group of, say, seven, would each have a different character. For example, if you went to a party with the seven dwarves, the vibe you'd get in a room with Grumpy, Sleepy, and Sneezy would be different from the one you'd get in a room with Happy, Bashful, and Dopey.

NO.	FEELING
1	Home/At-Rest
4	Happy/Upbeat
5	Waiting/Unfinished

Happy Major Chords

The 1 chord, shown in red, is of primary importance—it is the *home* chord. It provides the foundation and base against which all the other chords are heard. As mentioned earlier, in most cases songs start and end on the 1 chord.

The 4 chord, shown in orange, is loaded with energy and generally evokes an upbeat and positive feeling.

The 5 chord, shown in yellow, is second only in importance to the 1 chord. The interplay between the 1 and the 5 is what gives a song (and Western music in general) its basic structure, helping to create and resolve the tension that makes up basic musical statements. When the 5 chord is sounding, the music feels unfinished, incomplete, waiting for something to happen. The end of many very basic songs, like *Happy Birthday* or *Pop Goes the Weasel*, and countless other pieces of music, has the 5 returning back to the 1, bringing the tune home and setting things to rest.

NO.	FEELING
2	Shy/In-Transition
3	Heartbroken/Tragic
6	Sad/Nostalgic

Sad Minor Chords

The 2 chord is just a little sad, sounding almost shy, and is frequently used to convey the feeling of a gentle lift or transition. In some cases, however, a happy major variant of the 2, with a raised middle note, is used to create a positive or even comic feeling.

The 3 chord is an incredibly sad and heartbreaking chord, even tragic. Many very emotional songs, or parts of songs, make heavy use of 3 chords. You'll see in the chord palettes that the Beatles used lots of 3 chords, but generally mixed them in with the happier chords.

The 6 chord is sad and nostalgic. It is a mainstay in many sentimental pop songs and folk ballads, and is very often heard changing to or from its forlorn sibling, the 3, or moving to an upbeat 4 to evoke a feeling of hopeful change.

NO.	FEELING
7	Incomplete/Ephemeral

Oddball Tritone Chord

Named the *tritone*, the 7 is an unusual and less frequently heard chord. It can sound very tense, or even just plain wrong. Because the distance in piano key notes between the bottom and the top of the 7 stack is one less than the standard spacing used in the other six chords, it sounds jarring to our ears. For this reason, the 7, in its simple three-note stack incarnation, with the 7 as the root note, is usually avoided and has historically even been associated with the devil.

OTHER CHORDS

Things are of course, not so simple. The seven chords described above, built using only the seven notes in the major scale, are the most basic, but there are other kinds of chords that use notes from outside of the seven white-key scale notes. Three of these chords are shown here:

NO.	FEELING
-3	Heavy/Solemn
-6	Ominous/Foreboding
-7	Bluesy/Tough

Chords Built on Notes Outside the Major Scale

The −3 or flat-3 chord has a heavy pensive sound. It's a staple of a lot of hard rock and heavy metal songs, or in more solemn-sounding folk ballads, and often in the middle of a rising or falling progression.

The -6 or flat 6 chord has an ominous, foreboding, or mysterious feeling. Because of the very important relationship between 1's and 5's—the bottoms and tops of chord stacks—is so basic in musical structure, any change to it sounds a little unnerving to us, which is perhaps why this chord, which is just one note above the 5, sounds so unusual. The Beatles used this ominous chord in many of their songs.

The −7 or flat-7 chord is the most bluesy sounding chord. Earlier in the book we said that the −3 and −7 steps of the scale, described as *blue notes*, are the notes that you typically hear emphasized in blues harmonica and slide guitar playing. So, in some ways, you can think of the −7 chord, and its sibling, the −3, as *blue chords*.

THERE'S MORE TO IT

One reason that things are not quite as simple as what's been described here is that sometimes the middle note in a sad chord, like the 2, is raised a notch to make it sound happy or comical, or the middle note in a happy chord, like the 4, is lowered to make it sound sad or wistful. (See the sidebar *Chord Progressions and the Wistful 4*.) Chords can also be altered in all sorts of other ways, that are not captured in the chord palettes.

And to complicate things further, some chords are built using more than three notes in their stack. These are referred to as *extended chords*. As an example, one common extended chord uses the four-note stack of 1-3-5-7. These extended chords are rarely used in folk, rock 'n' roll, or blues, but are a mainstay in pop music and jazz. They generally give music more color and a wider variety of subtle sensations that can sound undecided, mellow, or ephemeral. Another simple way of thinking about these extended chords is that they are basically two or more simple chords being played at the same time.

While the Beatles did use these more complex kinds of chords in many of their songs, we won't go into much detail about them, as they're a bit too complex for the simplistic color-to-chord mapping system presented here.

THE FULL SET OF CHORD COLORS

The full set of chords used in the palettes is shown below. You'll note that we've described a chord for ten of the full set of twelve notes in the octave. The two not shown, the flat-2 and the flat-5, rarely show up in rock or pop music.

NO.	FEELING
1	Home/At-Rest
2	Shy/In-Transition
-3	Heavy/Solemn
3	Heartbroken/Tragic
4	Happy/Upbeat
5	Waiting/Unfinished
-6	Ominous/Foreboding
6	Sad/Nostalgic
-7	Bluesy/Tough
7	Incomplete/Ephemeral

Chord Palette Numbers, Colors, and Feelings

CHOOSING THE COLORS

The color mappings used for the vocal harmonies weren't too hard to assign; after all, harmony-wise there are basically three singing Beatles and three primary colors. The colors for the chords were more of a challenge. The reasoning went something like this:

- Use red for the all-important home chord, the 1, for its primacy, and yellow for the 5, which is next in importance after the 1. Together these two chords provide the musical framework for chords and harmony, so their shades are bright and close together in the rainbow.
- Use orange for the bright, happy, high-energy 4.
- Use blue for the sad 6, and a related purple for the 6's even sadder cousin, the 3.
- Running out of primary colors, use green for the 2.
- Use a darker, deeper blue for the bluesy and low-down flat −7, and a lighter gray for the heavy and pensive flat-3, which is the −7's rock and blues sibling. It's interesting that none of the Beatles'

twenty-seven hit singles use the flat-3, and in general, this heavy-sounding chord makes only a rare appearance now and then in the Beatles' catalog, such as the title song on the *Sgt. Pepper* album.
- Use gray for the ominous and mysterious -6.
- Lastly, we can use beige for the hardly-ever-used 7.

This color scheme allows for quick identification of the three major happy chords, the red 1, orange 4, and yellow 5, which comprise the brighter part of the rainbow, and as a group are in contrast with the three minor sad chords, the green 2, blue 6, and purple 3, the darker part of the rainbow.

CHORD PALETTES

Like the song maps in the main section of the book, the chord palettes are also broken up into song parts, but to keep things simple, only the verses, refrains, and bridges are shown (labeled V, R, and B, respectively). Intros, solos, and outros are not included. If a song doesn't have a refrain or a bridge, the space for that song part is usually left empty.

The individual parts in each song are shown as vertical columns of colored boxes, to show which chords are used. If there's a prominent use of the home chord's blue notes, either in the vocals or in an instrument, a blue dot follows the song part's initial. Each palette also has a title including its number, from 1 to 27, and an acronym for the song's name. Note that the vertical columns just show which chords are used and not detailed sequences or chord progressions.

As an example, the chord palette below shows the song parts and the chords for the 1964 hit single *I Feel Fine*. Note that the rock 'n' roll verse and refrain use the three standard chords of rock 'n' roll, the brightly colored red 1, the orange 4, and the yellow 5, and that they also use blue notes. In contrast, you can see that the more emotional pop-sounding bridge also includes the darker sadder purple 3 along with the three basic chords. You can also see that there are no blue notes in the bridge, which is typical when there are sad minor chords in the part.

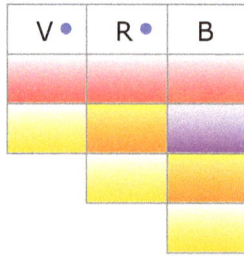

Chord Palette for *I Feel Fine*

One final complication, and something that presents a challenge to this simple chord palette system, is that sometimes a key change occurs during a song. This means that the home chord, or 1, actually changes to another note. As was briefly described in the Musical Terms in the Music 101 section, this type of key change is called *modulation*, in formal music terms. In most cases, the key change is temporary, and the song reverts back to the original home key. For example, the songs *From Me to You* and *I Want to Hold Your Hand* have temporary key changes in their very similar bridges. The home key changes to what is the 4 note in the original scale. This is a very common key change in popular music. However, some key changes are permanent, like the one towards the end of *Penny Lane* where the home key shifts up two notes. To capture these key changes in the chord palettes, an asterisk * is placed after the song part's initial, and the chord colors are applied as if the new home key is the 1, as is shown in the chord palette below, in the bridge of *From Me to You*. In some songs, as in the refrain in *Help* and the bridge in *Hey Jude*, it's not easy to say that a key change has occurred - it's a little subjective. In those cases, no asterisk or color changes were made.

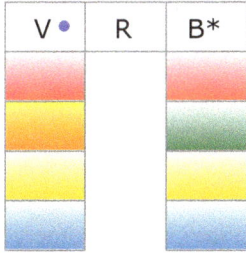

Asterisk (*) Used to Show Key Change in A Song Part

Note: Determining the correct chords for each song and part was even more subjective than figuring out who was singing what and when in the song maps. A number of different sources and methods were used including looking at *fake books* (simplified melody, lyrics, and chords) and web pages, looking at detailed scores, diving into scholarly descriptions of songs by musicologists, watching performance videos, and listening. There are no doubt a few spots where other musicians would interpret things differently. (See the *B Chord in I Want to Hold Your Hand* section in the Appendix for an example of what an ordeal it can be to just figure out what a single chord is.)

Beatles Chord Palettes 1962-66

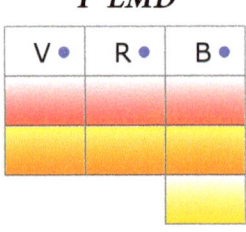
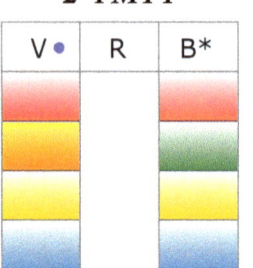
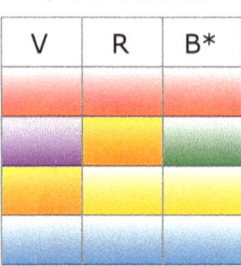

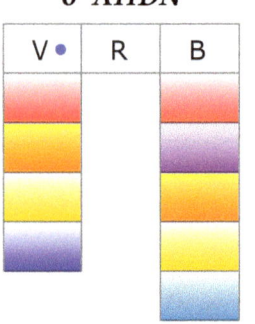
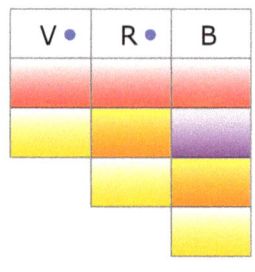
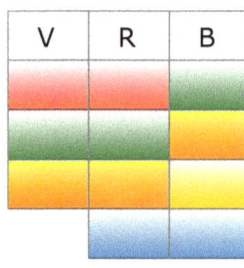
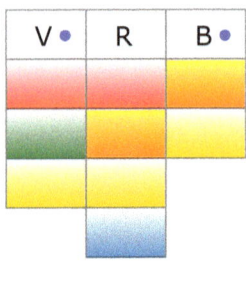
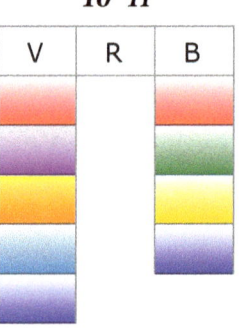

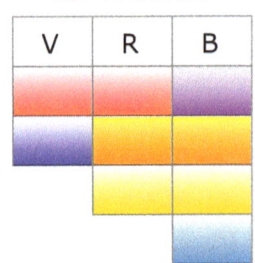
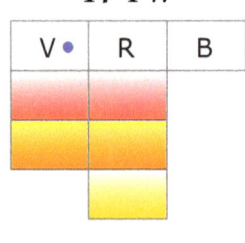
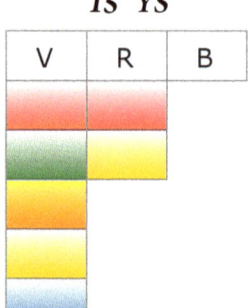
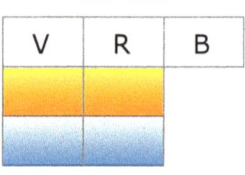

Beatles Chord Palettes 1967-70

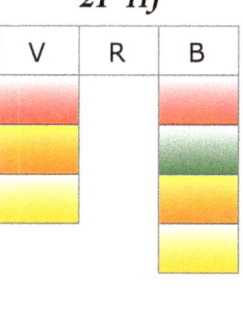
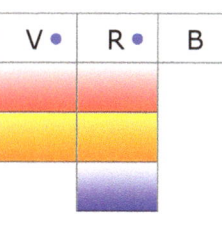
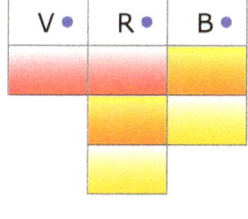

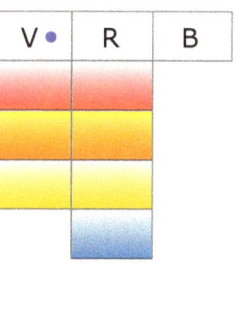
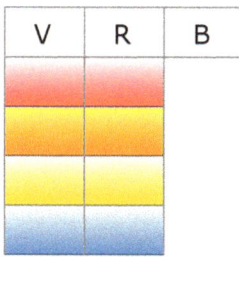

CHORD FEELINGS

NO.	FEELING
1	Home/At-Rest
2	Shy/In-Transition
-3	Heavy/Solemn
3	Heartbroken/Tragic
4	Happy/Upbeat
5	Waiting/Unfinished
-6	Ominous/Foreboding
6	Sad/Nostalgic
-7	Bluesy/Tough
7	Incomplete/Ephemeral

THE SONGS

1	Love Me Do
2	From Me To You
3	She Loves You
4	I Want To Hold Your Hand
5	Can't Buy Me Love
6	A Hard Day's Night
7	I Feel Fine
8	Eight Days A Week
9	Ticket To Ride
10	Help
11	Yesterday
12	Day Tripper
13	We Can Work It Out
14	Paperback Writer
15	Yellow Submarine
16	Eleanor Rigby
17	Penny Lane
18	All You Need Is Love
19	Hello Goodbye
20	Lady Madonna
21	Hey Jude
22	Get Back
23	The Ballad Of John And Yoko
24	Something
25	Come Together
26	Let It Be
27	The Long And Winding Road

SONG PARTS

V	Verse
R	Refrain
B	Bridge
•	Blue Note
*	Key Change

BEATLES NUMBER 1-HITS CHORD PALETTES

The preceding two pages show the set of chord palettes for all twenty-seven hit songs. (Like the song maps, they use a large layout size, to look like a two-page poster.) Take a few minutes to look over the songs as a set and see if you spot any patterns before you look more closely at the palettes for individual songs. Some things to notice are:

- Some songs are very simple and only use the bright 1, 4, and 5 chords, like *Love Me Do*, *Paperback Writer*, and *The Ballad of John and Yoko*.
- Other songs use lots of chords, like *Yesterday*, *All You Need Is Love*, and *Something*.
- Only the stark *Eleanor Rigby* and the galloping *Get Back* have no leaning yellow 5, and only *Eleanor Rigby* has no home red 1.
- All songs have the upbeat orange 4.
- The bridges in *From Me to You* and *I Want to Hold Your Hand* are the same.
- The palettes for *She Loves You* and *I Want to Hold Your Hand*, the two real Beatlemania songs, are very similar.
- Along with *Can't Buy Me Love*, *A Hard Day's Night*, and *I Feel Fine*, *Paperback Writer* suggests Blue Notes and Sad Chords with its bluesy verse but more pop refrain, as does *Ticket to Ride*.
- *Penny Lane*, *Hello Goodbye*, and *Lady Madonna*, all McCartney songs, all use the ominous dark grey flat 6. (It's interesting to note that *I Saw Her Standing There* also uses this chord.)
- No songs use the heavy light grey flat 3, so common in many rock songs, and there's not too many bluesy flat 7s.
- If we divide the set of hits into two halves, chronologically, with *Paperback Writer* in the middle, a few things stand out. Note that the first half is generally more colorful and has more song parts, especially bridges. The heartbreaking and tragic purple 3 chord is also much more heavily used in the first half.

In fact, this set of chord palettes, together with what we see in the song maps and an awareness of musical energy, explains much about the Beatles' music and how it changed over time. *Love Me Do*, released in October 1962, wasn't really a blockbuster when it came out, and it probably only became a hit, a year and a half later and only in the US, because the Beatles had had such amazing success breaking onto the world stage. So, skipping over *Love Me Do*, we'll break the first half of the song set out into three early-Beatles periods, by year.

1963 Songs—*From Me to You*, *She Loves You*, and *I Want to Hold Your Hand*
These three songs share a common formula; they are all high-energy, use lots of note-on-note vocal harmony, and have sentimental pop chord palettes, with plenty of blue, purple, and green in the mix. All three

were also co-written by John and Paul, in an early and highly collaborative period. These are the three singles that catapulted the Beatles to stardom, with *She Loves You* and *I Want to Hold Your Hand* giving rise to Beatlemania in the UK and the US. Another interesting characteristic of these songs is where the vocal harmony occurs. We can see in the song maps that the harmony frequently occurs in the bridges, which serves to heighten a song's emotional impact. If you study the songs in detail, you'll also see that the other notable harmony locations in these earlier and hugely successful songs is either on sad chords or when a happy chord changes to a sad chord, which, like the harmony in bridges, increases a song's pull on your heartstrings.

1964 Songs—*Can't Buy Me Love, A Hard Day's Night, and I Feel Fine*
The verses in these songs all use rock 'n' roll–style red, orange, and yellow chords, with lots of blue notes in the lyrics or guitar playing. But, in stark contrast to the verses, the refrain in *Can't Buy Me Love* and the bridges in *A Hard Day's Night* and *I Feel Fine* are heavily laden with purple sad chords and are very emotional. In each of these songs, the verses are rock 'n' roll, while the refrains and bridges are sentimental pop. These songs illustrate a key ingredient of the Beatles' music and provided the inspiration for this book's title, *Blue Notes and Sad Chords*.

While the energy is still high in this string of hits, it's a bit less than in the 1963 songs, and there are no more high-pitched and frantic mop-topped head-shaking *oohs*. At this time, the Beatles were enjoying unheard-of popularity as evidenced by the fact that, in April 1964, they had the top five spots on the Billboard 100, a feat never achieved before or since by any other artist.

1965 Songs—*Eight Days a Week, Ticket to Ride, Help, Yesterday, Day Tripper,* and *We Can Work It Out*
With a total of six number 1 hits in 1965, the Beatles continued to enjoy unprecedented success, as well as to evolve, with their songwriting changing and getting more sophisticated. The chord progressions were getting more complex, particularly in *Help* and *Yesterday*, and John and Paul were writing more independently. Also, including the tail end of 1964, this was a John-dominated period, which came to an end midway through the number 1s song set. Except for *All You Need Is Love, Come Together,* and *Something*, the entire second half consists of McCartney numbers. Lastly, the overall energy continues to come down and the lyrics were changing. The songs' stories became less romantic, more introspective, and, like the chord progressions behind them, less formulaic.

This early 1963–1965 period is characterized by readily identifiable formulas. It's marked by intense energy, John and Paul working closely together, lots of note-on-note harmony, and very high contrast between song parts. In particular, the heavily harmonized and sentimental bridges are a hallmark and high point of Lennon/McCartney collaboration.

1966 and after—With *Paperback Writer*, in 1966, there's a major change. The songs in the second half of the set are no longer distinguishable using a clearly identifiable formula. The Beatles weren't touring anymore and were working and experimenting much more in the studio. The energy came way down, probably in no small part because the band was no longer performing. There's less harmony in these songs, and it's more of the backing-vocals harmony type, and not as much of the note-on-note style of the early period. The Beatles' popularity had also declined a bit at this point. The double-sided A, *Paperback Writer* and *Yellow Submarine*, was the first single not to hit the top spot in the US. While the band still went on to enjoy amazing chart successes for both singles and albums, Beatlemania was over.

There are also fewer song parts, especially bridges, in this half, and a notable reduction in chord colors, and far fewer heartbreaking purple 3 chords. As we saw looking at the song maps, the second half of the set is dominated by Paul McCartney, with more sincere and slower numbers, like *Hey Jude* and *Let It Be*, as well as more music-hall-style numbers, such as *Hello Goodbye* and *Lady Madonna*. There's also a notable absence of John Lennon's word-biting and soulful bluesy inflections, and, except for *Something*, there are no more romantic love songs.

While breaking up the band's career into these sub-periods is an inexact science, the chord palettes and song maps do visually tell the story of how the Beatles changed over time, and how the essential ingredients that gave rise to their stardom—the high performance energy, rich vocal harmonies, and contrasting song parts, all stemming from close collaboration—gave way to more individual efforts and to a less formulaic kind of music.

SIDEBAR
CHORD PROGRESSIONS AND THE WISTFUL 4

The colored palettes present a simple generalization of the chords used in the twenty-seven hit singles. They provide a visual suggestion for the feelings a song or song part can evoke. The palettes, however, don't show the detailed sequence of individual chords that make up a song's *chord progression*.

The graphic below shows the chord progressions for both the verse and the refrain in *I Want to Hold Your Hand*, using the same chord-to-color mapping system as the palettes, laid out horizontally from left to right.

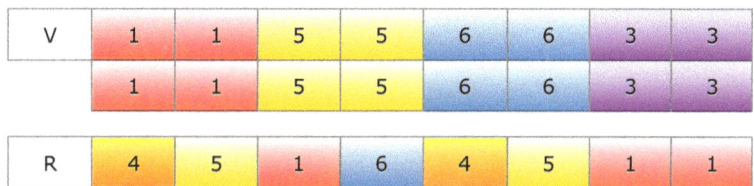

Chord Progression for Two-Line Verse and One-Line Refrain in I *Want to Hold Your Hand*

If a palette shows the set of colors or chords an artist has at their disposal for a composition, an ordered progression is more like showing the painting—what the artist actually assembled on the canvas with the colors they chose to work with.

The sensations and feelings that chords evoke are magnified and made more intense by the specific order they follow. For example, the blue 6 and the purple 3 are the saddest chords, and a 6 followed by a 3, as we see in the verse above, evokes a lonesome and forlorn feeling, but a sad blue 6 followed by an uplifting orange 4, as we see in the refrain above, results in a very hopeful feeling. So, this early Beatlemania blockbuster introduces an initially sad sensation at the end of the verse, but it's then quickly followed by a very feel-good, everything's-gonna-be-all-right refrain, bringing the song's mix and flow of musical feelings to a very happy end.

Although there are endless permutations and combinations of possible chord progressions, most rock 'n' roll and pop songs stick to a few basic formulas. There's the classic rock 'n' roll progression, using only the 1, 4, and 5, in songs like *Johnny Be Good, Kansas City, Roll Over Beethoven,* or the verse in *Can't Buy Me Love*. Lots of blues songs also use this same progression but slowed down. There's the archetypal 1950s tear jerker 1-6-4-5, used in songs like Wayne Cochran's *Last Kiss* (called by some the saddest song of the twentieth century). There's even a Wikipedia page dedicated to this chord progression:

https://en.wikipedia.org/wiki/List_of_songs_containing_the_50s_progression.

When played slowly, songs using variations of this progression can really pull on your heartstrings. When played up-tempo, they can be very uplifting and hopeful sounding. The Beatles' high-energy early period hits *From Me to You, She Loves You,* and *I Want to Hold Your Hand* can be classified in this category.

Another related and widely used sentimental feel-good progression, the 1-5-6-4, is used in songs like *Let It Be,* Train's *Hey, Soul Sister,* Jason Mraz's *I'm Yours,* Coldplay's *Viva La Vida,* Des'ree's *Life,* or Flo Rida's *Blow My Whistle.* This progression also has its own Wikipedia page, entitled *List of songs containing the I–V–vi–IV progression.* The band the Axis of Awesome did a great mashup video called *4 Chords,* which you can find at the YouTube link below, showing just how many big hits use this progression.

http://y2u.be/oOlDewpCfZQ

There are other common progressions. There's what you could call the rising or falling rockers, using the heavy flat-3 chord in the mix, in songs like Hendrix's *Purple Haze* or *All Along the Watchtower,* Deep Purple's *Smoke on the Water,* the Ventures' *Walk, Don't Run,* the Rolling Stones' *Under My Thumb,* the Yardbirds' *For Your Love,* or the Monkees' *(I'm Not Your) Steppin' Stone.*

One of the reasons many musicians who've never played together can just meet up for the first time and jam is that they instinctively hear and can play along with these commonly known chord progressions. This is particularly true for rhythm guitar, bass, and keyboard players.

THE BEATLES AND CHORD PROGRESSIONS

A lot of the Beatles' very early covers were standard rock 'n' rollers using classic 1-4-5 progressions, and the Beatlemania that followed is due, in large part, to a very amped-up energy used to deliver sentimental sounding progressions, like the ones used in *I Want to Hold Your Hand* and *She Loves You*. But in the latter part of their early career, starting with the album *Help*, the Beatles departed from tradition and started to write very original material that used unusual and fairly elaborate chord progressions. You can hear this in hits like *Help* and *Yesterday*. This is another key element in the Beatles' creativity and evolution, and one of the main reasons that it's often harder for musicians to figure out how to play these middle and later period songs.

The Wistful 4

The word wistful is defined as something like *having or showing a feeling of vague or regretful longing.*

There's a common pop-music chord change that goes from the happy energetic major-4 chord to the sadder minor-4 chord. It involves dropping a single note, in the middle of the stack, down a notch. It evokes a sad, lonesome, wistful feeling. It's a mainstay in many kinds of music, and the Beatles used this chord change in so many of their original songs that if you were looking for Beatles formulas, it would have to be included. Some of the songs that the wistful 4 shows up in are *Hold Me Tight, Anytime at All, I'll Follow the Sun, You Won't See Me, Nowhere Man,* and *In My Life,* and there are many more.

The wistful 4 is a specific example of a more general change between happy major chords and sad minor ones built on the same note and very colorful and noticeable to our ears. The Beatles did this a lot as well, and you can hear it on songs like *Things We Said Today, Penny Lane,* and moving in the opposite direction, in George's very last strummed chord change on a classical guitar at the end of *And I Love Her,* which goes from the weaker minor to the stronger major.

Like the high-energy, rich vocal harmony, and contrasting song parts, the wistful 4 is more a part of the early-Beatles formula, and isn't heard nearly as much in the second half of their career.

The 4 Chord and 4 Note

The 4 chord, almost always major in pop music, and rarely minor (it does show up in what's called the *minor blues*), plays such an important role in music. On the circle of 5ths (see Sidebar *Colored Music and Synesthesia*), it's next to the 1, but to the left and going counter clockwise. (Moving counter clockwise around a circle of fifths with just the seven scale note chords creates a beautiful chord progression that is frequently heard in classical music.) All that aside, 4 chords are a mainstay in rock and pop music. The Chord Frequencies chart in the Appendix show that the 4 chord is the second most commonly used, in the full set of Beatles' song, after the 1. This comes as no surprise, given how upbeat and happy the band was, like the 4 chord.

The 4 note, in some cases, can also load up a section of a song with some very special energy. This is done by holding the underlying chord to the 1, but singing or playing 4 notes in the melody. John Lennon does this in the verses of *I Feel Fine*, the first time around on the words *good*, and then *as*, and also in the verse in *You Can't Do That*, where he sings the words *say that might* in the first verse, and *caught you*, in the second verse. Hitting a 4 note in a spot like this, while still in a 1 chord, adds an amazingly bluesy and upward pulling energy to a song. This also occurs when Paul is singing the verses in *Back in the USSR*, when John Fogerty of Creedence Clearwater Revival is singing the opening words to the verses in *Born on the Bayou*, and when the Soggy Bottom Boys are singing the verses in *I Am a Man of Constant Sorrow* in the movie soundtrack for *O Brother, Where Art Thou?*

ESSENTIAL EARLY BEATLES: SONG MAP AND CHORD PALETTE TOGETHER

The twenty-seven song maps and chord palettes were presented independently, in sections 2 and 3 of the book, to help separate the reader's focus. The graphic below, using a slightly modified presentation style, shows the two lines from the verse and the one line from the refrain in *I Want to Hold Your Hand*. The graphic shows both the song map colors and chord palette colors, using units of half a measure. A measure lasts for 4 beats, and so the two verse lines last for 8 measures or 16 half measures, and the refrain lasts for 4 measures or 8 half measures.

The song map, with each half measure labeled with its sequential number, shows John and Paul singing in both unison, using a light purple, and harmony, using a red-to-blue fade, as well as guitar riffs, using gray. The chord palette graphic shows which chords are being played as a progression. You can see that in addition to the home-red-1 and leaning-yellow-5 chords, the sad-blue-6 and the heartbroken-purple-3 are prominent. Because the graphics are aligned, you can easily see corresponding song-map and chord-palette colors for the same half measure. For example, for half measures 15 and 16 in the song map, shown as John and Paul harmonizing, the corresponding half measures in the chord palette below show that a heartbroken-purple-3 is being played, and that for part of the last line in the chord palette, corresponding to half measures 3–6 in the song map, the classic 1950s sad-to-happy 1-6-4-5 chord progression is being played.

One thing the chord palette progression shows is that, as in many pop songs, the verse-refrain uses an A-A-B pattern, with the first two A verse lines using a slower 1-5-6-3 chord change, and the third B refrain line uses a more complex and faster set of chord changes involving the happy and upbeat orange-4-to-yellow-5 ending. (Increasing how fast chord changes occur is a classic method for injecting energy into a musical passage.) The chord progression also highlights the sad-blue-6-to-heartbroken-purple-3 chord change that John and Paul came up with for the verse in this song, sitting together at the piano in the basement of Jane Asher's London home. While not that common in pop music, *I Want to Hold Your Hand*'s verse 1-5-6-3 chord progression occurs in some well-known pieces of classical music, like Pachelbel's *Cannon* and Couperin's *Mysterious Barricades*, and in folk songs like Ralph McTell's *Streets of London*.

Note that there is some difference of opinion about the type of 3 chord used in *I Want to Hold Your Hand*. For a full exploration of this, see the dedicated section in the Appendix.

But the more important point to focus on here is that John and Paul's harmony in refrain half measures 3 and 4 occurs at the same moment as the sad 1–6 chord change, and the feel-good 4–5 chord change occurs just as they shift back into unison singing, in half measures 5 and 6. This combination of brilliant energetic harmony occurring at a heart-string-tugging chord change, which then resolves to a happy upbeat ending, is a hallmark early-Beatles musical moment. Simultaneously viewing the song map and chord palette progression sections here highlights the infectious combination of energy, alternating unison/harmony singing, and guitar playing that occurs in this song, as well as the use of a classic 1950s/60s sentimental chord progression, and helps explain why this Beatlemania blockbuster was so irresistible.

Song Map and Chord Palette Progression Aligned for the 12-Measure Verse and Refrain in *I Want to Hold Your Hand*

BLUE NOTES AND SAD CHORDS

The idea of Blue Notes and Sad Chords, exemplified by the string of three 1964 hits described earlier, when the Beatles were at the height of their success, refers to the mixing of bluesy rock 'n' roll and sentimental pop sounds and feelings in the same song. This is really just a specific example of something more general in the Beatles' music. This special something involves a high degree of contrast, in style and emotional feeling, between different parts of the same song. You can hear it on *It Won't Be Long*, the opening number to the *With the Beatles* album, where the title-words refrain, abruptly bursting with incredibly high early-Beatles energy, is in such sharp contrast to the bridge where everything slows way down, and John sings the heartfelt and hopeful lyrics (she left but she's coming back) against a smooth backdrop of long drawn-out and harmonized *oohs* and offset words in the backing vocals, sung by Paul and George. And to add additional contrast, the verse of *It Won't Be Long* also uses the ominous flat 6 described above. Contrast can be heard in *I Should Have Known Better*, where the bridge contains much more emotional material than the verse, or between the intro and the main body in a song like *If I Fell*. This contrast between song parts is a definitive characteristic of the Beatles' music, and something you won't hear nearly as much of in other bands. For just a few more examples in the band's early period, you can also hear this type of contrast in *I Wanna Be Your Man, I'm Happy Just to Dance with You, No Reply, Baby's in Black, I Don't Want to Spoil the Party, Norwegian Wood, Nowhere Man, Girl, Wait*, and *If I Needed Someone*. Additionally, this contrast between song parts didn't fall off as much as energy and vocal harmony did as the band evolved, and while it is perhaps more prominent in the earlier work, it can still be heard in second-half numbers like *Lucy in the Sky with Diamonds, I'm So Tired, The Continuing Story of Bungalow Bill, Julia, Hey Bulldog, I Want You*, and so noticeably, in *A Day in the Life*.

The Blue Notes and Sad Chords phenomenon is not only found in the contrast between vocals in the song parts; it's also delivered through guitar playing. For example, in the sentimental but high-energy pop number *She Loves You*, after the third time through *yeah, yeah, yeah*, between the refrain and verse, there's a jarring rocker guitar riff, or in *Please Please Me*, there's a heavy rising flat-3 rocker chord in the section separating the verse parts, and here, it's *within* the same song part.

A MUSIC GENOME FOR THE BEATLES

When you listen to music using streaming services like Pandora, Spotify, Apple, or Google, their computer programs guess what kind of music you like based on what you play and what you indicate you like or dislike. Behind the scenes, these programs rely on systems that classify music using hundreds of characteristics. For example, the "music genome" that Pandora uses includes over four hundred and fifty different characteristics to precisely describe the details in a piece of music. Using Pandora, you can see some of these details under the *Features of this Track* heading such as *prominent acoustic guitar, vocal harmony, rhythmic syncopation*, and so on, but they only expose some of them. The hundreds of musical characteristics that make up the music genome were once visible on the internet, but they have since been hidden. (You can still find a list of them on sites that historically archive content.) While a system like Pandora uses a computer program to identify the characteristics you like and then look for similar pieces of music, the initial characteristics of a piece of music itself are typically assigned by listening humans.

While highly simplified, the central premise of this book—that in addition to their looks and charm, the Beatles became so popular because of a special winning combination of three main musical ingredients, namely performance energy, vocal harmony, and song quality—is related to a system like the music genome. The song maps are a visual way of highlighting the vocal harmony ingredient, and the chord palettes a visual way of highlighting an element of song quality. And in addition to these main characteristics, we've gone into more detail, calling out more specific things like *soulful bluesy vocal inflections,* or *staggered drumming*, in the detailed walk-throughs of the twenty-seven hit singles. So in a way, we've described a set of key characteristics found in the Beatles' music, a mini-genome of sorts. We've also included some non-musical characteristics, like *high collaboration among songwriters*, and musical characteristics, like *unusual chord progressions*, or *combining rock 'n' roll and pop in the same song*, that systems like Pandora and Spotify are perhaps not, at this time, clever enough to identify.

It's obvious that the Beatles really did change over time. To look at the details of how they changed in a different way, and make use of something like a musical genome, the two word clouds on the following pages include characteristics of the two halves of the Beatles career, separated into early and late periods. The importance, or weight, of a given characteristic, is somewhat suggested by text size, while coloring is random (the later period cloud uses a wider range of colors). Note that there are some non-musical characteristics included.

These word clouds are highly simplified and subjective, but they do suggest a way to think about the Beatles' music and how it changed over time. In addition to comparing the early and late Beatles, you could also use them to compare the Beatles with other artists and their work.

EARLY AND LATE BEATLES MUSICAL WORD CLOUDS

Creative bass parts
Nostalgic lyrics   Motown songs   Introspective lyrics
Sentimental bridges   Country-western sounds
Ominous -6 chord   Romantic teen-love lyrics
Harmonized backing vocals   Live performances   Mixing major and minor chords
High-energy falsetto vocals   Time signature changes   Girl-group songs
Soulful bluesy vocal inflections   Sad 6 & 3 chords with happy 1 & 4 chords
Close note-on-note vocal harmony   The wistful-4 chord change
Harmonica   Writing songs together   Lennon songs
High-energy word biting   Vocal harmonies at chord changes   Original songs
Fast tempo   Screaming teen girls fan base   Blue notes and sad chords   Influence of drugs
Harrison songs
Harmonized bridges   Early rock 'n' roll sounds   Rock 'n' roll piano
Fractured early-rock style lead guitar breaks   Cover songs
Popularity   String quartets
High-energy multi-voice refrains
Sincere choirboy solo vocals

Early Beatles

Goofy lyrics Writing songs together
String quartets Raucous lyrics
Blue notes and sad chords Brass bands McCartney Songs
Bizarre lyrics Time signature changes High energy falsetto vocals
Strident rock guitar riffs Ad-libing Harrison hit songs
Early 20th century music hall sound Backwards music Creative bass parts
Long drawn out song endings Unusual adlibbing in outros
Popularity
Fast tempo Studio recording and experimentation Sentimental bridges
Writing songs alone Sincere choirboy solo male vocals
High energy screaming vocals Harmonized backing vocals
Choirs Unusual instrumentation Tender lyrics Ominous -6 chord
Original songs Introspective lyrics Indian influences
Orchestras Influence of drugs Hippie fan base
Close note-on-note vocal harmony Wistful-4 chord change
Unusual chord progressions

Late Beatles

THE ALBUMS

Are the twenty-seven hit singles representative of the full Beatles' catalog? Are the patterns and changes over time in the energy, vocal harmony, and song structure that we've see in the number 1s also found in the other 180-plus songs? Would it be fair to say that more thought went into the selection of songs for singles and that they're more purely representative of what the Beatles and George Martin wanted for their sound?

While a detailed overview of every song on every album is beyond the scope of this book, to help partially answer the questions posed above, this section provides a brief review of each of the thirteen albums the Beatles released between 1963 and 1970. Certain songs are called out within the context of the energy, harmony, and song structure that's been the focus of our discussion. To try to keep things simple, the tracks on the original UK released albums are reviewed here, and not the repackaged compilations sold by Capitol in the US and Canada. (To get the gist of these reviews, you need to be somewhat familiar with the Beatles' full song set.)

#1 *Please Please Me*
Recorded: September 1962—February 1963, Released: March 1963
Recorded in just 13 hours, *Please Please Me* includes seven covers and seven original songs that the Beatles had been playing at their live shows. The opener *I Saw Her Standing There*, an original, and the closer *Twist*

and Shout, a cover of the Isley Brothers' 1962 hit, are early-Beatles high-energy, although the overall energy on the album is a bit lower compared with what's to follow. The band uses harmony heavily in five of the songs including *Chains, Please Please Me, Love Me Do, There's a Place,* and *Twist and Shout*, and only three songs have no harmony at all. *Please Please Me, P.S. I Love You,* and *There's a Place* are all quintessential early-Beatles originals, with interesting contrast between song parts. *There's a Place* uses particularly unusual and contrasting chords following the verses in a bridge-like section, and *I Saw Her Standing There* features the use of the ominous/mysterious flat-6 chord when John and Paul's voices are raised in frantic *oohs* just before the title lyrics.

#2 *With the Beatles*
Recorded: July—October, 1963, Released: Nov 1963
With the Beatles opens with a definition early-Beatles hit, *It Won't Be Long*, featuring high energy, lots of harmony, and a sentimental bridge that contrasts with the rocker verse and refrain. As with their first album, there are seven originals and seven covers. *All I've Got to Do, Please Mister Postman, You Really Got a Hold on Me, Devil in Her Heart,* and *Money* are all awash in brilliant harmony, mostly in the backing vocals, although there is generally less contrast in chord palettes between song parts. *Till There Was You,* a cover from the 1957 musical play *The Music Man, Hold Me Tight,* and *Devil in Her Heart,* all make use of the *wistful 4* (see the Sidebar *Chord Progressions and the Wistful 4*) chord change. It's here that we first hear Paul McCartney's sincere-choirboy voice on *Till There Was You,* and many of John Lennon's leads are laden with his signature soulful and bluesy inflections.

#3 *A Hard Day's Night*
Recorded: January—June 1964, Released: July 1964
All thirteen tracks on *A Hard Day's Night* are originals, and it's a Lennon-dominated album. Seven songs feature harmony, including the beautiful *If I Fell* and the upbeat *Tell Me Why*, and *I'll Be Back*, a fully harmonized song throughout, which shifts back and forth between a brighter major home chord and a darker minor one. There is high contrast between song parts in *A Hard Day's Night, I'm Happy Just to Dance with You, Things We Said Today, You Can't Do That,* and especially between the upbeat verse and the heavily sentimental opening lines of the bridge in *I Should Have Known Better*. Overall, the energy is high, especially on *A Hard Day's Night, Can't Buy Me Love, Any Time at All,* and *When I Get Home*. The only songs without bridges are *Can't Buy Me Love* and *When I Get Home*.

#4 *Beatles for Sale*
Recorded: August—October, 1964, Released: December 1964
There are eight originals and six covers on *Beatles for Sale*. Except for the rock 'n' roll covers, Chuck Berry's *Rock and Roll Music* and Carl Perkins' *Kansas City*, sung by Paul in his Little Richard voice, the energy is a bit lower on this album. There's lots of harmony in the cover of Buddy Holly's *Words of Love, I Don't*

Want to Spoil the Party, and especially in *Baby's in Black,* where every line is full note-on-note Lennon/McCartney harmony. There's less contrast between song parts and fewer bridges on this album, and so, together with less harmony and energy, it's not quite as characteristic of classic early Beatles as the three albums that came before it.

#5 *Help*

Recorded: February—June, 1965, Released: August 1965

Help has ten originals and two covers. Except for the opening title song and the closing throat-ripping Lennon cover of Larry Williams' 1958 hit *Dizzy Miss Lizzy,* the energy has come down a notch. While harmony is featured in ten of the twelve songs, it's not as out front as it is in the earlier albums. There are lots of bridges, but less contrast between song parts. The lyrics are starting to change on this one, with John's *Help* and Paul's *Yesterday,* both retrospective and serious. The chord progressions, also on *Help* and *Yesterday,* and on *The Night Before* and *Girl,* are also starting to get much more sophisticated. All in all, it feels like things are evolving, with high-energy rock numbers and teen love stories making way for more creative, unique material.

#6 *Rubber Soul*

Recorded: June—October, 1965, Released: December 1965

The fourteen original tracks on *Rubber Soul* are an explosion of early-Beatles vocal harmony and melody, and a high point in the first half of the band's career. Every song is harmonized, and the melodies on tracks like *Norwegian Wood, Nowhere Man, Michelle, Girl,* and *In My Life* are unforgettably beautiful. There's significant contrast between parts, in at least half of the songs, and lots of bridges, and it's also on this album that we first hear George Harrison's exotic sitar work. Along with the chord progressions, the lyrics continue to evolve, with an unusually rich spectrum of emotions and colors. The *wistful 4* (see the Sidebar *Chord Progressions and the Wistful 4*) chord change is prominent in *You Won't See Me, Nowhere Man,* and *In My Life.*

#7 *Revolver*

Recorded: April—June, 1965, Released: August 1966

All fourteen tracks on *Revolver* are originals. Like the second track, *Eleanor Rigby,* is for the single hits, this album is at the midpoint of the Beatles' career, and the end of the beginning. There is still a good bit of energy and lots of harmony, especially in *Taxman, Good Day Sunshine,* and *Doctor Robert,* but there is less contrast between song parts and there are fewer bridges. There are no vestiges of early rock 'n' roll or blues, with the guitar playing more akin to what could be described as modern rock. There's more studio experimentation going on now, as with the backward guitar riffs in *I'm Only Sleeping,* and perhaps more influence from mind-altered states. If you were a young girl screaming away just a couple of years before, you may have been somewhat confused by the crazy jarring dreamscape in *Tomorrow Never Knows*. We're not in Kansas anymore.

#8 *Sgt. Pepper's Lonely Hearts Club Band*
Recorded: November 1966—April 1967, Released: May 1967
Sgt. Pepper is cited by many as a definitive high point in the Beatles' output. All thirteen songs are originals and incredibly creative. The energy, song structure, and harmony formula of the earlier Beatles, while still faintly detectable in a few spots, has given way to a new kind of rock and pop music. The opening title song, a slower driving rocker with good contrast between parts, and the reprise at the end of the album with things sped up a bit, less contrast, and more shrieking guitar, have the most energy. There's a lot of very unusual instrumentation, especially on the floating *Lucy in the Sky with Diamonds*, the circus soundtrack of *Being for the Benefit of Mr. Kite*, the mystically Indian *Within You Without You*, and the imposing orchestra crescendo and long loud reverberating chord in *A Day in the Life*. Paul's music-hall number, *When I'm Sixty-Four*, written years earlier, does have striking contrast between the upbeat and somewhat comical verse/refrain and the seriously darker bridge, and it's safe to say that, overall, this is a McCartney dominated album. The closer, *A Day in the Life*, like the album, is also often named as the best Beatles song. It's really two songs sewn together, and somewhat unusual for a Beatles best pick in that it has no vocal harmony. Generally speaking, vocal harmony is not a feature of the album.

#9 *Magical Mystery Tour*
Recorded: April—November, 1967, Released: December 1967 (UK), November 1967 (US)
Magical Mystery Tour was released in the UK as a six-song double EP, while the US release, a full LP, included A- and B-sides from the 1967 singles. *Magical Mystery Tour* wasn't really planned as an album by the band or George Martin, and with only five non-single songs, none of them Lennon numbers, it really came about as the result of the crazy little movie of the same name. The album is again somewhat McCartney dominated. *The Fool on the Hill* has unusual chords and a very dark, contrasting bridge. There's yet another McCartney music-hall-style number, *Your Mother Should Know*, along with a slow organ-laden 12-bar blues instrumental, *Flying*, credited to all four Beatles. George Harrison's eerie *Blue Jay Way* has high contrast in the bridge, both harmonically and rhythmically. The title song has a bit of energy and some bright harmony.

#10 *The White Album*
Recorded: May—October, 1968, Released: November 1968
The double *White Album* has thirty original songs. The energy is generally high, with some numbers, like *Why Don't We Do It in the Road*, *Yer Blues*, *Everybody's Got Something to Hide except Me and My Monkey*, and *Helter Skelter*, absolutely redlining the volume levels. There is significant contrast among song parts, particularly in Lennon songs like *The Continuing Story of Bungalow Bill*, *Happiness Is a Warm Gun*, *I'm So*

Tired, and *Julia*. And while more songs have bridges than don't, the most noticeable characteristic of the *White Album*, in the context of our inquiry, is the relatively low amount of vocal harmony. Harmony here, as in the case on *Sgt. Pepper*, is no longer a prominent feature of the band's music.

#11 *Yellow Submarine*

Recorded: May 1966—February 1968 (George Martin's score, October 1968), Released: January 1969
Yellow Submarine is a bit like *Magical Mystery Tour* in that it was never really planned as a full featured Beatles album. There are only four non-single songs on the album, supposedly just filler in order to comply with a contract, along with a full second side containing George Martin's movie-score tracks. *Hey Bulldog* is one great song that does stand out here, and it's a bit more early-Beatles formulaic, with great guitar riffs, intense energy, plenty of rich Lennon/McCartney harmony, and high contrast in the bridge (even if it ends with ad-libbed dog noises).

#12 *Abbey Road*

Recorded: February—August, 1969, Released: September 1969
Abbey Road has seventeen different original songs, a good number of them strung together in a medley on the second side. While much of the material, as in other latter-period work, is McCartney penned, there are still a few Lennon numbers, as well as most notably, the two beautiful Harrison songs, *Something* and *Here Comes the Sun*. And there's probably the closest thing we ever hear to a drum solo, with Ringo's work on *The End*. The energy is hard to pin down. There are bursts throughout, in many songs, but the overall feeling is a bit lower because of the many slower and calmer songs. There's still lots of harmony, particularly in the darkly lavish *Because*, and song maps of this album would be very colorful. In a return to an earlier style, especially after the more individually oriented *White Album*, there's a lot of contrast between song parts and quite a few bridges. Much of the material is a bit comical, even goofy, in a McCartney-esque way, and the song *Mean Mr. Mustard* stands out as something that, while John actually wrote it, could easily pass as a Paul number. A bit like in *A Day in the Life*, *I Want You* and *You Never Give Me Your Money* are really several songs sewn together.

#13 *Let It Be*

Recorded: January 1969—April 1970, Released: May 1970
Let It Be has twelve tracks, including eleven originals, four of which were single A- and B-sides, and the Liverpool ditty *Maggie Mae*. Many of the songs on *Let It Be* were actually recorded before *Abbey Road*, but it was too much of a challenge to put the album together at the time, so it was postponed. Notwithstanding his earlier and seminal work as a producer for so many successful artists, on this album Phil Spector famously added swirling Muzak-like backdrops to several numbers, including *Across the Universe*, *I Me Mine*, and *The Long and Winding Road*. Except for *I've Got a Feeling*, and parts of *Dig It* and *I Me Mine*, the overall energy is low. Only *Two of Us* and *One After 909* stand out as harmonized, as does the comical

Maggie Mae. The heaviest contrast is in George's *I Me Mine*, which also switches from waltz into straight time in the bridge. *Let It Be* is a little more of a hodgepodge than *Abbey Road*, and, along with the film, it's become famous as the musical backdrop for the Beatles' break-up.

ALBUM CHARTING

A look at the energy, vocal harmony, and song structure through the course of the thirteen albums does generally match what we see in the singles, with the early period more formulaic, and the latter period more disjointed, but nevertheless with continuing moments of creative brilliance. Another interesting thing to look at here is how album charting in the UK changed through the years. The table below shows the number of weeks each album spent at the number 1 position in the UK charts, along with the release year.

YEAR	ALBUM	WEEKS AT 1
1963	Please Please Me	30
1963	With The Beatles	21
1964	A Hard Day's Night	21
1964	Beatles For Sale	11
1965	Help	9
1965	Rubber Soul	8
1966	Revovler	7
1967	Sgt. Pepper's Lonely Hearts Club Band	28
1968	Magical Mystery Tour	0
1968	The White Album	8
1969	Yellow Submarine	0
1969	Abbey Road	17
1970	Let It Be	3

Beatle Album Charting in the UK, Source: www.officialcharts.com

We can see that the Beatles burst onto the scene in 1963 with an amazingly high 30-week run for their very first album, never to be repeated. While things dipped a bit, 1963 and 1964 showed incredible chart success. 1965 and 1966 saw a bit of a more of a decline which was then abruptly reversed in 1967 with *Sgt. Pepper*. Things again declined, with the *White Album* having some success, and the pseudo-albums *Magical Mystery Tour* (an EP in the UK) and *Yellow Submarine* not hitting the top spot (although *Magical Mystery Tour* as an LP did hit number 1 in the US). But the Beatles were always full of surprises, and *Abbey Road* showed another spike, with a swan-song run of 17 weeks.

What kind of a story do these numbers tell? Note that 1963 and 1964 accounted for a record-breaking 83 weeks with an album at the top spot, while the remaining years, 1965–70, total up to slightly less, at 80 weeks, meaning that about half of all the Beatles' UK album weeks at number 1 occurred in the first two years.

US album charting is not shown here, as in the early period it would rely on repackaged albums with slightly different mixes of songs. That said, US chart numbers did somewhat mirror the UK's, particularly showing a very strong start and an overall decline with fewer albums as the decade wore on, but with two major spikes from *Sgt. Pepper*, and *Abbey Road*.

THE BEATLES AND OTHER ARTISTS

After reviewing the Beatles' albums, we have another important question to ask. Is the combination of high energy, beautifully arranged vocal harmonies, and creative song structure, as seen in the twenty-seven number 1 hits, really unique to the Beatles? Can these same musical elements be found in the songs of other successful artists of the 1960s? Comparison can be a great way to get to essentials, so here we'll take a brief look at energy, harmony, song quality, and other musical elements in the work of other 1960s artists.

1960s Hit Singles

The two tables below list the artists, number of songs, weeks at the top spot, and year range for any artist with more than a single hit, from 1960 to 1970, in the US and the UK. Note that Elvis had a slew of hits, most of them in the 1950s, that are not shown here, and that the Stones, like Diana Ross on her own, had some big hits in the 1970s and later.

NO.	ARTIST	HITS	WEEKS	FROM	TO
1	The Beatles	20	54	1964	1970
2	The Supremes	13	19	1964	1969
3	Elvis Presley	6	20	1960	1969
4	The Rolling Stones	5	13	1965	1969
5	Bobby Vinton	4	12	1962	1964
6	The Four Seasons	4	15	1962	1964
7	Chubby Checker	3	6	1960	1962
8	Connie Francis	3	5	1960	1962
9	Ray Charles	3	8	1960	1962
10	Simon & Garfunkel	3	5	1966	1968
11	The Beach Boys	3	5	1964	1966
12	The Jackson 5	4	10	1970	1970
13	The Monkees	3	12	1966	1967
14	Young Rascals	3	10	1966	1968
15	The Byrds	2	4	1965	1965
16	The Doors	2	5	1967	1968
17	The 5th Dimension	2	9	1969	1969
18	The Righteous Brothers	2	5	1965	1966
19	Roy Orbison	2	4	1961	1964
20	The Shirelles	2	5	1961	1962
21	Petula Clark	2	4	1965	1966
22	Herman's Hermits	2	4	1965	1965
23	The Four Tops	2	4	1965	1966
24	The Temptations	2	3	1965	1969
25	Tommy Roe	2	6	1962	1969
26	Brenda Lee	2	4	1960	1960
27	The Association	2	7	1966	1967

US Billboard Singles, Artists with More Than One Hit, 1960–1970

SECTION 3 : BLUE NOTES AND SAD CHORDS

NO.	ARTIST	HITS	WEEKS	FROM	TO
1	The Beatles	17	63	1963	1969
2	Elvis Presley	13	50	1960	1970
3	The Rolling Stones	8	18	1964	1969
4	Cliff Richard and The Shadows	7	17	1960	1963
5	The Shadows	5	16	1960	1963
6	Frank Ifield	4	17	1962	1963
7	Roy Orbison	4	7	1960	1964
8	Gerry and The Pacemakers	3	11	1963	1963
9	Manfred Mann	3	7	1964	1968
10	Sandie Shaw	3	9	1964	1967
11	The Everly Brothers	3	12	1960	1961
12	The Kinks	3	5	1964	1966
13	The Searchers	3	7	1963	1964
14	Anthony Newley	2	5	1960	1960
15	Bee Gees	2	5	1967	1968
16	Billy J. Kramer and The Dakotas	2	5	1963	1964
17	Cilla Black	2	7	1964	1964
18	Cliff Richard	2	3	1965	1968
19	Engelbert Humperdinck	2	11	1967	1967
20	Georgie Fame	2	3	1965	1968
21	Helen Shapiro	2	6	1961	1961
22	John Leyton	2	4	1961	1961
23	Marmalade	2	3	1969	1969
24	Petula Clark	2	3	1961	1967
25	Rolf Harris	2	12	1969	1969
26	The Beach Boys	2	3	1966	1968
27	The Hollies	2	3	1965	1965
28	The Scaffold	2	4	1968	1969
29	The Seekers	2	5	1965	1965
30	The Spencer Davis Group	2	3	1966	1966
31	The Walker Brothers	2	5	1965	1966
32	Tom Jones	2	8	1965	1966
33	Tommy James and the Shondells	2	3	1968	1968

UK Singles Chart, Artists with More Than One Hit, 1960–1970

The Beatles are at the top of this lists in both tables (double A-sides are only counted once). We can also see that Elvis and the Stones are at the top in both lists. Maybe we can also see some differences between musical tastes in the US and the UK, with the Supremes and Bobby Vinton successful in the US, and the Shadows and Cliff Richard in the UK.

Note that while the tables above show singles, some artists not listed did have number 1 albums in the same timeframe, including, in the US, the Kingston Trio, Herb Alpert's Tijuana Brass, Led Zeppelin, and in the UK, Bob Dylan, Simon and Garfunkel, the Seekers, Cream, Led Zeppelin, Jethro Tull, and the Moody Blues. It's also important to remember that albums began to outsell singles and get more play time on FM radio in the later part of the 1960s.

Elvis
Without Elvis, there probably would have been no Beatles. He came along in the mid-1950s, had his first number 1 hit in 1955 with *Heartbreak Hotel,* and broke the mold. With his raw sexual energy, good looks and sincere charm, wide stance, gyrating hips and eggbeater legs, and deep quivering, hiccupping, and soulful voice, not to mention some great songs and bandmates, he changed everything. With a new and unique combination of pop, blues, and gospel, the King changed music and performance in a striking way. He didn't write many of his own songs, and you wouldn't necessarily say that there's something unique about their construction, as it was more a question of how he delivered them that set him apart. As with the Beatles, a key factor in Elvis's success was stage presence and energy, and especially the way he pumped this energy into a new wound-up hybrid of southern black and southern white roots music, during his wild early performances. And it is this energy and stage presences that the Beatles inherited, from Elvis and from other hit 1950s rock 'n' rollers, that was so much a part of their early star-bound incarnation.

The Supremes
The Supremes had major singles success in the 1960s in the US, second only to the Beatles. Along with so many other Motown acts, they brought a new kind of music to the scene, again and in some ways like Elvis, a hybrid mixture of black and white ingredients. In this case however, the black and white mix is a lower energy and sentimentally laden kind of pop music, delivered with chiseled stage performance, choreography, and vocal arrangements, with lots of melody and beautiful but understated harmony in the backing vocals. Like lots of good pop music, these songs, penned by Motown's formidable Holland-Dozier-Holland team, often include bridges that contrast with the main verse and refrain parts. It's the combination of this song quality, along with Diana Ross's beautiful sweet-girl-melodic-yet-soulful voice, that made these queens of the girl groups such a bit hit.

Cliff Richard and the Shadows
The Shadows, an instrumental electric guitar group, while probably not very familiar to most Americans, were incredibly popular in the UK. If you're not familiar with the Shadows, listen to *Apache*, which spent

5 weeks at number 1 in 1960, and *Wonderful Land*, which spent 8 weeks there in 1962 (there are plenty of recordings online). The Shadows were also the backing band for Cliff Richard, also a chart topper and incredibly successful act in the UK, and perhaps at times a little bit like the clean-cut and sincere American Bobby Vinton. If you're not familiar with Cliff Richard, listen to *The Young Ones* and *Summer Holiday*. On their own, the Shadows were a bit like the Ventures, both becoming popular in the early 1960s, although perhaps because of their association with Cliff Richard as a front man, the Shadows had much more chart success.

(We'll get to the Rolling Stones in a separate section below.)

All the Others
What about all the other artists in these lists? There are over one hundred hits in each of the tables above, and a combined total of over fifty artists, so while we won't go into too much detail, we can pose some basic questions. What can we say about what made these artists successful and how the key ingredients in their music compare with those of the Beatles? Scan these lists of artists and think about energy, vocal harmony, song quality, and the other musical elements that led to their success. What would their song maps, chord palettes, and musical word clouds look like?

There were crooners and other great vocalists, more groups than solo artists in the US, a more even balance in the UK. There's a little rock, but it's mostly pop (these are pop charts), and it's generally not about instrumental prowess. Along with Elvis, and the Stones, there are clearly some high-energy acts in the lists, but it's not quite the same kind of frantic energy that we heard in the early Beatles, which was really a brief resurgence of Little Richard and Jerry Lee Lewis–style 1950s over-the-top rock 'n' roll energy. The music of these artists is also not generally as spirited as what was to come when bands like Cream and Led Zeppelin appeared on the scene and set the stage for heavy metal and arena rock.

The key element in most of the chart-topping songs, as with the Beatles, is a combination of great vocals and high-quality, memorable melodies. Simon and Garfunkel's songs and harmonies are truly amazing, and rich harmony is a main feature in the work of artists like the Everly Brothers, the Shirelles, and the Association, but it's usually delivered at lower energy levels. Many of the bands that are guitar groups with harmonizing singers, like the Bee Gees, the Beach Boys, the Hollies, and the Byrds, have lineups like the Beatles, but again, their energy levels are generally lower. The Beach Boys of course had that special, clean-cut harmonic energy, and a good number of blue notes in the mix, but it's so sweet and polished that it sometimes comes across a little bit like a barbershop quartet on steroids. For a combination of energy, harmony, and the mixing of lighter and darker parts within the same song, the Hollies came close with hits like *Bus Stop* and *I Can't Let Go*, and the 5th Dimension really belted out some truly spirited energy through a solid wall of multi-part harmony in their hit *Aquarius (Let the Sunshine In)* but in terms of the sheer number of songs with high-energy harmonic blasts, the Beatles are in a class by themselves.

While looking at just pop chart singles is informative, it's still limiting. There are of course lots of other great artists with songs that didn't become number 1s and album work to consider. It's hard to imagine anybody having more energy than the collapsing cape-covered James Brown, or than Barry McGuire biting into the words on *Eve of Destruction*, or the Who's driving energy with Peter Townshend's windmill guitar strumming and Roger Daltrey's gutsy delivery. There is wonderful harmony in the work of the acts like Peter and Gordon, Chad and Jeremy, the Mamas and the Papas, and many others. The quality of Bob Dylan's songs is legendary, with top artists covering songs like *Blowin' in the Wind, Mr. Tambourine Man,* or *All Along the Watchtower,* and Ray Davies of the Kinks and Jim Morrison of the Doors, to name just a few, were brilliant and very original songwriters.

Energy and vocal harmony are very physical, noticeable characteristics of a piece of music. Determining how the different parts of a song and interesting lyrics come together to contribute to an overall quality is subtler and requires closer listening. One specific thing you won't hear as much of in the work of many of these other artists is the high contrast between musical chord palettes used in the different parts of the same song, the type of contrast we've identified as a key ingredient of many Beatles songs. However, because it's such a basic element in so much music, this type of contrast does show up in a good number of songs. Take a few minutes to go online and listen to the following set of songs from the mid-1960s. Listen for the basic feeling laid down at the beginning of each song, either in the vocals or the instruments, and then for a significant change, typically going from the dark or bluesy to the emotional or sentimental, along with the shifts in energy, that come in a refrain or bridge.

SONG	ARTIST	YEAR
Doo Wah Diddy Diddy	Manfred Mann	1964
Oh, Pretty Woman	Roy Orbison	1964
It's Gonna Be All Right	Gerry and the Pacemakers	1964
The Last Time	The Rolling Stones	1965
We Gotta Get out of This Place	The Animals	1965
Lies	The Knickerbockers	1966
Li'l Red Riding Hood	Sam the Sham and the Pharaohs	1966
96 Tears	Question Mark and the Mysterians	1966
The Letter	The Box Tops	1967
Happy Together	The Turtles	1967

Songs with High Contrast Between Parts

The main point is still that while so many artists shine in their use of energy or vocal harmony or interesting song construction, and some bands do bring them all together in a few numbers, it is only in the work of Beatles that we consistently hear each of these musical elements brought to new heights, each element on its own, and especially all three in wonderful combination.

SECTION 3 : BLUE NOTES AND SAD CHORDS

The Beatles and the Rolling Stones

It's an essential and definitive question about musical taste: who do you like better, the Beatles or the Stones? On one hand, it's a fair question to ask, given that if you had to pick two headliners for the decade of the 1960s, these are the two, but on the other hand, while earlier on they had some elements of rock 'n' roll in common, they were clearly far apart on a pop-rock spectrum. To help illustrate this, we can compare the two groups in the context of this book's main themes—energy, vocal harmony, and song structure, in number 1 hits.

Over their long career, the Stones have had twelve number 1 hits in either the US or the UK.

HIT SINGLE	YEAR
It's All Over Now	1964
Little Red Rooster	1964
The Last Time	1965
Satisfaction	1965
Get off of My Cloud	1965
Paint It Black	1966
Ruby Tuesday	1967
Jumpin' Jack Flash	1968
Honky Tonk Women	1969
Brown Sugar	1971
Angie	1973
Miss You	1978

Rolling Stones Hit Singles

From the song list, we can see that the Stones started to top the charts a year after the Beatles, and, like them, had their best year in 1965. We can also note that, in contrast to the Beatles, the first two Stones hits were covers. In terms of sheer volume, the Beatles have outsold the Stones by a significant margin, and one simple reason to explain this is that the Beatles catered to a much wider pop music audience, and didn't limit themselves to playing just blues or rock 'n' roll, as the Stones somewhat did, by choice. In fact, while the Beatles covered a good many rock 'n' roll classics early on, they rarely played the blues.

It's not quite that simple though, because the Stones did record many great numbers that were not blues or rock 'n' roll, including songs like *As Tears Go By, Play with Fire, Lady Jane, Ruby Tuesday, Paint It Black*, and *Angie*. It is safe to say, however, that most of their hits, nine of the twelve in the above table, were indeed bluesy rock numbers.

In terms of energy, the two bands were clearly different, and both of their energy profiles changed over time. A good example that demonstrates this difference in their early careers is the song *I Wanna Be Your Man*, which incidentally was written by John Lennon and Paul McCartney and given to the Stones.

The song, released in November of 1963, was the Stones' second single, and ended up as their first entry in the charts, making it up to number 12 in the UK. In the Beatles' version, which moves along at a very fast tempo (about 98 bpm), Paul joins in to harmonize with Ringo during the refrain, and he's really singing his heart out, so it's very high energy of a certain kind, with lots of Beatles screams thrown in just before and during the fractured guitar solo. In the Stones version, the tempo is slower (about 82 bpm), and the overall feeling is more of a steady driving freight-train rock number, with Brian Jones taking a break to wail away on the slide guitar, and there's no vocal harmony. Mick Jagger does really lay into some hyped vocals at the end of the song, so it's not really a question or more or less energy, but it's clearly a different kind. In classic Beatles fashion, the song's verse is rock 'n' roll, but the refrain is pop-sounding, and it's in the refrain that we hear some of the sharpest contrast between the Beatles pop vs. Stones rock energy. Citing a difference about contrast in energy based on this one Beatles-penned single is certainly not conclusive, but it does provide some indication of a basic difference.

In terms of harmony, while Keith Richards does join in to sing along with Mick Jagger on quite a few numbers, like *It's All Over Now, The Last Time, Jumpin' Jack Flash*, and *Honky Tonk Women*, it's probably again safe to say that vocal harmony is not a prominent feature of the Stones' music, and, because of the lineup, it's the note-on-note type of harmony and never really in the backing vocals type. So, while we would see some harmony in song maps of the Stones' hits, there wouldn't be as much color blending, and there would be much less of the constant alternating between unison and harmony that we see in Beatles songs. This is also due in no small part to the fact that the Stones, vocally, had a single front man, while the Beatles had two, and even sometimes three.

While there are clearly differences in terms of energy and vocal harmony, it's in song structure that we see one of the biggest differences between the two bands. If we made chord palettes of the Stones' hits, while we'd see some darker colors, outside of the basic three chords of rock 'n' roll (the red 1, orange 4, and yellow 5) in more pop-sounding songs like *Ruby Tuesday* and *Angie*, or in the very darkly minor-laden *Paint It Black*, there is much less contrast between song parts, and there are far fewer bridges.

There are, of course, other non-musical differences between these two groups, not the least of which was in looks and stage presence, stemming from the direction provided by their managers, Brian Epstein and Andrew Loog Oldham. The arguably more handsome Beatles broke onto the world stage in cookie-cutter fashion with their smart collarless Pierre Cardin suits, taking deep bows after each performance, making all the young girls go so crazy. This is in stark contrast to the Stones, who very purposely cultivated a bad boy image as direct opposites of the Beatles. In some ways, these differences are a bit like the clash between mods and rockers that swept the UK in 1964. In his great book, *Beatles vs. Stones*, John McMillian points out the irony in the widely held public perception that the Beatles were clean-cut lads and the Stones were dangerous stuff that you'd need to protect your daughters from. In fact, the early leather-jacket-clad Liverpool Beatles came from much rougher working-class origins, and then came to age in a very decadent Hamburg, Germany, whereas the Stones came from relatively more upscale London surroundings, with

Mick Jagger actually planning on studying at the London School of Economics before changing careers in favor of music.

It's not really fair to make a comparison between the two bands in this way, citing a lack of the Beatles' pop elements in the Stones. The kind of energy the Beatles exuded, with their high-pitched *oohs*, deep vocal harmonies, highly contrasting song parts, and wider array of song styles, would simply not have been *cool* or fitting for a band like the Stones. Another thing that shouldn't be overlooked when comparing the two bands' musical styles, evolution, and output is that, while the Stones had some very gifted recording engineers and producers, including Glyn Johns and then Jimmy Miller later on in their peak period, they never had anybody like a George Martin.

The energy in Stones hits like *Gimme Shelter*, with the amazing Merry Clayton crying out the words *rape* and *murder* in the backing vocals, is truly awesome, in the original sense of the word. And in terms of the guitar playing and rhythmic grooves in songs like *Jumpin' Jack Flash* and *Street Fighting Man*, there are really no foot-tapping or ass-shaking parallels in anything the Beatles ever did. If you listen to the first five tracks on the second disk of the compilation album *Hot Rocks*, which along with the three songs just mentioned also include *Sympathy for the Devil* and *Honky Tonk Women,* you could probably be convinced that the epithet "greatest Rock 'n' Roll Band" is fitting and well deserved, but musically, and in terms of enthusiasm, pure creativity, and variety, there are just many more dimensions to the Beatles—there's just more color.

SIDEBAR
SYNESTHESIA AND COLORED MUSIC

Synesthesia is a cross-wiring of the senses that causes people to experience such things as seeing sounds, hearing lights, or tasting shapes. The first sentence on the Wikipedia page describes it like this:

> **Synesthesia** *is a perceptual phenomenon in which stimulation of one sensory or cognitive pathway leads to automatic, involuntary experiences in a second sensory or cognitive pathway.*

The key words in this definition are *automatic* and *involuntary*. This means that real synesthetes don't consciously decide how sounds appear visually or sights as sound. It's effortless and just how they perceive things.

There are many kinds of synesthesia. At a very basic level, most people have a sense of warm and cool colors. But there are some exotic varieties. If you want to learn more about synesthesia, and understand what a strange expression like "there aren't enough points on the chicken" means, read Richard Cytowic's interesting and entertaining book *The Man Who Tasted Shapes* (the cover alone is worth it).

The most common form of synesthesia is when people associate colors with letters and numbers, and another related common form is a mapping of sounds to colors, or *chromesthesia*.

There's quite a list of famous musicians, composers, artists, and writers who claim to have, or are said have had, synesthesia, including Duke Ellington, Billy Joel, Pharrell Williams, Franz Liszt, Vincent Van Gogh, and Vladimir Nabokov.

The Clavier à Lumières

In 1915, the Russian composer Alexander Scriabin had his musical work *Prometheus: The Poem of Fire* performed in New York City. The performance featured a keyboard instrument, called a *clavier à lumières* (keyboard of lights), that projected differently colored lights depending on what notes were being played. The following graphic, from the Clavier à Lumières Wikipedia page, shows how the colors and notes were associated.

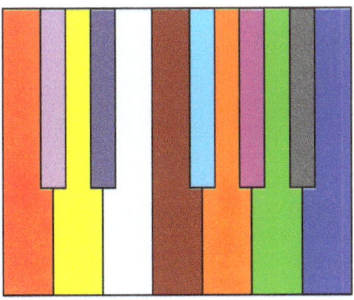

Scriabin's Note-to-Color Mapping

In Scriabin's system, the C note is colored red, its 5th, G, is colored orange, and *its* 5th, D, is colored yellow. So, Scriabin was mapping what is called a *circle of fifths* to the colors as they are ordered in the rainbow: red, orange, yellow, green, and so on. The graphic below, again from the Clavier à Lumières Wikipedia page, shows how the order of colors in the rainbow and the circle of fifths are aligned.

Scriabin's Colors as a Circle of Fifths

The distance in notes, or the *interval*, between a note and its 5th is of primary harmonic importance in music. One famous partial circle of fifths (moving clockwise) familiar to rock music fans is the chord progression used in Jimi Hendrix's first single, *Hey Joe* (whose authorship is disputed), released in 1966. The chord progression, known by many guitarists, is C-G-D-A-E, or, using steps in the scale, 1-5-2-6-3, and because it's in the key of C, it overlaps with Scriabin's system.

There is general agreement that Scriabin was not actually a synesthete because he purposely designed his system of mapping musical notes to colors—it was contrived and did not occur automatically and involuntarily in his perception.

Song Maps and Chord Palettes

Both systems of mapping sounds to colors used in this book, because they were purposely designed for specific reasons, are technically not synesthesia. In the song maps, the three singing Beatle voices are mapped to the three primary colors, red, blue, and yellow, so that when they combine in harmony they produce the secondary colors, purple, orange, and green.

The chord-palette system assigns a color to a relative step of the scale using the three bright warm colors red, orange, and yellow, to represent the three strong, happy major chords, the 1, 4, and 5, and using darker, cooler colors to represent the three weaker, sad minor chords, the 2, 3, and 6. Along with a few other chords, a blue dot to represent blue notes, and an asterisk to show when the home key changes, the chord palette system allows us to visualize the contrast between song parts in vivid color, and especially how the Beatles mixed happy or bluesy rock 'n' roll with sadder and more sentimental pop sounds in the same song.

The Beatles and Color

Scriabin's colored graphic keyboard could have come right out of *Pepperland*, the brilliantly colored fantastical world featured in the film *Yellow Submarine*. The association of the Beatles with color is a recurring meme of the 1960s. From Richard Avedon's famous psychedelically touched-up photos of each Beatle, to the band's colored uniforms on *Sgt. Pepper* and even to John Lennon's crazily painted Rolls Royce, there is no shortage of color in our memories of the Beatles. And as an aside, LSD trips are often associated with colorful synesthetic experiences.

Light and Sound

Whether involuntary or contrived, people have long been fascinated with the relationship between light and sound. In his 1704 work *Opticks*, the renowned English scientist Sir Isaac Newton included a wheel diagram showing how the seven colors of the spectrum are associated with seven musical notes of the major scale, and in 1810, the famous German philosopher Goethe published his *Theory of Colours*, saying that musical tones and color tones shared common frequencies. And Scriabin wasn't alone as a musician interested in color. All through history musicians and artists have been fascinated with associating colors and musical notes, and the Wikipedia page *Color Organ* includes a great list of them.

Note that Newton originally had only five colors in his system, but he expressly expanded it to seven to be a rainbow, and match the musical scale, the order of colors recalled by the acronym ROYGBIV (Richard Of York Gave Battle In Vain)—red, orange, yellow, green, blue, indigo, and violet. (The indigo seems pretty iffy as a separate color and goes to show what happens when you try to shoe-horn one system to match another.)

Whether it's Scriabin's clavier à lumières or a dish of colored water placed on an overhead projector to light up the walls of a high school gym in a 1960s dance, the associations and mappings between sound and color spectrums is a complex and fascinating phenomenon. And while the contrived sound-to-color mappings featured in this book are not technically considered synesthetic, could a young child in the midst of abstract sensory development, if presented with the colors from the song maps and chord palettes while listening to music, possibly develop a similar form of synesthesia?

SO WHERE DID IT COME FROM?

Merseybeat

What are the origins of this magical combination of performance energy, vocal harmony, and song quality? While the Beatles were clearly unique, and enjoyed unprecedented success and popularity, they were not conjured up out of thin air. Their music had its origins in a time and a place and a scene, and that place was Liverpool, that time was the late 1950s, and that music scene was *Merseybeat*. (Bill Harry, who attended Liverpool Art College with John Lennon, launched a local music newspaper called *Mersey Beat* in 1961, and may have coined the term.)

The association between place and sound has occurred many times throughout the course of music history. Think about spirituals and gospel singing in the southern slave states; Dixieland Jazz and New Orleans; the blues and the Mississippi Delta and Chicago; rock 'n' roll and the southern US; country and Nashville; Texas Swing; the punk scenes in New York and London; grunge and Seattle; and the list goes on. So, why Liverpool and why the early 1960s?

Liverpool, with just about 1 million inhabitants in 1960, was in sharp industrial decline. The city had been one of Britain's major shipping ports and industrial centers since the early nineteenth century, and was famously the home port of the Titanic, the Lusitania, and the Queen Mary. Earlier, in the eighteenth century, it had also been a major hub for slave ships and the slave trade, and later on during the American Civil War it had been a major market for southern American cotton. As a strategic port city, Liverpool was the target of countless German air-raids during World War II, and had been heavily bombed. It was also home to a large number of Irish immigrants. Some speculate that Merseybeat originated in Liverpool because of an influx of American records and musical instruments brought back on the transatlantic ships, or because there were so many Irish, or so many urban working-class poor. Whatever the reasons are, Liverpool became the epicenter for an amazingly vibrant and thriving new music scene, which at the height of the Merseybeat period could boast some 350 to 400 bands, a strikingly high number for a city of its size.

Merseybeat was the musical descendant of many different ancestors. It sprang from a rich mixture of ingredients including American doo-wop, rhythm and blues, rock 'n' roll, and British Skiffle. Skiffle, thought to have originated from the southern American jug-band and country-blues scene, underwent a wildfire revival in the UK in the late 1950s, when Glasgow-born Lonnie Donegan scored number 1 hits in the 1957 UK Singles Chart with a rehash of the Appalachian folk song *Cumberland Gap* and a cover of American country singer Vernon Dalhart's 1920 hit *Puttin' on the Style*. This second number is notorious as one of the songs played (and for which a famous scratchy low-quality recording exists) by a young John Lennon and his Quarrymen at a church fair in the Woolton suburb of Liverpool, on that fateful summer day in 1957, when John met another teenage rock 'n' roll enthusiast named Paul McCartney.

By 1963, Merseybeat bands including the Beatles had broken onto the national scene and scored some number 1 hits in the UK charts. The first hit came, not from the Beatles, but from another band being managed by Brian Epstein and produced by EMI's George Martin. Gerry and the Pacemakers landed a chart topper in April with the song *How Do You Do It* and held the top spot for 3 weeks. George Martin had initially wanted the Beatles to release this same song as their first single, and while they did record it, they thought it was too pop-sounding, and opted instead for the bluesier *Love Me Do*. Gerry and the Pacemakers would go on to release two more number 1 hits in 1963, *I Like It* and *You'll Never Walk Alone* (as part of Gerry Marsden's legacy this popular show tune from the 1945 Rodgers and Hammerstein musical *Carousel* would be adopted, and continues to this day, as the anthem for the Liverpool F.C. soccer team). Like the Beatles, as part of the British Invasion, Gerry and the Pacemakers appeared on the Ed Sullivan Show several times and produced their own attempt at a *Hard Day's Night* like film, *Ferry Cross the Mersey*, in 1965. While they still had a number of charting singles in 1964 and 1965, they would never again score any number 1s after their initial burst in 1963, and so their popularity declined and they broke up in 1966.

The other chart-topping Merseybeat acts include the groups the Searchers, Billy J. Kramer and the Dakotas, and solo act Cilla Black. There were also dozens of other groups that were highly popular in and around Liverpool, and, like the Beatles, also played stints at clubs in Hamburg, Germany, like Rory Storm and the Hurricanes, the Big Three, Derry and the Seniors, and the Swinging Blue Jeans.

It's instructive to listen to songs recorded by some of these other Merseybeat top acts. You can definitely hear similarities with the Beatles, especially in songs like Gerry and the Pacemakers' *It's Gonna Be All Right* or the Searchers' *Needles and Pins* or their cover of the rock 'n' roll number *Sweets for My Sweet*. Many of these tracks also typically feature bright sparkling guitar work and some fairly unusual chord changes. Billy J. Kramer's *Little Children* stands out as having a very unusual, and somewhat dark but loping, chord progression, and the Lennon/McCartney team actually wrote another one of their hits, *Bad to Me*. But while there are similarities, in contrast to the early Beatles, most of these other Merseybeat songs are generally medium energy, have less harmony, and most importantly, have a crooning lighter-fare sentimentality.

The Beatles' first hit, *From Me to You*, did end up knocking Gerry and the Pacemakers' *How Do You Do It* out of the top spot, hitting number 1 in early May 1963, and staying for an impressive 7 weeks—*She Loves You* would be four months away. So, we can again see that, even among their Merseybeat siblings, the Beatles stood out. Their special brand of infectious energy and vocal harmony were clearly signs of something extra, something more and lasting, something that led to Beatlemania.

Merseybeat artists enjoyed a burst of popularity in the UK, with musical business types flocking to Liverpool to scoop up as many artists as they could find, but after the 1963–64 time period, other than the Beatles, there were no more chart toppers. However, the rest of the UK was hardly quiet—hugely successful bands were springing up all over, including the Animals from Newcastle, and Herman's Hermits and the Hollies from Manchester. And with the likes of the Rolling Stones, the Kinks, and the Yardbirds, there was a general southward shift in the center of gravity to bluesier London. It's safe to say that Merseybeat, from which Beatlemania sprang, was both an important factor in the burgeoning UK rock and pop scene, and a spark that helped light a fire called the British Invasion.

The British Invasion

In addition to launching themselves onto the world stage, the Beatles' appearance on the Ed Sullivan Show and their popularity in the US charts also gave rise to a new craze in the US for bands from the UK. Dubbed the *British Invasion*, this 1964–66 frenzy would see Peter and Gordon, the Animals, Manfred Mann, Petula Clark, Freddie and the Dreamers, Wayne Fontana and the Mindbenders, Herman's Hermits, the Rolling Stones, the Dave Clark Five, the Troggs, and Donovan all hit the top of the charts in the US. And while they didn't score number 1 hits, many other artists would have great success in the US in this time period: Dusty Springfield, the Searchers, Billy J. Kramer, the Bachelors, Chad and Jeremy, Gerry and the Pacemakers, the Honeycombs, Them, Tom Jones, the Yardbirds, the Spencer Davis Group, and the Small Faces would all enter the US charts. At one point in May 1965, nine out of the ten Billboard Hot 100 acts all hailed from the UK or the British Commonwealth, and by the end of 1965, they accounted for half of all the year's chart toppers.

The British Invasion never really ended, but it did fade as things evened out between the two sides of the Atlantic, with a host of US bands crowding into the charts at the end of 1965 and especially in 1966, including the Byrds, the Young Rascals, the Mamas and the Papas, the Lovin' Spoonful, the Association, and the Monkees, to name only a few. However, British bands like the Who, Cream, and Led Zeppelin, would go on to make a deep impact on the world of rock, and help create new branches in its ever evolving and growing family tree.

Things fade because their novelty wears off, fads come and go, and in this context we can see that, even after the earlier hype of Merseybeat, and after the onslaught of the British Invasion, the Beatles went on and continued to be hugely successful, always evolving, always coming up with something new. It's significant to note that at the same time as the British Invasion was peaking in 1965 and then dying down in 1966, the Beatles, always ahead of the game, produced the seminally creative albums *Rubber Soul* and *Revolver*.

BLUE NOTES AND SAD CHORDS: A DEEPER LOOK

Music and Contrast

The idea of Blue Notes and Sad Chords describes the mixture of driving, bluesy, rock 'n' roll and sentimental heartstring-tugging pop in the same Beatle song. With a verse rendered in rock 'n' roll, a refrain or bridge rendered in pop, and a repeating sequence of this pattern, the contrast between the genres is heightened, and the feelings evoked by each type of music are intensified. The rock 'n' roll parts sound *bluesier*, and the pop parts sound *sadder*, when we hear them mixed together this way. This comes about in much the same way that multiple colors appear more brilliant, their hues more distinctive, when we see them together in a sequence—the blue is bluer and red is redder when we see them side by side.

The Beatles used other kinds of contrast in many of their songs, not just bluesy rock 'n' roll and sentimental pop. In the song *You Can't Do That*, John Lennon's verses are hard core blues, but the beginning of the bridge is not sentimental at all— it uses an angrier and darker sounding 3 chord, which isn't minor. We could call this a case of Blue Notes and *Mad* Chords. (This song is also the first time we heard George's 12-string Rickenbacker as well as John stepping out front to take a lead break on the guitar.)

This use of contrasting chord palettes in the different subsections of the same piece of music, has always been a hallmark of popular music, and in a much more general sense, along with variations and changes in tempo and energy, is a fundamental feature of Western classical music. Sonatas, concertos, and symphonies are all structured to include significant contrast between their various subsections. Listen to Beethoven's symphonies, or Bach's *Brandenburg Concertos*, for a great reminder of this. Contrast and variation are cornerstones of the change that is built in to a single piece of music and what keeps it interesting. For a more high-brow, in-depth, but concise description, the following line, from the Wikipedia page for 'Contrast (music)', says it all:

> *Contrast is not only a way of adding interest, but is essential to the aesthetic illusion of dramatic resolution of conflict.*

Another great example of contrast in classical music that you may have heard is in the opening overture of Tchaikovsky's *Swan Lake*, which was also incidentally used by Heinz Roemheld for the soundtracks of the horror movies Dracula (1931) and The Mummy (1932). It starts off slow, lonely, and mysterious, then switches gears into a shorter but very intensely heartfelt and tender section, before going dark and dramatic again. The little hopeful part, sandwiched between and in sharp contrast to the beginning and end material, is certainly interesting in its use as the music in a horror film.

Black and White

The kind of contrast that the notion of Blue Notes and Sad Chords describes, while in a general sense a basic characteristic of so much music, has a more specific origin. It stems from the deep mixing of black African and white European musical elements, over the four-hundred-year course of American history. A cruel and terrible irony, if the word *irony* can even be used in this sense, is that the main branches in the family tree of American popular music, and among America's most significant cultural contributions to the world including ragtime, the blues, jazz, swing, and rock 'n' roll, all have the institution of slavery as their common ancestor.

The continuous combination and juxtaposition of black on white, and white on black, in American popular music is all-encompassing. Consider minstrel shows, a surreal combination of mockery and fascination with black culture, speech, and especially music and dance, the use of burnt cork to actually blacken a white man's face, virtually changing his race. Consider those most American songs of Stephen Foster, like *Oh! Susanna* and *Suwannee River,* featured in these minstrel shows. Then there's ragtime, where melodies from popular marches, like those of John Philip Sousa, and other European classical music elements are rendered in 'ragged' black time, with an irresistible syncopated snap, a leader of the pack in

America's long-standing habit of putting people in a crazed frenzy to tap their feet and shake their asses. Then we have the blues, from the lonesome sound of Robert Johnson's Mississippi Delta, to W.C. Handy's Beale Street in Memphis, to the raucous electrified offspring of Muddy Waters' Chicago. There's the blues' more sophisticated cousin, jazz, born in the saloons of New Orleans, a combination of many ingredients (African, Latin, and European), and given to such sophisticated improvisation and a never-ending evolution. Consider, too, the Scots-Irish tunes and ballads of Appalachia, played on the black African banjo and the white European fiddle, and the pre-rock-'n'-roll swing era, when the flush harmonies of the Andrews Sisters and their *Boogie Woogie Bugle Boy* set a world at war to cut a serious rug. All the dance crazes contributed, too: the Foxtrot, the Charleston, the Lindy Hop, the Jitterbug, the Twist. And of course we can't forget gospel-rooted Elvis and the mixture of black and white southern roots music that spawned rock 'n' roll, and the crossover success of the earlier girl groups and all the Motown acts that followed. This black and white concoction permeates everything. Even Micky Mouse, with his white gloves and comic antics, is the offspring of an archetypal minstrel character, and you can hear all that incredible early jazz from the likes of Cab Calloway in the cartoons of the 1930s, along with those crazy black crows and the many other over-the-top racially stereotyped characters. Many suggest that the mixing of peoples, the American "melting pot," is a myth, but this is certainly not true where music is concerned. American popular music is a rich mixture, it's chocolate milk, it's gumbo, from minstrel shows to Eminem.

Texicana Vaudeville Tin Pan Alley Stride Piano Hawaiin Steel
Fiddle Bluegrass Doo Wop Cajun Americana Stage Irish Tremonisha Soul
Honky Tonk Rain Dance Dixieland Jump Blues Folk
The Blues Rhapsody In Blue Gospel Negro Spirituals
Barbershop Quartet The Lindy Hop Country Western
The Twist Minstrel Show Rhythm and Blues
Latin The Charlston Swing Rock 'n' Roll Slave Songs
Cakewalk Appalachian Scots-Irish Boogaloo
Race Music Tap Dancing
The Two-Step Ragtime Boogie Woogie Cartoon Jazz Salsa
Jazz Hip Hop Big Band Beebop Banjo The Foxtrot Pop
Jug Band Souza Marches Clawhammer Texas Swing

Word Cloud for Popular American Music and Dance

216

Some have said that the Eskimos have dozens of words for snow. In this same context, there are hundreds of words for popular American song and dance. The word cloud above shows some of the more prominent words and phrases that were used to describe these musical genres, dancing styles, and works. Unlike the early and late Beatles' word clouds shown earlier, the size and coloring of each word or phrase shown here is somewhat random.

This word cloud, in a way like the set of musical genome characteristics used to describe a song being played on Pandora, is used here to show a collection of related musical styles and elements that would be too complicated to portray in a specifically detailed family-tree or cause-and-effect way.

The Genesis of Rock 'n' Roll and Charting Crossover

Nothing tells the story of the black and white mixing in American popular music, and how a hodgepodge of primarily southern musical elements came together to define rock 'n' roll, better than the way musical charting changed in the second half of the 1950s. This period also produced some of the main strands of musical DNA that would lead to the Beatles and the British Invasion.

While Jackie Brenston's *Rocket 88*, and an earlier hit by Goree Carter called *Rock Awhile* (listen to this for a great early preview of Chuck Berry's guitar sound), are often cited as the among the first rock 'n' roll songs, musical historians generally agree that 1955 is the year rock 'n' roll went mainstream, when Bill Haley and his Comets' *Rock around the Clock* hit number 1 on the Billboard Top 100. (This is also the year that, incidentally, Scottish-born Lonnie Donegan's Skiffle number *Rock Island Line* hit number 1 in the UK.)

At this time, the musical charts were still segregated. In 1955, a different Billboard chart, called Rhythm and Blues hits, or R&B, listed such luminary blues and rock 'n' roll names as Little Walter, Etta James, Bo Diddley, Ray Charles, Fats Domino, and Chuck Berry, along with doo-wop stars like the Penguins, the Moonglows, and the Drifters. Before being dubbed "R&B," this chart had at first been called the "Harlem Hit Parade" and then the "Race Records Juke Box" chart. Also, in 1955, another separate Billboard chart of number 1 country singles hosted hits by artists like Webb Pierce (*In the Jailhouse Now*), Eddy Arnold (*The Cattle Call*), and Tennessee Ernie Ford (*Sixteen Tons*). In 1955, all the artists with number 1s in the R&B chart were black, and all the artists in the country chart were white.

Then in 1956, something unusual happened. This crazy white kid named Elvis Presley had a major hit with his double-side *Hound Dog/Don't Be Cruel*, and Billboard ended up listing it on the top of the R&B singles chart. It hit number 1 in September and stayed on top for 6 weeks. In this same year, Elvis also had hits in both the country chart and the mainstream top-100 chart. This charting confusion continued over the next few years, when hits by Jerry Lee Lewis and the Everly Brothers were getting listed in both the top 100 and the country singles charts.

It's not a coincidence that all this crossover between black and white and between country and mainstream was happening right as early classic rock 'n' roll was at its high point, in the middle and late 1950s, when a mix of explosive, high-energy number 1 hits by Elvis, Little Richard, and Jerry Lee Lewis shared the spotlight with more moderate or lower-energy numbers by Bill Haley and his Comets, Chuck Berry, Buddy Holly and the Crickets, the Everly Brothers, and Danny and the Juniors (*At the Hop*).

The black and white mixing in musical charting for this period was unprecedented. It is said that many people thought Elvis was black and that Chuck Berry, who definitely had some country atoms in his musical molecules, was white. And more and more white artists were showing up in the R&B charts. In 1957, along with Elvis (*All Shook Up, Jailhouse Rock*) and Jerry Lee Lewis (*Whole Lotta Shakin' Goin' On*), Paul Anka (*Diana*), Jimmie Rodgers (*Honeycomb*), and the Everly Brothers (*Wake Up Little Susie*), were added to the list. It is unknown whether this commercial-cultural confusion was the reason, but at the end of 1958, Billboard rechristened The *Top* 100 to The *Hot* 100, and began to include top-selling black R&B charters in the list. This is why the 1959 Hot 100 number 1s include hits by the Platters (*Smoke Gets in Your Eyes*), Lloyd Price (*Stagger Lee*), Dave "Baby" Cortez (*The Happy Organ*), and Wilbert Harrison (*Kansas City*). While a speculation, this racial-musical identity crisis may have led to the fact that, for a little over a year (from November 1963 to January 1965), there was no Billboard R&B singles chart at all, and all black artists' hits were listed in the mainstream Hot 100. It's also been noted that this gap in the R&B charts occurred when Berry Gordy's Motown, *the* seminal crossover hit factory, was really coming into its own, with number 1 singles by Mary Wells, the Temptations, and especially the Supremes.

Black artist charts were reinstated with the "Hot Rhythm and Blues" hits in 1965, which was renamed "Best Selling Soul Singles" in 1969. This renaming continued over the years, adjusting to the times, to use "Black Singles" in 1982, back to "R&B" in 1990, and then to "Hot R&B/Hip-Hop" in 1999.

Yank and Brit

With all this focus on one side of the Atlantic, it would be a mistake to ignore the cultural ping-pong that has always gone on between the US and the UK, and especially the musical back-and-forth that occurred in the 1950s and 60s. In the genesis story of 1960s rock, we have to say that British pop and jazz, along with American folk, begat Skiffle, then Skiffle, doo-wop, and early American rock 'n' roll begat Merseybeat, while the London scene and American blues begat the British blues guitar virtuosos. Liverpool's Beatles, Newcastle's Animals, Manchester's Hollies and Herman's Hermits, and London's Dave Clark Five and Rolling Stones begat the British Invasion. The British Invasion was answered by a resurgence of American bands as the 1960s wore on, including the Supremes, the Byrds, the Turtles, the Monkees, and many others. This all then begat the San Francisco psychedelic/acid rock scene. And it goes on and on. Led Zeppelin, Cream, and other psychedelic/acid rock bands begat heavy metal and 1970s rock. 1970s rock begat punk rock, punk rock begat grunge, etc. There are now too many sub-genres of rock to list. But to be clear, without this original transatlantic musical conversation, there would have been no Skiffle, no Merseybeat, no Beatles, and no British Invasion.

Music, Evolution, and the Beatles

The bottom line is that the explosive mixture of rock 'n' roll and pop that we find in some of the best early-Beatles songs is at the tail end of a long line of mixing and melting of black African and white European musical elements, along with the rich exchange of musical influences that occurred between the US and the UK in the 1950s and 1960s. In this way, the phenomenon of Blue Notes and Sad Chords in the Beatles' music is just one very special descendant from a very hybrid family tree. If you could capture the DNA in just about any hit single and send if off to some lab, let's call it MusicalAncestry.com, to see where it comes from, you'd find traces of many different musical ancestors that thrived in many different geographic locations.

Darwin's theory of evolution, involving complex elemental combinations, geography, time, and survival of the fittest, can readily be applied to the atoms and molecules that comprise cultural artifacts, including literature, art, and music. These forces, these ever-changing systems, give rise to golden eras, when things like sonnets, concertos, and painting styles attain their highest points. The Beatles provided the critical moment in such a golden age, when rock 'n' roll and pop came together to create rock in the 1960s, and in doing so helped define the decade's substance and style, its sights and sounds, its themes and memes.

CONCLUSION

PERFORMANCE ENERGY, VOCAL HARMONY, AND SONG QUALITY

One of the primary musical elements we hear in the early Beatles hits, in the singles and albums that launched them to fame and fortune, and that provided them with so much unpressured room to experiment creatively in the studio, is really a comeback, a brief resurgence, of the ultra-high energy heard in the music of the late 1950s rock 'n' roll stars, including Elvis, Jerry Lee Lewis, Chuck Berry, and especially Little Richard. And it's probably safe to say that this over-the-top energy was originally more of a McCartney than a Lennon ingredient. When Paul is belting out *Long Tall Sally, I'm Down, She's a Woman*, and even later on some of the more raucous numbers on the *White Album*, we can hear this type of energy in its purest form. And while his cover of *Johnny B. Goode*, which can be heard on the early BBC hits collection, is hardly as amped-up as many McCartney numbers, we can hear in songs like *Twist and Shout, Mr. Moonlight, Rock and Roll Music*, and *Yer Blues* that John Lennon too had his high-energy moments. But John's more important gift was his ability to infuse his singing with such amazingly soulful and bluesy inflections, such as we hear in his cover of Smokey Robinson's *You've Really Got a Hold on Me* or in his own *All I've Got to Do*, which are both really more soulful doo-wop and pop than rock 'n' roll. So, a key characteristic of the early Beatles is the combination of these two types of energy, McCartney's toned down Little Richard rock 'n' roll with Lennon's Smokey Robinson soul, coming together in perfect harmony to form the magical and irresistible music that we hear in *From Me to You, She Loves You, I Want to Hold Your Hand*, and so many other songs.

When you think harmony, you think duos, like the Everly Brothers, Simon and Garfunkel, Peter and Gordon, Chad and Jeremy, and Sonny and Cher. In a sense, John Lennon and Paul McCartney can be seen as an embedded and dominating duo within a group. And one thing to note is that in all those early high-energy rock 'n' roll hits of the later 1950s that so inspired the Beatles, there is never really any harmony. The Beatles' rich voice blending, something they layered over their foundational energy, is more a child of doo-wop, pop, and folk music than it is of rock 'n' roll, and it is here again, that the Beatles stand out as a rare exception, combining the two very physical characteristics of bluesy rock 'n' roll energy and vocal harmony to create such a distinctively new type of music. The sound created when two, and very often three, Beatle voices were joined together in vocal harmony was a quintessential and incredibly pleasing part of the band's appeal. The sound of their beautifully blended voices coming into our ears, as with any vocal harmony, resulted in our vibrating along with them. Their frequencies became our frequencies, we were all resonating, in one very intense and intimate performer-listener shared experience.

The driving energy of bluesy rock 'n' roll musical passages, along with the emotional pull of pop and sentimental chord palettes, are made significantly more intense when constantly alternating, switching back and forth, through the different verses, refrains, and bridges that make up the band's catalog. In their songwriting, the Beatles brought this special musical ingredient to dramatic new heights. While not as readily and physically identifiable as performance energy or rich vocal harmony, the phenomenon of Blue Notes and Sad Chords in their music, along with the melodic tunefulness in so many of their songs, was a distinctly defining element in their ability to pen so many high-quality songs, clearly separating them from the pack.

The three elements we've focused on - energy, vocal harmony, and contrasting song parts - are certainly not the only characteristics that made the Beatles great. One thing that has not been covered in these pages, and that could fill several books, is the melodic quality of so many of the band's songs, and how the melodies fit in with underlying the chord progressions. Beautiful songs like *Blackbird* or *Across the Universe* can hardly be described as high-energy, and they have no vocal harmony, but they are certainly representative of a yet another key quality in the Beatles' superbly crafted music. One can imagine another kind of graphic analysis, coloring the notes in the melodies with the chord palette spectrum, and seeing how they did or didn't match the colors in the underlying chords, but musical detail like that would require obtaining permission from the owners of the music, which would probably be difficult if not impossible.

People love tight bands with high musical performance energy, beautiful vocal harmonies, and good songs. The special combination of these elements that magically came together in the Beatles' music, particularly in the first half of their career, when measured by hit single and album popularity, has never been matched by any other artist and probably never will be. By blasting beautiful and rich Everly Brothers–style harmonies through a high-energy jet engine of Little Richard rock 'n' roll and Smokey Robinson soul, and at the same time using the striking contrast of Blue Notes and Sad Chords to combine and heighten an intense rhythmic desire to tap your feet with sentimental, heartstring-tugging emotion, the Beatles created the most infectiously irresistible popular music the world may ever know.

AND IN THE END

I hope you've enjoyed this audio trip down memory lane and that you can now hear, and perhaps even see, music so familiar to you in a new and enjoyable way.

These abstractions, the calling out of energy, harmony, and song structure as separate things, is faulty in some ways. These things don't exist on their own; they are different elements of the same whole, and greater than the sum of their parts. This type of analysis would probably also have turned the Beatles off, just as ridiculously complex interpretations of their lyrics did. These things came naturally to them; they didn't know how to read music or have any formal music training. The fact that, especially early on, they came across as so innocently charming, relaxed, and funny, and that this music seemed to spring from them so effortlessly, and in such a great quantity, will always be a great irony in their story.

What's next? You have new ways to listen to, and visualize, music, and this can help understand it better. You might want to re-listen to more Beatles music or that of your other favorite artists. As enjoyable homework, maybe you want to see how this set of the twenty-seven hit singles has held up by looking at the popularity of different Beatle songs on sites like iTunes. Or maybe you'll listen to the material the Beatles each produced on their own, after they broke up, and see if you hear or don't hear bits of the energy, harmony, and song quality that put them on top when they started off. And without needing to get caught up in analysis-paralysis, you can try your own different ways of hearing, seeing, and thinking about music and music theory, simplifying it through the use of graphics and your choice of colors, or through some other way. The techniques used in this book are just a few in a myriad of synesthetic possibilities.

A Last Personal Note

Life fundamentally changed for so many of us on the night of February 9, 1964, when the Beatles first appeared on the Ed Sullivan Show. The sound and the sight of them … you just couldn't get enough of it. How could any group ever sound so good, any performance be so enjoyable? It was one of the most ecstatic popular music entertainment moments the modern world has ever experienced.

It wasn't the first time the world had been so taken with a musical act. There was of course the gyrating, hiccupping Elvis a few years back, and old blue eyes Frank Sinatra before him, both at the tail end of a long succession of American music stars and dance fads, and even back in nineteenth-century Europe the long-haired piano-playing Hungarian Franz Liszt made women faint. But did these other artists, with their new and amazing sounds, really have the same impact as the Beatles? The same impact on a decade, a generation, a culture, a world?

The late John McGann, a professor at the Berklee College of Music in Boston and my friend, music teacher, and mentor, who sadly passed away in 2012, knew *every* chord, melodic line, vocal harmony part, instrumental riff, and drum beat in *every* measure of *every* single Beatles song. I'm not kidding—he really did. He used to say these details were what comprised his musical DNA. What kind of artists can inspire such study and make up such a deeply meaningful part of one's life? What other artists have left multiple generations of musically minded people with such an obsessive desire to describe, catalog, and analyze every last chord, lyric, or note in a body of popular music? There are hundreds of books about the Beatles out there, and other forms of analysis, study, and tribute just seem to continue on, with no end in sight.

SECTION 3 : BLUE NOTES AND SAD CHORDS

The Beatles helped define, and in turn were defined by, the tumultuous 1960s, inexorably tied to the decade and providing the foundation for its soundtrack. Their first single, *Love Me Do*, was released in October 1962 and hit the airwaves in the UK during the Cuban Missile Crisis. On Friday, November 22, 1963, the day JFK was assassinated, the band released their second album, *With the Beatles*, the album that would help bring Beatlemania to the US. The day after their first appearance on the Ed Sullivan Show, the US Congress passed the Civil Rights Act. In March 1965, when the first US ground force marines landed in Vietnam, they would have heard *Eight Days a Week* on their transistor radios, and *Help* came out in July, just a few weeks before the Gulf of Tonkin incident and the Watts riots in Los Angeles.

In 1966, *Eleanor Rigby* and *Yellow Submarine* were released just a week after Stokely Carmichael delivered one of his first black power speeches, and a year later, *Sgt. Pepper* famously came out during the Summer of Love. In 1968, *Lady Madonna* came out a day before the My Lai massacre in Vietnam, and a couple of weeks before Martin Luther King Jr. was assassinated. *The Ballad of John and Yoko* was on the airwaves for the Apollo moon landing in July 1969, and in October, *Something* and *Come Together* were released in between Woodstock and Altamont. In May 1970, the shootings of students by the National Guard at Kent State occurred in between the releases of the last two singles, *Let It Be* and *The Long and Winding Road*.

The Beatles' music was playing the whole time all these things were going on—the continuing civil rights movement, US involvement in Vietnam, the protests, the assassinations, the riots, the flourishing counterculture, sex, drugs, and rock 'n' roll, and, like so many other things in the 1960s, the Beatles also seemed to break into pieces and unravel as the decade came to its close. But they were aware of and part of it all, refusing to play to segregated audiences in the southern US during their early tours, taking part in the drug culture with unwilling but public admissions, deliberately not talking about the Vietnam war until later days with John and Yoko's anti-war chanting and bed-ins, and in the end, dissolving before our very eyes, as so many things had, in the film *Let It Be*.

It was enlightening to do this book. I started out knowing that I wanted to color code the Beatles' vocal harmony, using the lyrics in the hit singles to highlight one of the most pleasing aspects of their music in a different and highly focused way. And I had always been aware of their exceptional energy, but decided not to try and incorporate that using anything visual. But it was only after listening again and again to the songs, and thinking about how Beatles music was so different from anybody else's, that the contrast between song parts, the idea of Blue Notes and Sad Chords, became so obvious. It was more of a realization of something that had sort of gone unnoticed, but had always been there right in front of me, and then became very clear and definitive, especially after going through and re-listening to so many other artists' work, trying to find the same thing.

You can probably tell, because of the book's basic themes, that I'm a bit more of an early period fan, and I do *so* wish they had done another album, say between *With the Beatles* and *A Hard Day's Night*, full of soulful bluesy vocals and rock 'n' roll, rich harmonies, high energy, and contrasting song parts. But they could never keep still. They were always changing, always looking around the corner for something new, some new sound.

One purpose of this book has been to explain how and why Beatlemania came about—that it stemmed initially from a combination of the high energy, rich vocal harmonies, and hybrid song structures found in the band's earlier 1963 and 1964 songs. This theory may not resonate as much with some fans who favor the Beatles' latter work, for example those fans who consider *Sgt. Pepper* to be the height of the band's musical achievements. While the singles and albums the Beatles produced in the second half of their career, starting with *Revolver*, are truly remarkable and exhibit a creative genius rarely if ever seen in a music studio, it must be kept in mind that none of this work would ever have enjoyed its well-deserved popularity if the Beatles hadn't first taken the world by storm with their earlier and incredibly infectious Beatlemania formula.

I don't think John Lennon had it right when he said that the Beatles were just a rock band that made it very big. They were much more. Maybe it's because some of us were all so young and impressionable that their music meant, and still means, so much—growing up with them, and at the same time having them a key part of such crazy changing times. So many of my most basic and early Proustian childhood memories conjure up the sound and sight of the Beatles and vice versa—the smell of a newly mowed lawn, the wind in the trees, an early winter snowfall, or thinking back to junior-high dances, adolescent love, first cigarettes smoked, all my coming-of-age adventures ... practically everything.

As time goes on and the 1960s and Beatles slip more and more into the past, we are constantly reminded of their impact, hearing their wonderful songs on the radio or coming from some cyber-stream, seeing them in documentaries, web pages, newspapers, or magazines, both in the earlier black-and-white images and in the rich and floral day-glow colors of their latter incarnations, and especially at the present moment, when every month seems to bring a new it-was-50-years-ago-today remembrance. And it's not just the older die-hard baby-boomer fans that won't let go—there are many younger people, the children of boomers and others, who know all the words to all the songs and have much interest in figuring out why and how the Beatles did what they did.

So, it will never really be over. The Beatles are embedded in our memories, our sounds, our sights. Their music is part of the woodwork now, and so it will go on and on, as will our love for this infectious harmonic energy, all these beautiful songs, and the four so-likable lads that gave them to us.

APPENDIX

MUSIC 301

This section goes into a little more detail to explain some elements of sound and music theory that were presented in the highly simplified Music 101 and 201 sections, and also shows what the original full-lyrics song maps looked like.

Notes, Harmonic Ratios, and Overtones

When you pluck a string on a guitar, or hit a piano key (also a string), it vibrates and you hear a sound. For example, when you pluck the A string on a guitar, it vibrates 110 times a second, or 110 Hertz (Hz, named after Heinrich Rudolph Hertz, a German physicist). Humans can hear sounds in the range of 15 Hz to 20,000 Hz. Dogs can hear up to 45,000 Hz, which explains dog whistles, and cats even more, up to 79,000 Hz.

Because of physics and the way things vibrate, when you pluck the A string on a guitar, a lot of other notes also sound, but at lower volumes. One name for these other notes is *harmonic overtones*. When you pluck the A string, the next loudest note you hear mixed in is another A, but an octave higher than the main note. For the A string, the note an octave higher vibrates 220 times a second, or twice the frequency. The ratio of this note's frequency, an octave higher, to the main or *fundamental* note, is 2:1.

The next note you hear, after the octave, is an E, or the fifth note of the A scale (the E is the *so* in the do-re-me-fa-so of the A scale). This E note is higher than the higher A and vibrates at about 332 times a second. The ratio between this E and the second A is 3:2 (332 divided by 220 is about 3/2) This vibrating fifth in the second octave above the fundamental, and this basic 3:2 ratio, are hints about why the relationship between the 1 note and the 5 note (and the chord stacks built on them), is so important. It helps explain why this *interval* of the fifth provides the musical backbone for harmonic structure in the music we hear.

The next note you hear, after the E-332, is yet another A, this time two octaves higher than the fundamental A-110. This next A vibrates 440 times a second, and is the note orchestras use to tune up. It just so happens that the ratio between this A-440 and the last note in the series, the E-332, is 4:3. This is another special ratio that explains why the 4 note in the scale, and its chord stack, is so important. Another way of putting it, and something that every rhythm guitar player and many other musicians learn without knowing music theory, is that the E is the fifth of the A, and the A is the fourth of the E.

If you keep going through all the notes that sound when you pluck that A string, in higher and higher octaves, at lower and lower volumes, and look at their harmonic ratios, you end up with a list that basically describes the importance of musical intervals, in descending order. So far, we've covered the 1-5-4 notes and intervals and their repeating pattern 2:1, 3:2, 4:3 ratios (which helps explain the three strong happy chords of rock 'n' roll), but if you keep going, you hit the major third with a 5:4 ratio, then the minor third with a 6:5 ratio, then the seconds, etc. This list also helps describe how harmony evolved over the course of Western musical history, first using stronger and more basic octaves, fifths and fourths, then more sophisticated and subtler thirds, sevenths, ninths, and so on.

It's easy to play some these harmonic overtones on a guitar. When you just lay your finger lightly at the twelfth fret of a guitar string, which is exactly halfway along its length, and pluck the string, you'll hear an overtone one octave higher than the open string. When you do this on the seventh fret, at a third of the string's length you hear the fifth harmonic. When you do it a quarter of the way along the string, at the fifth fret, it produces an overtone two octaves higher. If you do it at the fourth fret, you'll hear a third. If you do it halfway between the second and third frets, you'll hear a flat-7. If you want to prove these ratios to yourself, use a tape measure. For example, a Fender Mustang electric guitar has a twenty-four-inch string, and you can hear an octave halfway at twelve inches, a fifth at eight inches (a third of the length), and so on.

Another interesting fact is that if you create a series of notes produced by taking consecutive fifths, say starting with C and then hitting G-D-A-E, you're listing out the notes in the *pentatonic* scale, a basic staple of music all over the world.

The Chinese and the ancient Greeks, and in particular the famous philosopher Pythagoras, knew all about how vibrating strings, or columns of air in instruments like the flute, were mathematically related. It turns out that these natural and perfect harmonic frequencies and ratios work fine if you're only playing music in a single key. But, if, for example, you need to tune a piano so that things will sound in-tune in any of the twelve keys, these perfect ratios don't work. Because of this, the musical world has adopted a system for tuning instruments that doesn't use the perfect ratios in any one key, but instead, using a system called *equal temperament*, ensures that playing in any key sounds okay, even though there are slight and barely perceptible imperfections. This is interesting because it shows how humans practically solved a sticky problem, when applying purely physical and mathematical principles didn't work. The reasons for all this are somewhat complex, but if you'd like to learn more about it, there's a great book by Stuart Isacoff entitled: *Temperament: How Music Became a Battleground for the Great Minds of Western Civilization*.

APPENDIX

The mathematical relationships between the notes in the scale, their frequencies, the intervals between them, and their harmonic ratios are fascinating topics that can fill many pages. It ultimately explains why there are seven notes in our Western *diatonic* scale, and why there are twelve notes in our *chromatic* octave. We've only just touched on it here to provide a notion of the basic physics underlying music, and why some notes, like the 5 and the 4, and their chord stacks, hold such relative importance.

The Relative Minor Key and the Church Modes

In the Music 101 and 201 sections, the only scale presented was the seven-note *do-re-me-fa-so-la-ti-do major scale*, which goes from the 1 note, up through the other six notes, and lands back on the 8 note, which is an octave higher than the 1. So, for example, in the key of C, using only the white keys on a piano, this major scale would have the notes C-D-E-F-G-A-B-C. But things are not that simple. You can actually keep the same spacing between the notes, say using only the white keys on the piano, but start and end on a different note, to play a different kind of scale. The most common example of this is to use a scale that starts and ends on the sad 6 note. Because this scale has the sad 6 as its base home note, it's called a *minor scale*. So, using only the white notes on a piano, this scale would be A-B-C-D-E-F-G-A. Because the C major scale and the A minor scale use exactly the same set of white-key notes, they are related, and the A minor in this case is referred to as the *relative minor*, of C major.

Using the sad 6 to start and end a scale is only one example. You can start and end a scale on any of the seven basic notes. Each one of these scales, referred to as *modes*, has a Greek name. The major and relative minor scales just discussed are called the *Ionian* and *Aeolian* modes. If you start and end a scale on the 2 note, it's called the *Dorian* mode, and if you use the 5, it's called the *Mixolydian* mode (the jigs and reels heard at an Irish session, include lots of tunes in the *Dorian* and *Mixolydian* modes). The scales started on the 3, 4, and 7 are called the *Phrygian, Lydian,* and *Locrian* modes, and are used much less than the other four. You already know that the oddball 7 has a flat or *diminished* 5 note and the other scales, built on the 3 and 4 can sound jarring, eerie, and just downright wrong. However, they do rarely show up. For example, some musicologists suggest that the Lydian mode (3 note based) is used in George Harrison's *Blue Jay Way*, which definitely sounds a little different, and Jefferson Airplane's atmospheric *White Rabbit* is often described as Phrygian (4 note based) or the even stranger Locrian (7 note based).

Historically, these seven different modes formed the system that was used in medieval church music, and for that reason they are sometimes referred to as the *church modes*.

Because of the spacing of the notes, both the *Dorian* and *Mixolydian* modes have a flat, bluesy sounding 7 notes. This explains why lots of rock or blues music, making heavy use of flat-7s and flat-3s, sounds a little like some Celtic music, including many Irish reels and jigs, which use the *Mixolydian* mode. Many of these Celtic tunes also alternate between using a major and minor 3 note, which is a hallmark of the blues.

Blue Notes and Extended Chords

In the Music 101 section, blue notes were described as the flat-3 and flat-7 in the set of major scale notes, running from 1 to 7. Things are again not so simple. In fact, in rock 'n' roll and blues, in addition to the 1 chord, the 4 and 5 chords are also sometimes played with their own blue notes, and in particular, their flat-7s. This means that in the case of the 4 chord, its flat-7 will be the flat-3, and in the case of the 5 chord, its flat-7 will be the 4 note.

It's also interesting to see that if you make an extended chord stack with four notes starting on the 5, you end up with 5-7-2-4. This turns out to be a very important chord—it's called the *dominant seventh*. It contains the flat-7 so fundamental to the blues, but still only uses notes from the diatonic major scale. A great layered example of this chord in Beatles' music is in the song *Twist and Shout*, when John starts with a long drawn out *ahh* on the 5, then George comes in to harmonize with a 7, then Paul with a 2, and then somebody adds in that bluesy 4, and then they all start screaming, and their voices joining together to sing this 5-7-2-4 chord creates an incredibly energetic buildup of tension, before crashing down and coming back to the home chord for the verse.

Four-note stacks like this are called *seventh chords*, because if you built one on the 1, the fourth note in the stack would be the 7.

Chord Degrees and Function

One of this book's goals was to use simple numbers, colors, and familiar feelings to describe the set of chords built on the notes of the scale, and to avoid the specialized vocabulary typically employed by musicologists and scholars. The graphic below shows the chords that we've used in the chord palettes, but the numbers have been changed to roman numerals and the chords have been changed from feelings to their harmonic function names, frequently used by music theorists in books describing the Beatles' and other music (the roman numerals are part of what is called the widely used *Viennese* system, there are others). The upper and lowercase roman numerals are handy for distinguishing between strong happy major chords and weak sad minor ones. The chord names, on the other hand, are probably unfamiliar to most people.

NO.	CHORD NAME
I	Tonic
ii	Supertonic
bIII	Flat Mediant
iii	Mediant
IV	Subdominant
V	Dominant
bVI	Flat Submediant
vi	Submediant
bVII	Subtonic
vii*	Leading Tone

Chord Roman Numerals and Function Names

Formal music theory involves an extended and complex vocabulary. Here are some examples:

- The word *ostinato* is used to characterize a repeating melody line, such as the guitar riffs in *I Feel Fine* or *Day Tripper*.
- The word *melismatic* is used to describe multi-syllable singing, such as when John and Paul are singing the word *hand* in four descending syllables in the refrain in *I Want to Hold Your Hand*.
- The word *diatonic* is used to describe the basic seven-note major scale *do-re-mi*..., the relative minor scale, and the other related *church modes*.
- The words *perfect cadence* describe the settling V to I (*dominant* to *tonic*) chord change at the end of many musical passages.
- The word *coda* is used to describe a song's outro.
- The roman numeral *iv* and the words *minor subdominant* describe the chord that we've called the *wistful 4*, which appears so frequently in the Beatles' music.
- The word *diminished* is used to describe the oddball 7 chord (7-2-4), because the 4 note at the top of its stack is a flat 5, not a full 5, above the root note. When the 5 is sharp, the chord is called *augmented*.
- The term *note*, which actually refers to written music representing musical sounds at different pitches, and at different spaces apart (*intervals*), is more appropriately called *tone* or *half-tone*.

Understanding Musicology

The chord symbols and names shown above are often used to untangle Beatles' songs in books written by music scholars. Consider the paragraph below, describing the song *Can't Buy Me Love*, taken from Terence J. O'Grady's wonderful book, *The Beatles: A Musical Evolution*, published in 1983. Here Professor O'Grady describes what we've been calling Blue Notes and Sad Chords, the mixing of bluesy rock 'n' roll and sad sentimental pop, in the same song, and calling attention to its uniqueness:

> "… Here, diatonic minor chords (including ii, iii, and vi) are included in the refrain-like bridge of a song which is also characterized by the chord progression and flatted thirds and sevenths of the blues tradition. These two harmonic characteristics—the free use of minor chords and the blues-like harmonic activity—had seldom been combined into one song previously. In "Can't Buy Me Love," however, there exists what amounts to an alternation between the two harmonic styles with the introduction and coda sections emphasizing a free use of minor chords, the verse demonstrating a strict blues style, and the bridge combining both within a few measures …"

Below are just a few notable books describing the Beatles' music, most using formal music theory language:

> *The Beatles: A Musical Evolution* - Terence O'Grady
> *The Beatles as Musicians, Volumes 1 and 2* - Walter Everett
> *Tell Me Why, The Beatles: Album by Album, Song by Song, the Sixties and After* - Tim Riley
> *The Songs of John Lennon, The Beatles Years* - John Stevens
> *Twilight of the Gods, the Music of the Beatles* - Wilfred Mellers
> *Revolution in the Head, The Beatles' Records and the Sixties* - Ian MacDonald

There is also a great set of Beatles' song descriptions and other materials, on Alan W. Pollack's *Notes On … Series*, available at the following link:

> http://www.icce.rug.nl/~soundscapes/DATABASES/AWP/awp-notes_on.shtml

In addition to the cited books and website, many scholarly papers have been published to describe various aspects of the Beatles' work. In the following graphic, I've taken the liberty of coloring a chart from KG Johansson's fascinating paper *The Harmonic Language of the Beatles,* and have substituted specific chord letters with roman numerals. Here Johansson has detailed the frequency of chords used in the Beatles' full catalog of 200+ songs. The vertical column of numbers on the left indicates the number of times a chord has been used in the song set, based on chord change counts. The chart readily shows the prominent use of the strong and brightly colored I, IV, and V chords, (the three chords of rock 'n' roll), and the less frequently used minors and other flattened chords, not all of which have been included in our chord palette system. (The colors chosen for the chords are an approximation, based on the colors used in the chord palettes.)

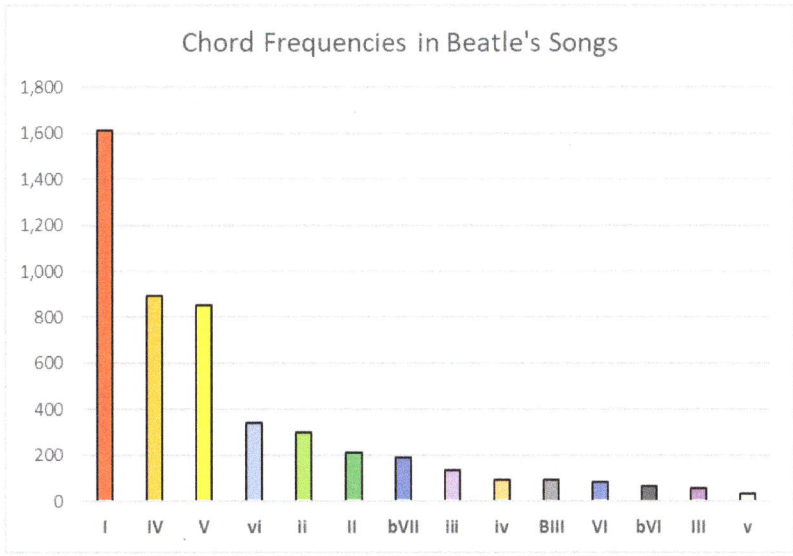

KG Johansson's Chord Frequencies in Beatles' Songs

Professor Johansson, a Swedish rock 'n' roll scholar, in *The Harmonic Language of the Beatles*, has written an illuminating paper, which uses the basic foundation of the *circle of fifths* (mentioned in the Sidebar *Colored Music and Synesthesia*), to describe how the Beatles extended the practice of traditional chordal harmony. This paper is well worth the effort for those interested in the deeper details of the Beatles' music.

The type of writing used in the books, website, and paper cited above is generally only comprehensible to those initiated in music theory. But perhaps, with the simplified explanations and color-laden depictions of harmony and chords used in this *Blue Notes and Sad Chords* book as a stepping stone, some readers will venture forth and tackle some of the more formal and esoteric descriptions of the Beatles' music.

The B Chord in I Want to Hold Your Hand

People really get carried away when studying the Beatles' music. The special magic in their music drives people to try and figure out every last little detail. Here's an example of how you can wonder about just one chord in one song, and how far you can go to figure something out. It's the B chord in *I Want to Hold Your Hand*.

I Want to Hold Your Hand is in the key of G. The catchy chords in the verse use a progression suggesting I-V-vi-iii (1-5-6-3)—note that in the major scale, the 6 and 3 chords are minor, as shown with the smaller roman numerals, and the 3 chord in the scale of G is built on a B note.

When on a pilgrimage to Liverpool in 2006, I acquired a prize possession. It's a score book called *The Beatles Complete* that had all the Beatles' songs, with lyrics, chords (using those little dots on the fretboard diagrams), and generalized melodies written out on the staff—what people often refer to as a *fake book* (at the time it wasn't available in the US or Canada). If you look up *I Want to Hold Your Hand* in this book, you'll see that the 3 chord in the verse we're talking about here is shown as a B minor. Likewise, if you look at the chord in Hal Leonard's official *1* CD fake book, with all twenty-seven hit song scores, you will also see a B minor here. BUT, if you dig into some detailed musicology descriptions of the song, for example from the list in the previous section, in O'Grady or Pollack, you'll see that they call attention to the chord as being a B major. Using a B major here is somewhat unusual because the middle note of the B major chord stack is a D sharp, and the D is the all-important 5 note in the key of G, so the sharp 5 sounds a little unusual to our ears. Now if you look up the complete score for the song in the book *The Beatles Complete Scores* (Hal Leonard again), which has every chord, instrument, vocal, etc., you'll see that they mark the chord as a B seventh, and this sounds even more jarring than the B major. So, which one is it? We have three different versions of a B chord, from multiple sources. There's even another possibility, which would be a *power chord*, which is a chord with only 1s and 5s, no 3rds at all.

I really wanted to get to the bottom of this, so I did two things. First, I looked at the YouTube video of the Beatles playing the song during the second set of their first and so famous US appearance on the Ed Sullivan show, on February 9, 1964. (It's interesting to hear how prominent Paul's voice is in the mix, you can hardly hear John at all.) If you freeze the video at the spots where George and John are playing the chord, you can see that they are both playing what's called a grand-bar chord, with their index fingers stretched out up across the 7th fret, and their other three fingers playing notes just above that. If you look closely (do a screen copy, save it as an image, crop their hands, and zoom in), you'll see that it does look like they are both playing B major chords, because their middle fingers are pressing down on the 8th fret of the 3rd string and hitting that D sharp note. If they were playing minor chords, their middle fingers would be off the fretboard, and if they were playing B sevenths, their fingers would be using yet a different pattern.

But to really confirm that it was a B major, I used Audacity software and OOPS (see the Sidebar *Out of Phase Stereo*) to cancel out the vocals in the middle of the stereo image, and to hear what the more detailed instrument tracks on the right and left sounded like. When you do this with *I Want to Hold Your Hand*, you can really hear some great details in George's sparkly little lead fill-ins that are not so noticeable in the regular mix (and the arpeggios at the very end of the song are really great). Anyway, if you listen to the several sparse notes he's playing at about 1:16 on the right track, you can indeed hear a two-note passage, D sharp down to B, so in this sense the answer is yes, it is a B major.

But the thing of it is, if you're just noodling along on your guitar, playing chords and humming the song, the chord that seems to fit the best is the B minor—our ears sort of want to make it a B minor, to fit in with the diatonic scale we're so used to. And while we do see George and John playing B majors on Ed Sullivan, and we can indeed hear the D sharp in George's playing in the OOPS version, the truth of it is, those little major 3rd D sharp notes are so buried down in the mix, they're barely audible, which is the reason so many people filling out fake books just write in the B minor.

As an aside, many fake books are notoriously full of errors. Hal Leonard's *1* CD fake book, which otherwise has correct keys, shows the key for *Penny Lane* as C, which is incorrect—the verse opens in the key of B, as well as not showing the right modulation in the refrain, from an A chord up to a B chord, at the end of the song. This reminds me of all the times, when as a young guitar player in the mid-1960s, I couldn't wait to get out of church and get my hands on the Sunday paper, which always featured a trendy pop song, and spelled out the chords, but which were so very often not the right ones.

In any case, that's just one example of thinking about only one chord in one song, there's so much more—it's endless. If you added up all of the chord changes that KG Johansson counted in his paper mentioned above, it comes to about 5,000. There's just not enough time.

FULL-LYRICS SONG MAPS

As stated in the preface, the original idea for the song maps was that they'd contain the full lyrics to each song, but then SONY/ATV and Hal Leonard changed their minds (argh). So, for the book's plan B, the song maps contain only song part names.

The figure below shows the full-lyrics map for the song *For He's A Jolly Good Fellow*. In this fictitious rendition, John sings the first line of the refrain, Paul the second, John and Paul sing in harmony for the third, then George joins in on the last line, in full three-part harmony. For the middle section, which we'll call a bridge here, Ringo sings the first line alone, then all Beatles sing in unison for the second line. The refrain repeats at 0:16.

For He's A Jolly Good Fellow—Example of a Full-Lyrics Song Map

Next, the simplified song parts only song map is shown, along with its legend.

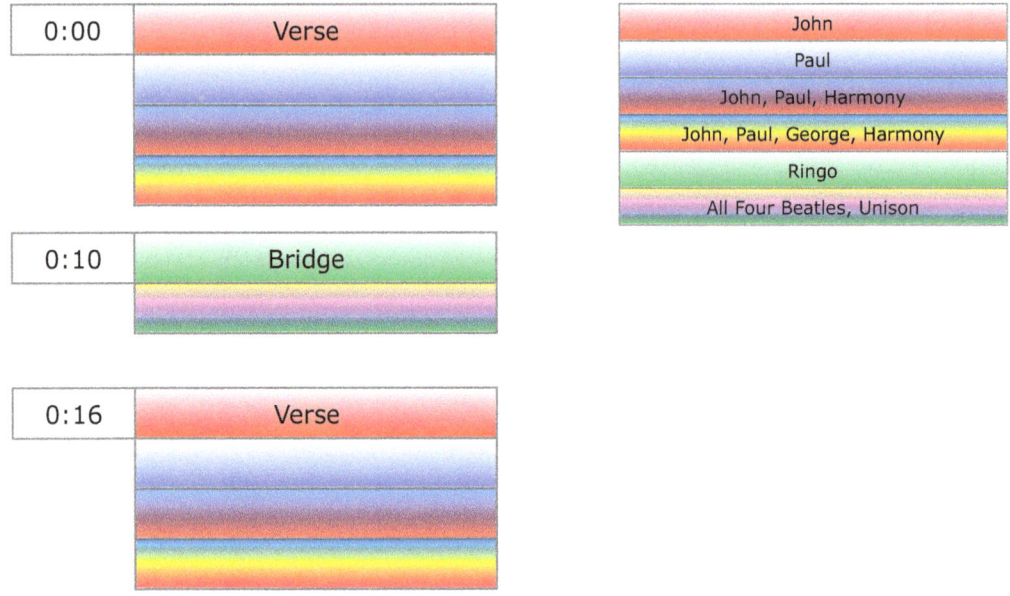

For He's A Jolly Good Fellow, Song Parts Song Map and Legend

So, while the full lyrics song map looks busier, it's easier to follow if you're listening along with the music, but the simplified song parts song map is still in a way more pleasing to the eye, because the colors stand out more.

WRAP UP

In this Appendix we've taken a more detailed and accurate look at the musical elements suggested in the song maps and chord palettes. These concepts, and the study of music in general, can be fascinating and very rewarding. There are so many patterns and details that come into play. For example, the happy 1, 4, and 5 chords together contain all eight notes in the scale. The sad 6, 2, and 3, are all relative minors of the majors, respectively. The eight-note major scale can be seen as two four-note scales put together, called *tetrachords*. A three-note chord stack, or *triad*, can be seen as two thirds stacked together, and so on.

An excellent musical primer, to help prepare for the more complex writings cited above, which uses very readable language and readily understood diagrams is *Hearing and Writing Music, Professional Training for Today's Musician*, by Ron Gorow.

Another great resource for learning more about music theory and pop songs, using a relative scale step and colored approach a little bit like the one used in this book, is Hooktheory (I and II) which you can install on your cellphone, tablet, or computer. Unlike the chord colors used in this book, which were chosen to show happy major chords as bright, and sad minor chords as dark, Hooktheory's interactive books and app use a color system which maps the notes in the scale do-re-me, etc., to the rainbow-ordered colors, red-orange-yellow, etc. You can learn more about the Hooktheory app at the following link:

https://www.hooktheory.com/

And if you don't already, some day you might even go as far as to try and understand the London Times' music critic, William Mann, in his 1963 article praising the Beatles where he uses phrases like *chains of pandiatonic clusters*, *flat submediant key switches*, and *Aeolian cadences*, which John Lennon thought sounded like exotic birds.

ABOUT THE AUTHOR

Brian Hebert is a cartographer, computer programmer, musician, and author living in the Boston area. After hearing the Beatles on Ed Sullivan in 1964, he started to play the guitar. Over the years his musical interests broadened to include blues harmonica, classical guitar, keyboards, Appalachian claw-hammer banjo, Strumstick, and especially traditional Irish and Scottish tunes played on fiddle, tenor banjo, and octave mandolin. In recent years his interests have turned to morphing and arranging Beatles' songs and both old and new popular music, into Americana and Celtic instrumental tunes, on both acoustic and electric tenor guitar, and cello. The music of *Brian Hebert and Friends* can be found on Amazon, iTunes, Pandora, CD Baby, Spotify, and YouTube.

ABOUT THE GRAPHICS

The colored song maps and chord palettes shown in this book were generated as Scalable Vector Graphics (SVG) images, using several customized markup languages and computer programs developed by the author.

www.ingramcontent.com/pod-product-compliance
Lightning Source LLC
Chambersburg PA
CBHW061810290426
44110CB00026B/2843